David Saul, MD

SEX
FOR LIFE

THE LOVER'S GUIDE TO
MALE SEXUALITY

David Saul, MD

SEX
FOR LIFE

THE LOVER'S GUIDE TO
MALE SEXUALITY

Canadian Catalogue in Publication Data
Saul, David. 1951–
        Sex for life: the lover's guide to male sexuality

Includes Index.
ISBN 1–896817–18–1

        1. Sexual disorders.   2. Men–Sexual behavior.   3. Sex
1. Title.

RC889.S38 1998   616.6'9   C98–901–440–1

Published by **APPLE PUBLISHING COMPANY Ltd.**
220 East 59th Ave., Vancouver, British Columbia, Canada V5X 1X9
Tel: (604) 214-6688   Fax: (604) 214-3566
e-mail: books@applepublishing.com

Printed in Canada

Praise and Acclaim for
Dr. Saul and *Sex For Life*

"Dr. Saul has been able to integrate a mind-body approach to medicine that really works in a traditional family practice office setting. Dr. Saul's insights into disease alleviation through the use of new and beneficial techniques have changed my style of practice for the better. The patients I refer to Dr. Saul (chronic pain and erectile dysfunction - ED) always come back with a practical therapeutic approach to the road of recovery."

- Gordon Ko, MD, CCFP, FRCP (C)
Medical Director, Canadian Center for Integrative Medicine, Markham, Ontario; Associate Professor, Senior University Lecturer, Dept. of Medicine, University of Toronto

"I know I can count on Dr. Saul to write fresh and stimulating perspectives on a variety of traditional medical issues. Dr. Saul has a common sense approach to medicine and is always looking for ways to improve the practicing of medicine for family doctors."

- Vil Meere, Managing Editor, Family Practice Medical Newspaper for Family Physicians

"For over 20 years, Dr. Saul has been on the forefront of innovative cognitive therapy techniques. Dr. Saul brings to men's health valuable insights on the interaction of the mind and sexual performance."

- Herman Gelber, MD, FRCP, former Chief of Psychiatry, Scarborough General Hospital, Scarborough, Ontario

Acknowledgments

The inspiration for this book came in October 1997 at the end of a meeting I had with Matthew James, Continuing Health Education Coordinator for Quest Vitamins. "Write a book about men's health," he told me quite casually. "But make it comprehensive, to include traditional and complementary approaches to men's health care."
Not so casually I replied, "It's not that easy to write a book." But the seed was sown, and you are presently looking at the harvest.

Also at that meeting were Stuart Thorburn, Continuing Medical Education Coordinator for Pharmacia and Upjohn, makers of Caverject™; David McCready, product manager for Andriol™, from Organon Canada; and David's assistant, Patricia Cadeau. We were all finalizing arrangements for my "NEW APPROACH TO MEN'S HEALTH" public health seminar. Thank you to Matthew, Stuart, David and Patricia.

A special thanks goes to Maria Besant, owner of Homelife Remedies Health Food Store in Markham, Ontario. Maria was always ready with energy, commitment and fresh ideas to help me run group programs in her store for breast cancer prevention, chronic pain and fibromyalgia.

Some other people I would like to thank are Daun D'Cunha Ph.D. for her inspiration; Bonnie Brownstein, Head Librarian at Scarborough General Hospital for her help in securing research articles from Medline; Vil Meere, Editor of Patient Care Canada medical journal for publishing my first journal article, *"If he's too shy to seek help for failing sexual performance,"* (November 1997); Dr. Alvaro Morales, one of the most respected urologists in Canada, for having the confidence in me and my work in men's health, to invite me to join the Canadian Male Sexual Health Council as the only family doctor among a group of 12 top Canadian urologists; and an additional thank you to Patricia Cadeau from Organon Canada for her help in printing the many hard copy versions of my book.

To Apple Publishing President, Alexander Pazitch, and to my editor and the Project Manager, Lucretia Schanfarber – thanks for your confidence and for giving my original manuscript a second reading.

Thanks also to James Slater for his editorial assistance, Richard Bakker for his design and layout and Karina Meléndez for her illustrations.

Finally, to my wife, Judy and my two sons, Daniel, age 18, and Michael, age 14, for their support, tolerance and encouragement in the evolutionary process of this book. Judy helped with her editing skills and everyone had to listen to my concerns, provide me with suggestions and rate the closing jokes for laugh appeal.

Preface
Let's get something straight.

hy did I write **Sex For Life**? Because in my men's clinic that's what the men tell me is truly important – having a firm erection they can count on to last for a lifetime of sexual intercourse. But that information of course is only from a tiny fraction of the three million Canadian men who have erectile dysfunction (abbreviated to ED and formerly called impotence).

Sex For Life might reach out and help those men who have been traditionally embarrassed to discuss their sexual difficulties.

A man's ability to produce and maintain an erection is an integral aspect of who and what he is. For a sizable portion of a man's life, especially during the fertile "baby-making" years, this sexual ability can be counted on day after day after day.

As Jerry Seinfeld, the American comedian said, "Men are like firemen. To us, sex is an emergency, and no matter what we're doing we can be ready in two minutes."

But can a 50- or 60-year-old man today feel as sexually virile as he did when he was 20? And can he have the same physical and intellectual capabilities as his 20-year-old counter-part? The sad truth is that many older men cannot hold a candle to the young bucks. What went wrong?

Heart disease, diabetes, prostate cancer, stress, testosterone hormonal declines and ED have all taken their toll on millions of middle-aged and elderly men. Once strong, virile and active men are now tired, all hunched over and *unable to get it up anymore.*

For some of these former athletic and vibrant men, it may be too late, *but for the vast majority of men, it is not too late to change.* You can definitely regain some (or a lot) of your lost muscles, stamina, mental capacity and sexual ability. How? By reading and following the guidelines in this book.

I also wrote **Sex For Life** for women who love their men – their husbands and boyfriends; women who are having sexual relationships with men and want to maintain or improve their own and his sexual enjoyment. My hope is that women who read this book will appreciate this universal message about men: *A man needs to count on his erection every time, without fail, or his sense of manhood is jeopardized.*

As a woman you do not have to understand *why* the ability to produce an erection is so important to a man. Men do not necessarily understand the reason either, but that still does not negate its importance. When a man is really hot for sex, he cannot hide his excitement, and *does not wish to hide it.* A man feels intense pride in a powerful erection.

Ernestyne White was very astute to say, "Eventually, all men come out of the bathroom dressed as a majorette."

Please consider **Sex For Life** as a source of recognized medical and psychological treatments for any existing erectile dysfunction. But more important, for you men who do not have difficulties with sex at the present time, you can benefit immensely from the protective and preventive aspects. Then all men can subscribe to the motto I use in my men's clinic:

SEX – WHENEVER YOU WANT IT, FOR AS LONG AS YOU WANT IT.

What's truly important to a man? To be *able* to make love with passion tonight and every night with the woman he loves.

Moms Mabley said it best, "A woman is a woman until the day she dies, but a man is a man only as long as he can."

Table of Contents

Table of Contents *continued*

Introduction

Men: are you having trouble with sex?

Mr. G. answered the advertisement I regularly placed in the local newspaper and came in to see me.

MEN: ARE YOU HAVING TROUBLE WITH SEX?

Find out how new medical treatments can help you regain your sexual vitality when the opportunity is present, but the desire or the ability is lacking.

Call Dr. David Saul, director of North Scarborough Men's Health Center.

Mr. G. appeared to be around 60 years old. He shook my hand and sat down. Before I could give him my sexual dysfunction questionnaire to fill out, it happened. I have witnessed it several times as well with other men in my clinic – Mr. G. started to cry.

Not wanting to lose complete control, Mr. G. stopped himself from bawling. But there was no mistaking it, this man broke down and quietly wept in front of a doctor who treats male sexual problems.

Mr. G. stopped crying, but could not erase the anguish and despair from his face. He quietly told me he lost his erections and said, "This is very embarrassing. I feel ashamed." Mr. G. went on, "I feel bad talking about it, but I know I have to do something. I can't go on living like this."

Those four words, "This is very embarrassing," which I heard from man after man after man, told me that men were hurting. *This book is an attempt to ease the hurt many men are feeling today and prevent further pain tomorrow.*

WHAT'S WRONG?

The medical journals were revealing incidence statistics for ED (Erectile Dysfunction, the inability to develop and/or maintain an erection) to be a minimum 30% of *all* adult men in North America. But why was it that in over 20 years of practicing family medicine only a handful of men ever complained to me about any sexual dysfunction? Why not one third of all my adult male patients? My colleagues reported similar findings. Something was obviously wrong.

I began researching medical reports, journals and textbooks. I finally figured it out. The statistics were correct alright, or likely even under-estimated. However, the doctors treating men with ED were all urologists (specialists in the genito-urinary system). But when it came to family doctors, three things were happening:

1. Family doctors were not asking their male patients enough direct questions concerning ED and other sexual functioning. And because the doctors were not asking the right questions, they were only seeing one icicle of a titanic iceberg.

2. Patients were not aware that effective medical treatments were available for ED. They assumed they were stuck with their ED permanently and chose a typical male solution to their dilemma – to suffer in silence.

3. Many doctors were not up to date with recent medical improvements in the treatment of ED. Many were still stuck in the old medical dogma that 75% of ED is due to psychological problems and 25% to medical (physical) problems. In the past 15 years the medical literature consistently and conclusively has been showing the reverse to be true: 75% – 85% of ED is due to medical concerns and 15% – 25% is due to psycho-social concerns.

❝ *75% – 85% of ED is due to medical concerns and 15% – 25% is due to psycho-social concerns.* ❞

It was only after repeatedly hearing those four words, "This is very embarrassing," that I finally understood what was wrong. Not only was ED embarrassing but the embarrassment was universal and pervasive among men. It became the main reason preventing men with ED from seeking treatment by the family doctor.

WHAT DID I DO ABOUT IT?

For every advertisement I placed in the newspaper, about 10 men with ED responded. I then developed my own ED flow chart questionnaire. This enabled me to rapidly elicit their medical, sexual and psychological history. Armed with this information, I could then establish a diagnosis and plan a course of treatments.

Next, I began to consider all my middle-aged and elderly male patients as if they were suffering from ED but were just not telling me. I looked closely at their medical conditions and the various treatments, which I had prescribed for their diseases and syndromes. I was searching for the answers to two questions:

1. Could the disease itself be a cause or at least a contributing factor to ED?
2. Could the medications that my patients were taking be *inadvertently* causing or contributing to ED?

WHAT HAPPENED?

With some indirect questioning I was able to discover a few men with ED. Their initial responses were very similar. They all hesitated before saying,

"Now that you mentioned it, Doc..." or

"Well, as a matter of fact, Doc..." or

"To tell you the truth, Doc...."

However, I still recorded only a small fraction (1% – 2%) of the 30% incidence statistics quoted in the medical studies. It finally dawned on me that when it came to sex and sexual functioning, men could be good poker players. In other words, they were lying straight to my face.

How did I know they were lying? The answer is in the story of Mrs. P.

MRS. P.'S STORY

Mrs. P. was a 51-year-old patient of mine who complained of menopausal symptoms. We discussed the advantages and the drawbacks of HRT, hormone replacement therapy. Inevitably the subject of sex came up.

I told Mrs. P. that with supplemental hormones, especially estrogen, she would likely experience an increased sex drive along with better vaginal lubrication.

It was then that Mrs. P. told me to have a talk with Mr. P. "Why?" I naively asked.

"Because Mr. P. has suddenly lost his interest in sex and he's having trouble getting it up," she said.

I did not tell Mrs. P. that I had just seen her husband in the office only two weeks earlier for his annual physical. Since I was using my new interviewing skills searching for potential ED, I used them on Mr. P.

Guess what his reply was? That's right, typical, locker-room bragging. "No problem here!" was part of Mr. P.'s response.

That's when I realized that men will lie about ED and will do an excellent job of it, too.

GETTING STARTED

I knew that the services I had to offer for correcting ED would help these men. I had extensive experience with stress management skills during the four years I was running group therapy sessions for patients with chronic pain and chronic fatigue syndrome. I exhaustively researched and studied medical books and journals. Soon I had absorbed a wealth of knowledge on causes and treatments of ED.

I even researched medical journals and textbook sources for complementary and alternative medicine to obtain the latest research on vitamins, nutritional supplements and herbal preparations. The field of complementary medicine was also very active in treating ED and other male urological conditions, such as prostate problems. In addition, many of my patients preferred to begin with vitamins or other herbal supplements instead of prescription medications.

Finally, I took additional one-on-one training with a urologist in Toronto who was actively involved in treating men with ED. He was only too glad for me to take over some of the patient load, as his waiting period for seeing new patients with ED was already over six months long.

I'M READY NOW

I devised individualized treatment programs for the men who answered my ads. The results were highly successful. I knew I was doing something effective and gratifying for everyone. However, I was still far away from that 30% figure quoted in all the research. I realized I would have to take a new approach with my middle-aged and elderly patients. I was able to coax out more information about sexual functioning in three ways:

1. I held three public seminars about men's health in general. They were all held in the evenings and free of charge. One of the topics covered was ED. I promoted these events to my patients and to the neighboring community. The turnout numbers were 75, 100 and 250. We were all surprised by the larger-than-expected attendance. Feedback questionnaires revealed that over 90% of the men who attended the seminars did so because of personal erection concerns and not because of heart or prostate concerns.

2. I began looking for symptoms in my middle-aged male patients of male menopause (lowered testosterone levels). If their symptoms fit the medical picture, I would order the appropriate blood tests to corroborate the findings. Often a lowered testosterone blood level meant there was some degree of ED also occurring or brewing.

3. I devised a few more unique questioning strategies which were innocuous and not embarrassing, but would definitely lead to answers pertaining to sexual performance. In other words, the questions did not suddenly pop out of the blue. Instead, they easily fit into a routine medical inquiry.

These three action plans – the public seminars, the blood testing and the indirect questioning – began to bear fruit. I then went one step further. I wrote to the editor of a local medical journal primarily for family doctors. I commented on an article written by urologists on the management of ED published in that journal during the previous year. I noted that it was clearly organized and well-referenced. But I also pointed out that the article was not particularly useful to family doctors because we were not seeing a sufficient number of ED cases (1% as opposed to 30%). It was the old story of the cart before the horse.

What the family doctors needed most (before any discussion on treatment) was the ability to bring these men forward. I volunteered to write an article for the journal outlining the questioning techniques

I had developed. I also wanted to include some ED preventive management strategies for family doctors to use in a typical office setting.

The editor of the journal contacted me and was very enthusiastic about my idea. My article, "If he's too shy to seek help for failing sexual performance" was quickly accepted and published in the November 1997 issue of *Patient Care Canada*.

I went on to present that article, retitled, "Erectile Dysfunction – A touchy subject. A guide for the family doctor. How to ask and how to treat," at the First World Congress on the Aging Male, a medical conference held in Geneva, Switzerland in February 1998.

WHAT WILL YOU GET FROM THIS BOOK?

Look through the table of contents and see if you find a description of yourself. You should. I have included every cause of ED. You may never have heard or even thought of many of them. I tried to make this book as comprehensive and as up to date as possible with the latest medical and psychosexual research.

Each chapter begins with a true excerpt from one of my case files (such as Mr. and Mrs. P.) I use only the patient's initials when describing each case to ensure confidentiality.

Every chapter has a detailed evaluation of the pertinent medical and scientific information for each ED problem. This will follow with straightforward, step-by-step and ready to use solutions to enable rapid resolution of ED, if you have it now. However, if you do not have ED or you feel a particular section does not apply to you, it will still be in your interest to read this book for its preventive value. Finally, every chapter ends with a sexually oriented joke for added entertainment.

There is nothing in the life of a man more relevant or profound than the ability to achieve and maintain an erection. *Sex For Life* gives you the ways and means to "keep it up" for life.

❝ There is nothing in the life of a man more relevant or profound than the ability to achieve and maintain an erection. Sex For Life gives you the ways and means to 'keep it up' for life. ❞

PART ONE
MEN AND SEX:
THE MIND

*When the mind is in gear,
get ready for something big*

CHAPTER ONE
The Brain

A man's largest sex organ!

The erection process is an organized yet complex phenomenon, consisting of vascular (blood and blood vessels), hormonal, enzymatic and neuromuscular interactions. Throughout this book, at each appropriate chapter, I will present detailed descriptions of these specialized processes. For now, let's just concentrate on the neurological effect the brain has on ED (erectile dysfunction).

THE PROCESS

Human sexual functioning involves two processes:
1. The mental process – desire, i.e., feeling horny, hot, lustful and excited.
2. The physical process – performance, i.e., erection and ejaculation (orgasm) in men, vaginal lubrication, vaginal and uterine contractions (orgasm) in women.

The process does not always require your active or willing participation. Don't laugh, it can happen while you are asleep. There are sexually arousing dreams and "wet dreams" involving erections and ejaculations in teenage boys and in some adult men also.

The sensory nerves from the penis, scrotum and surrounding skin areas travel to the spinal chord, where they make a connection. A reflex system of nerve pathways allows for direct functioning of the erection and ejaculation process sometimes without any input from the brain. In addition, there is a special switching system in the spinal chord which connects the nerve fibers traveling from the penis to the nerve fibers coming down from the brain. This gate-like operation is called the spinal erection center (SEC).

THE BRAIN'S INPUT

The human brain is unique to the erection process because it has the ability to enhance or diminish it. Let's examine how the brain can influence erections – either up or down. First, we need some basic neuroanatomy. The human brain is composed of three major sections, with the higher brain overlying the mid- and lower centers:

1. The lower or hind-brain is responsible for basic body functioning, such as respiration (breathing), cardiac (heart) function, digestion, and temperature regulation.
2. The limbic system is responsible for all the emotions and many important memory functions.
3. The higher brain (cerebrum) with its neocortex cover called gray matter comprises 80% of total brain mass. The cerebrum is responsible for thinking, sensory and motor skills, and all higher mental functioning.

The brain sends sexual nerve impulses down the spinal chord to the spinal erection center. These nerve tracts have two influential properties when it comes to sex:

1. Enhancement: "Ready or not, here I come!!"
2. Inhibition: " Whoa, slow down, big fella!!"

THE BRAIN AND ED

The psychological component of ED is usually but not always related to stress and the stress response. In the next chapter I will describe the typical stress response and how it can interfere with sexual enjoyment. Other specific psychological problems, also presented in the following chapters, do not necessarily elicit a stress response such as psychosexual trauma, depression, castration syndrome and an "old" mindset. These problems still result in ED but are caused by more involved psychological disturbances in the brain.

The psychological impact on ED is not as profound as the physical causes are. Both can be sudden and devastating, but the physical causes have been shown to be much more prevalent. Psychological troubles directly account for 15% – 20% of all cases of ED. However, these troubles can also augment some physical problems. As a result, the impact of a man's psychological health is far more influential than the simple 15% – 20% incidence quoted in most of the recent studies of ED.

❝ The psychological impact on ED is not as profound as the physical causes are. ❞

CLOSING JOKES

Here's a joke by Beverly Mickins, an American comedienne:
"I love the lines the men use to get us into bed. 'Please, I'll only put it in for a minute.' What am I, a microwave?"

Did you hear about the magic elixir that can restore youthful sexual potency in men with one swallow? It is so effective and works so fast that you have to swallow it right away, otherwise you can end up with a stiff neck.

Did you hear about the man that wanted a vasectomy?
The doctor asked him, "Did you talk about it with your wife and family and are you really sure you want to go through with it? You know it is irreversible."
"Oh yes," replied the man. "To tell you the truth, I don't really want to have it. But my wife asked the children and they all voted on it."
"What was the result?" asked the doctor.
"Those in favor won, 12 to two."

CHAPTER TWO
Work Stress

Remember, it's _just_ a job.

"I lost my job and I lost my erection," said Mr. A. during our initial interview. "I don't know what I'll do now. I'm only 57, too young to retire."

I asked about any coincidence in the timing of losing the erections and the firing from his job.

Mr. A. said, "After about a week, the shock and realization kicked in that I was really out of work, and this was not going to be a holiday. That's when it started. I was making love with my wife, and it just went soft before I could enter. I'll tell you, it's gone soft a little from time to time before, but I could always get it hard enough for intercourse, and once I entered, it always got firmer. This time it just deflated and went limp. My wife made a little wise crack, and that was it."

He went on, "We tried it a few times after that, and the same thing happened. I got hard right away, but after about five minutes I lost it completely." He quietly added, " We haven't done it in over a month. Losing my job was bad enough, but losing my erections, that's another story."

66 The longer the problem manifests, the more entrenched it can become in the man's mindset and the more difficult it is to fix. 99

The rest of the history and physical examination from Mr. A. did not reveal any major causes of ED. His blood pressure was marginally high, but that was to be expected and he had no past history of high blood pressure. Mr. A. was suffering from a transient, stress-related cause of ED. It was lucky for him that he came into my clinic soon after the onset of ED. The longer the problem manifests, the more entrenched it can become in the man's mindset and the more difficult it is to fix.

STRESS – THE SHORT COURSE

Many books are written about stress and the influence stress has on the human body. In the past 10 years the medical and local libraries have seen an explosion in sheer numbers of volumes written on the subject of stress. An excellent resource book, which began this researching and documenting craze, is *Stress Without Distress,* by Hans Selye.

What I will present now is the short course on stress. Stress is defined as a perceived threat. Whether to a real or an imagined stress event, the body responds instinctively with the fight or flight response. The stress response is an automatic mind and body program, which is ingrained in all humans, but designed biologically only for protection and survival. When the stress button is pushed to either real or imagined events, the body responds instantly with the following:

- Increased heart rate and blood pressure
- Increased breathing rate
- Sweating, "hot under the collar"
- Digestion ceases due to blood shifting towards the large muscles of the arms and legs
- Pupils dilate, eyelids tighten
- Increased mental alertness
- Hormonal changes, especially an increase in adrenaline and noradrenaline coupled with a decrease in testosterone

The stress response (fight or flight) is also referred to medically as the sympathetic nervous system (SNS). When the SNS is engaged, it is designed to run non-stop for 20 to 30 minutes. Every time. And remember, it operates for real or imagined events. Also once engaged, there is no backing out. The body is primed for action, to either run for your life or to fight for your life. All the bodily changes must then run their course until they can be stabilized again.

A BALANCING ACT

The sympathetic nervous system (the fight or flight system) is in a constant balancing act with its opposite, the parasympathetic nervous system, PSNS (the relaxation system). The physiological responses described and listed in the previous section for the sympathetic nervous system, all revert to the exact opposite when the parasympathetic nervous system is dominating. Some of these PSNS changes are:

- Slower heart rate and lower blood pressure
- Slower breathing rate
- Cooler body temperature, relaxed muscles
- Good digestion
- Feeling relaxed, calm and sleepy
- Hormonal and immune shifts, with increases in testosterone

The body's two nervous systems are always operating within a certain ratio of two chemicals, adrenaline and acetylcholine. These two chemicals help to transmit information between cells and are referred to as neurotransmitters. When the SNS is dominant during a stress response, there is more adrenaline released than acetylcholine. When the PSNS is dominant during a relaxation response, there is more acetylcholine released than adrenaline.

> **❝ Thinking about a stressful situation or actually being in a stressful situation has the same effect on your physiology. ❞**

Sometimes, more than we would like to admit, SNS is called into action to deal with *unnecessary* stresses. Since both real or imagined threats will trigger a stress response, simply *thinking* about a stressful situation or actually *being* in a stressful situation has the same effect on your physiology.

For many people today, the SNS is working overtime with too much adrenaline production and not enough acetylcholine to counterbalance it.

IT'S EITHER UP OR IT'S DOWN

The PSNS promotes the nerve and hormonal stimulation for proper erectile function. The SNS promotes the nerve and hormonal stimulation for proper ejaculation function. Right after ejaculation, the erection rapidly fades because of sympathetic dominance.

The two systems cannot operate at the same time. Can you see what the problem is? If the SNS is operating longer than it should, then there cannot be any decent erections. The nerves and the hormones are directing the opposite to occur – a limp penis.

For most men, the PSNS is dominating in the late evenings, leading to a sleepy state and an erection. This promotes a desire for sexual relations and then a good night's sleep. Also, throughout the night there are erections occurring during dream states. Sleep is under strong parasympathetic control, which helps to explain the firm and usually prolonged erections.

Another theory suggests that these nocturnal (nighttime) erections are specifically designed to provide blood (and the resulting oxygen) to the cells that actually produce the erections. Because of sustained SNS stimulation in the daytime leading to a limp penis for the majority of your waking hours, hypoxic (no oxygen) damage can occur in these cells. Perfusion of blood at night with nocturnal erections can reverse this lack of oxygen to help maintain the integrity and function of the erection system.

66 *Being more relaxed leads to better erections and better sex, and sex itself results in a more relaxed mental state. 99*

During the daytime, the sympathetic system has the edge, and therefore, no erection. However, too much adrenaline production from too much stress can lead to an over expression of the SNS and result in ED. Sometimes, depending on the extent of the stress response and the over-expression of the hormone adrenaline, other troubling medical conditions, such as cardiac or digestive troubles can occur.

JOB STRESS

To have good erections and good sex, the mind has to be focused completely on sex, which is not usually difficult for men, in general. However, sometimes life's stresses can seem overwhelming. When that happens it is important to assess your emotional response to the current stresses. If the stress response appears too high, try to cool off a little before engaging in sex or possibly avoid sex for the time being. On the other hand, as a result of their caveman heritage, men have the ability to tune out stresses from their minds when a specific task (such as sex) is at hand.

Right after a sexual encounter many men often find themselves in a more relaxed and focused mental state. Therefore, both conditions apply – being more relaxed leads to better erections and better sex, and sex itself results in a more relaxed mental state.

A major area of stress for men today centers around the work they do. Family relationships, car trouble, politics and health concerns are also stress inducers in men's lives. But for most men, the job, career, business, work, (whatever it's called) ranks higher than everything else does. I am not comparing job stress to the death of a loved one or a similar one-time tragedy. I am simply stating that the job is on the mind of most men, everyday, all day.

It doesn't matter if it is right or wrong, good or bad, for men to have work on their minds to such an extent. What is important for our purposes here is to accept this phenomenon about men and to deal with it, *so that men do not get sick or lose their erections due to job stress.*

LET'S RECAP

It's not the stress but the stress response (either more than is necessary or going on for too long) that can lead to ED trouble. Prolonged stimulation of the SNS leads to an increase in adrenaline, leading to vasoconstriction (tight arteries and high blood pressure), leading to inadequate blood flow to the penis, leading to ED. The SNS is designed to promote ejaculation, not erections.

More involvement of the PSNS results in an increase in acetylcholine, leading to vasodilatation (open arteries and decreased blood pressure), in turn leading to more blood flow to the penis. The end result is the ability to have erections that are big, hard and sustained. The PSNS promotes erections, not ejaculation.

The stress response (SNS) is a natural protective phenomenon that is pre-programmed in all humans. Too often, we overplay the stress response to imagined and not actualized events. A good example of this comes from a quote by Mark Twain: "I've been through a lot of troubles in my life, and some of them have actually happened."

66 *Losing a job ranks as one of the highest stresses for men.* **99**

Stressful stimulation comes in all shapes and sizes. Being involved in a car accident is stress. The car not starting is stress. Buying a new car is stress. A scratch on a new car is stress. Looking for a car wash without a line-up is stress. And remember, even just thinking about all of the above events makes the same alterations to your SNS/PSNS balance and your stress response.

Work is a major area of stress for men. Men have been conditioned since they were cavemen to be the breadwinners, the leaders and the protectors. In ancient times, a man did not return home without food or without success on the battlefield. If he did, the family would starve (without food) or would be taken into slavery (losing the war). Therefore men feel the need to succeed at work everyday. Losing a job ranks as one of the highest stresses for men.

ARE WE DOOMED?

The pressure is on men to produce financially, protect physically and perform sexually. The reality, however, for all men, is the inevitable failure in business, the bedroom, the boardroom, on the boulevard, the battlefield, the baseball diamond and finally, in building something. Failures, mistakes and rejections – these are all part of life. They are also part and parcel of work for men.

In days gone by, how did men react to the work-related stress of unemployment? Here are six different coping styles that men developed over the centuries:
1. The cap in hand approach – beg or borrow
2. The immoral, illegal approach – cheating, stealing, conniving
3. The stoic approach – take any job available, just to put food on the table
4. The ostrich approach – get drunk and try to forget it
5. The cowardly approach – run away and try to escape from it
6. The suicidal approach – jump out the window, to really escape from it (like the stockbrokers did in the 1929 stock market crash)

THAT WAS THEN, THIS IS NOW

We are no longer living in the Dark Ages, the Middle Ages or even the Industrial Age. We are now at the dawn of the Third Millennium. As modern men, we need to have better mechanisms available to cope with unemployment than the ones used in previous centuries. And not only that, we need more effective, stress-reducing skills for other life stresses besides losing our jobs.

> **❝As modern men, we need to have better mechanisms available to cope with unemployment than the ones used in previous centuries. ❞**

Therefore, in the next section, I will present five specific strategies that today's men can apply to this age-old problem of work stress. I will then outline five stress-reduction mechanisms that are beneficial for any type of stress, large or small.

1. Reality is staring you in the face

Wake up and smell the coffee. The days of working for "the man" or "the company" for 30 years straight with a gold watch at retirement are gone. Estimates from the business sector reveal the majority of all jobs available today have a time limit of only six years, not the 25 to 30 years from Dad's era.

Tom Peters, author of *Thriving on Chaos* and half a dozen other business management books, issues sober warnings to his readers and seminar participants:

- Information technology is changing so fast, that if you don't at least keep up, you will be left behind.
- Emerging Third World markets are now major business competitors and not captive markets as before.
- The factory industrial system in North America is outdated and obsolete. More people will be working from their homes, linked via their computers and cell phones.

Peters and other business-forecasting gurus advocate the need to keep your resume current and to review it every three to six months. Other advice for those hit or threatened with downsizing and restructuring (fancy names for firing) include:

- Constantly upgrade your work skills
- Go to courses and seminars on new work–related technology and procedures
- Read job-related texts, manuals and journals
- Invent new programs or improve old programs in your existing job environment

Another suggestion is to diversify your opportunities, such as: networking contacts in different lines of work, studying and taking courses in fields unrelated to your present work and always being inquisitive and open to unique possibilities. In these ways you can protect yourself should the axe fall. Having other fallback positions, such as people to call on to return a favor or some other contingency plan will also help.

Successful people are rarely surprised by downturns in the economy. They have already planned ahead and even anticipated them. And sometimes they have even begun a pre-emptive strike (to borrow a military term).

I remember the time when my lawyer left a thriving practice working with clients injured in motor vehicle accidents to work for a large real estate and land development firm. He saw the writing on the wall. One year after his move, the government abruptly changed certain laws, essentially removing the ability to sue for car accidents. The majority of his legal buddies were suddenly out of work, all scrambling at the same time for crumbs from the big firms.

2. The ladder of success

Men grow up climbing the ladder of success. We want to make the team, then we want the local championship, then the regional championship, the national championship and finally, all-star status. We want to be the best. Okay, not all of us want to be the best, but the competitive spirit is an integral part of almost all men.

Competition fuels the drive for success. It helps to establish goals, develops commitment and promotes perseverance. Sure, sometimes we lose. Someone has to lose. We can't always be the winners. Babe Ruth struck out more than twice the number of home runs he hit. Competition is a driving force that helps men feel the awesome thrill of victory.

However, there is an inherent danger with the ladder system, of always wanting more and/or better. Reaching and climbing to the top can sometimes backfire for men. Besides causing stress to always produce more, when the workplace does grind to a halt with seasonal slowdowns or other economic downturns, there is a huge letdown. It's like the day after Christmas.

However, there are other effective ways out of the endless treadmill of success. One concept for you to consider is to plateau. That means to stop the treadmill, get off and stay at that level for a while. Enjoy the view, relish your work and be satisfied with your level of achieve-ment. If you feel happy at this level, then by all means dig in for a while and coast.

Another option for some men who are nearing that certain age (retirement) is to cash out. Early retirement is an option being pre-sented to many aging (55+) men in today's marketplace. Cashing out can also involve selling the big house, the big car, and the expensive lifestyle too. Simpler needs and a slower pace are excellent ways of cashing out of the rat race. Do you know the joke about the rat race? Whoever wins, you're still a rat.

3. Life after work

Is there life after work? Or, at the end of the workday, do you get ready to do more office work at home? Many men become worka-holics and work day and night until they die (sometimes from over-work). Two important areas of life to consider getting involved with besides work are family relationships and personal growth. Men's health and longevity are directly tied into the quality and quantity of their family relationships.

A sobering statistic for elderly men reveals the following: widowers who were married for over 30 years and have not remarried within two years of their wife's death are almost all dead themselves. It's frightening but it's true. So nurture your love relationships; they have health-promoting benefits for men.

The next avenue for men to pursue is personal growth. I will be outlining detailed, personal growth and development mechanisms quite frequently throughout this book. Some activities to concentrate on include dieting, weight training and other exercising, hobbies and creative talents. Finally, there may be other neglected challenges to consider such as piano, tennis, chess, and running for politics.

4. Don't kill yourself over a job

A job isn't everything. It's something, it's important, but it isn't every-thing. Jobs come and go. They always have and they always will. Was there any benefit for the stockbrokers to jump out of their office win-dows on Wall Street in 1929? There is always another way out.

Remember, tomorrow is another day, and to borrow some more cliches:

- The sun always rises in the morning.

- The rain will always end.
- Don't sweat the small stuff; it's all small stuff.
- The phoenix will rise again.
- It's not the end of the world.

As long as you have your health, you can always get another job, pay off your debts and keep going.

5. Look for the silver lining

In the middle of a job loss, it seems like the end of the world. However, could this obvious tragedy be a blessing in disguise? Many times, better opportunities present themselves (call it fate or good luck) only because we were in the middle of a bad experience.

One way to enhance this way of looking at unemployment is again found in a cliché; "Is the glass half-full or half-empty?" Remember, it's the same glass. The only difference is in your attitude. If you look for and expect something good to come your way, then you have a greater chance for that to occur. Look for and expect continued trouble and you will likely find it.

GENERAL STRESS MANAGEMENT TECHNIQUES

It's not *what* happens to us in life, but *how we handle what happens* that determines the quality of our lives. Here are five simple but effective ways to change your perspective:

1. Laughter

As the saying goes, "laugh and the world laughs with you." "Laughter is the best medicine" is yet another saying used extensively in the healing profession. When you are laughing, you cannot be crying and you won't have an excess of adrenaline coursing through your veins. Your biochemistry becomes more balanced and as a result, your world appears more than tolerable but accepting and maybe even friendly. By actively promoting laughter, telling jokes, reading comics, and watching sitcoms on television, the benefits for stress reduction on an ongoing basis will be readily available.

2. Eyes on the prize

Goal-oriented behavior is a way of life inherent in most men. Having the bottom line clearly in your mind is all it takes to direct your brain to establish the mechanisms for its attainment. One effective way to get your mind in gear is to use verbal affirmations. Two things to keep saying to yourself, over and over, are: "I'll handle it" and "What do I do now?" Just say the words and your brain will come up with the necessary answers that you need for effective stress reduction.

3. One day at a time

This is another way of saying to just be in the here and now. Thoughts about the past or the future have very little relevance to our lives right now. The past is done and cannot be changed. The future is never ours to see. All we have is right in front of us.

Think about driving a car and looking in the rear view mirror the whole time or looking exclusively out the front windshield. When driving we need to frequently check the gauges, side mirrors, rear mirror, road conditions and status of the vehicle. However, most of our attention should be and is, directed out the front (the present), not the rear view mirror (the past) and not over the next hill (the future), thereby establishing a full awareness of the present state.

4. Slow it down

We are a rush, rush, rush society. Did I mention rush? I see many men in my practice hurrying to their graves! It's necessary to go full out, but only when it's called for. And when it's not, we need to be able to slow down, re-evaluate and maybe recharge our batteries. Two ways that will consistently and quickly slow us down are meditation and prayer. Prayer is an activity everyone knows about but is an activity many don't always do. Most people know very little about meditation and are even more reluctant to start. The following is a list of books and cassettes available to enlighten you on the brain-stabilizing benefits of meditation:

- *How to Meditate,* by Lawrence LeShan M.D.
- *Breath by Breath,* by Larry Rosenberg.
- *Wherever You Go, There You Are: Mindfulness Meditation in Everyday Life,* by Jon Kabat-Zinn.

- *Don't Just Do Something, Sit There: A Mindfulness Retreat with Sylvia Boorstein,* by Sylvia Boorstein.
- *The Miracle of Mindfulness, a Manual on Meditation,* by Thich Nhat Hanh.

5. Rev it up

Here is a tried and true way to speed up your system, stabilize and balance your hormones, and also reduce your stress – it's called exercise. You will also achieve a sharper brain, more energy and vitality, and an increased desire for cooperation and reconciliation.

There are two types of exercise: aerobic and anaerobic. Aerobic exercise involves running, biking, stair-climbing, swimming, skipping or finally, anything to make you sweat and breathe fast (yes, sex is an aerobic exercise). Anaerobic exercise involves weight and resistance exercises. With weight-training you won't breathe as hard but you will definitely sweat and feel the muscle action. The benefit of both kinds of exercise for stress reduction is not necessarily during the exercise but afterwards.

REMEMBER THIS

Work stress has had a negative impact on men, their sexual desires and their performance abilities. Only men who are proactive in their approaches to career opportunities and stress management skills can prevent any disruption in their sexual functioning.

“ Remember, it's not what happens to us in life, but how we handle what happens that determines the quality of our lives. ”

CLOSING JOKE

Here's a funny one from Dave Barry:

"As a rule, women would like to devote as much time to foreplay and the sex act as men would like to devote to foreplay, the sex act, and building a garage."

CHAPTER THREE
Depression

Climbing out of the depths.

Mr. B. came into the office. He was in his early forties, tall, well dressed, but moved slowly and looked very tired.

"I've been in a state of depression for over a year," he told me. "It all started with my new boss. Nothing I did was good enough. He wanted more production and kept piling the work on. I tried my best but it was never enough for him."

He smiled a tired smile. "Then my work began to suffer. It was just too much pressure. I made more and more mistakes and I fell farther and farther behind. I was yelling at my wife and my kids. I was a mess."

Mr. B. went on, "One day, I just stayed in bed and could not go in to work. I just gave up. I couldn't take it anymore."

Mr. B. told me that he sought help from his family doctor who prescribed antidepressant medications. Mr. B. was also given a leave of absence from work, and in fact had not returned to work in the past year.

"I went to a psychiatrist, who just gave me more pills." said Mr. B. "They helped a bit. I could sleep better with the pills, but I felt tired a lot. I had no desire to do anything except eat. I gained 30 pounds."

I asked about the specific medications he had taken and if he was taking anything at the present time. Then we talked about his sex life.

"I started having trouble concentrating on sex during the trouble with my boss, but I could still do it. My desire was down. I was tired a lot, and had headaches too. My wife was very understanding, and didn't push me for sex, so we just had less and less."

I then inquired specifically about his ED.

"When I went on the pills, I began having trouble with my erections. It wasn't as hard as usual for me. And when we had intercourse, sometimes I couldn't ejaculate. It was very frustrating, so we just stopped having sex. We haven't done it in over six months."

Mr. B. could not look at me. He looked at his shoes. Mr. B. had no diabetes, no high blood pressure, nor a low testosterone blood level. He had no other medical problems aside from being a little overweight. Mr. B. was taking no other medications, just his antidepressant drugs. His prostate was normal.

BEWARE OF THE CURE

Depression is a common mental condition. It affects almost 10% of the population in North America, is seen in children and adolescents, and troubles women four times more frequently than men. Symptoms of depression include various degrees of fatigue, sleep disturbance, change in appetite (increased or decreased), memory loss, poor concentration abilities, lack of motivation, sexual dysfunction, and often profuse crying spells. What are some of the causes?

- Depression can be a reaction to a loss, such as a job, spouse or pet.
- It can be related to emotional disturbances or trauma from the past, such as sexual abuse, survivor syndrome, or post-traumatic stress disorder.
- It can be related to a genetic predisposition, such as a family history of depression.
- It can be related to absolutely nothing external, and may instead be caused by a chemical imbalance in the brain.

❝Depression can cause ED directly. However, ED is a common side effect of the antidepressant medications prescribed by doctors. ❞

Depression can cause ED directly. However, ED is a common side effect of the antidepressant medications prescribed by doctors. These medications (Prozac™ being the first and most popular medication for depression) have up to a 30% incidence of sexual side effects, such as ED and decreased desire.

With depression, the pharmacological cure is very effective. However, the potential sexual side effect of medication is something that must be considered before initiating treatment. Some of the newer antidepressant medications have less of a sexual side effect profile and could be as effective as traditional Prozac™.

IS THERE ANOTHER CURE?

If your doctor feels that antidepressant medications are inappropriate for you, due to either side effects, cost or compliance, is there anything else that can be done? Check out *Beyond Prozac* by Michael Norden, M.D. It's an excellent book on alternative therapeutic modalities, which can be tried instead of, or in addition to, medications for depression.

Also, intensive traditional psychotherapy from a skilled psychiatrist or psychologist can be helpful in many cases. Finally, there is a new psychotherapeutic approach available to help patients with depression. It is the use of cognitive therapy. Cognitive therapy employs systems to change thinking habits and language behavior. The results are often extremely rapid and permanent. Some excellent resource books on cognitive therapy are:

- *The Feel Good Handbook,* by David Burns, M.D.
- *Rational Emotive Therapy,* by Albert Ellis, Ph.D.

MY VERSION OF COGNITIVE THERAPY

In the work I have done with patients suffering from chronic pain and chronic fatigue syndrome, I developed a unique cognitive therapy approach in addition to medications to help alleviate my patients' depressions.

The first part of the approach follows from the presumption that there are three basic negative emotions – anger, sadness and fear. All the other negative emotions are variations of these three. In my therapeutic system their definitions are:

- Anger means something is wrong
- Sadness means something is gone
- Fear means something could be wrong, or could be gone

And that's it. I know it sounds very simplistic, but by using this concept all that is required for correction of a negative emotion is to:

- Make a wrong into a right – no more anger
- Make a gone into a found – no more sadness
- Make a could be into a will not be – no more fear

When you think about this cognitive approach, you will see not just how simple it is, but how true it is. If nothing is wrong, you can't be angry. If nothing is gone, you can't be sad. If nothing could be wrong or could be gone, there is no fear.

Here's the next aspect of the cognitive approach to anger management:

- Anger is designed to push you into correcting a problem.
- Sadness is designed to show you what is important for you, and what you might have taken for granted.
- Fear is designed to protect you from getting into trouble.

We need these negative emotions for our survival. However, problems arise when we stay in these negative states for too long and begin to develop an imbalance in the brain's neurochemical levels. This often leads to other stress-related diseases and dysfunctions.

Take a lesson from young children. When they are angry, sad or afraid, they are fully in the emotion. And very soon (within a few minutes) they are completely out of the negative emotion, back into a happy, peaceful state again. Too many adults can stay angry and depressed for years at a time.

WHAT IF IT CAN'T BE FOUND?

I said that sadness or depression means that something is gone. To find it or to replace it will instantly remove the sadness. That's fine with appliances, shoes, car keys, or broken equipment, but what about the loss of a child? Obviously you cannot and should not replace the lost child. But in these types of situations, there is something else you can do. Let me tell you the story of one mother in California.

This mother's teenage daughter was killed in a drunk driving car accident. The driver was convicted and sent to jail. Justice was served. However, it did not bring the daughter back from the grave. The mother went into a deep depression. She contemplated suicide. Nothing was helping. Then one day the mother thought about other teenage daughters and sons who could be killed by drunk drivers.

The rest, as they say, is history, and Mothers Against Drunk Driving (MADD) was born. MADD did not bring the daughter back but it did change society's acceptance of driving while drunk. This one woman has single – handedly started an international organization that is influential in changing and enforcing traffic laws, speed limits, and breathalyzer tests. All this was accomplished with the initial desire to make the roads a safer place for children.

What this mother did was try to replace what was lost in some way, or at least in the best way available. She still gets sad and angry when she thinks about her daughter. However, she does not dwell on it anymore; she is too busy saving other lives.

This mother made the best right she could out of a tragic wrong and made the best found she could out of a bitter loss. It worked for her. If you are depressed presently, can you compare your depression to hers? Try this cognitive therapy approach. It can work for you too.

REMEMBER THIS

The bad news is that depression *and* the drugs most commonly prescribed to treat depression can *both* cause ED. The good news is that the use of cognitive therapy, traditional psychotherapy, and the judicious use of low-dose antidepressant medications and testosterone hormone replacement can help men with depression. Don't forget the importance of a good diet, nutritional supplementation and regular exercise in overcoming depression.

❝ Men can climb out of the depths of depression and begin to enjoy life and sex again. ❞

CLOSING JOKE

A husband and his wife were having a conversation about their future. The wife asked casually, "Honey if I died, would you remarry?"

The husband responded, "Why would you ask me such a question?"

The wife said, "I just want to know, would you remarry?"

"Well I guess I would," said the husband.

"Would she live in the same house?" asked the wife.

The husband replied, "You fixed up the house so nice, I guess she would."

"Would you let her drive my Oldsmobile?" asked the wife.

"I guess so," said the husband. "The car runs well, I don't see why not."

"Well, would you let her use my golf clubs?" asked the wife.

"Oh no. Definitely not!" The husband said emphatically.

"So wait a minute," asked the wife now a little confused. "You would let her stay in the house and drive my Oldsmobile but you would not let her use my golf clubs?"

"That's right" exclaimed the husband, "she's left-handed."

CHAPTER FOUR

Old Mindset

***Sex is not over at
50, 60 or even 90.***

M r. C. came into the office. Mr. C. was 62 years old, and definitely looked his age, and more. He had lost most of his hair, and what little there was left was now grayish white. Mr. C.'s face was all wrinkled. His back was all hunched over and he walked with a cane. Mr. C. looked very tired.

"Tell me about your problem." I said.

Mr. C. then began to explain, "I have no more erections, Doc. Not even when I wake up. I haven't had sex with my wife for a few years, now."

He had a sad look on his face. His eyes were moist but he held back the tears. Mr. C. went on, "It's like this, Doc. I always liked to have sex but my wife never did. It was as if she was doing me a favor. Then when she went through her change, she really didn't want it anymore. I'm not the type to run around, I don't like to masturbate, and so over the years, I just lost interest. That was fine with my wife, but it never really sat well with me."

Mr. C. continued, "But you know what is worse than not having erections, Doc? It's not having any interest in sex anymore. I used to get aroused when I saw a pretty young woman dressed in a short skirt. It doesn't do anything to me now."

I did some blood tests on Mr. C. and was not surprised to see that his testosterone level was quite low. He had no blood pressure or heart problems. His blood sugar was normal, and he was not taking any medications. Mr. C. was suffering from insufficient testosterone, also referred to as male menopause. (I will discuss in detail the male menopause syndrome [andropause], in the next chapter.)

Mr. C., in addition to or because of lowered testosterone, had the manifestations of the psychological syndrome I have termed the "old" mindset. It might be one of the causes of lowered testosterone, or it might be a result. The blood levels and the physical appearance correlate strongly with each other. However, medically we cannot determine which came first.

WHAT IS IT?

"Old" mindset is basically a mental awareness in a person to think and act old – not vibrant, lively or young at heart. The person (whether a man or a woman) usually looks elderly, like Mr. C., and has many of the following physical characteristics:

- Hunched upper back due to osteoporosis. This leads to a loss in height, sometimes quite significant. Generally there is arthritis in the back and knees, which requires medication and sometimes surgery.
- Aging skin, with thin, wrinkled and blotchy discolorations, especially on the face.
- Muscle loss in the arms, legs and chest. Increased fat accumulation around the stomach in men, and the stomach and hips in women.
- Mental deterioration, with poor short-term memory, less concentration ability, sometimes errors in judgement and finally, deficits in eye-hand co-ordination and reaction time.
- Shrinkage of the penis and testicles in men, and vaginal atrophy in women.
- Significant loss in sexual desire, referred to as lowered libido.

HOW DOES IT HAPPEN?

As I mentioned, lowered sex hormones for men and women can be the cause and/or effect of an "old" mindset. For men, this psychological profile can be the accumulation of many years of either thinking "old" (on their own) or being encouraged to think "old" (by others). For example:

- Having a desire for sex, maybe getting stimulated and aroused and then being told, "You're a dirty old man. Act your age!"
- Guilt or bad feelings about masturbation.
- Life-long rejections from a wife concerning sex. Feeling many times like he had to beg for it.
- Prostate trouble, usually benign prostate overgrowth, leading to trouble urinating and less fluid in the ejaculate.
- A heart attack almost always "ages" men, in their appearance and demeanor, often 10 to 15 years within three months of the heart attack.
- Equating sexuality with youth through advertising psychs men (and women) into believing that they are only sexy if they are young.

WHAT CAN BE DONE ABOUT IT?

Aging is a natural part of the human condition. Premature aging, however, is a combination of heredity, environment, pollution, nutrition, diseases, hormonal imbalances and finally, as I have presented in the preceding section, psychological factors. Sometimes, premature aging cannot be helped, no matter what the circumstances are. On the other hand, if you don't want to grow old in mind and body before your time, consider the following suggestions:

Fix any physical problems

First, have your testosterone level checked. If your doctor feels you are suffering from a low level, he/she may want to supplement it. Second, your doctor might want to prescribe antidepressant medications for clinical depression. Next, have your doctor evaluate and treat any cardiovascular, arthritic or osteoporosis problems. Finally, if ED is due to a physical problem, the use of "hardware" might come into play. Penile injections (Caverject™), penile insertions (MUSE™), vacuum constriction devices, and surgical implants (all of course, if sildenafil [Viagra™] does not work).

Find a partner

If you are older and single due to divorce or the death of your spouse, consider ways of pairing up with a woman. Go to dances, singles groups, matchmaking and dating services. While prostitution is illegal in most parts of the world, that doesn't stop the brisk activity in this field. Perhaps the payment for sex without love, termed the world's oldest profession, is a way of satisfying men's sexual urges and possibly postponing the aging phenomenon. However, practicing safe sex is strongly encouraged if this route is chosen.

Learn self-pleasure

Masturbation has so many curses associated with it, I'm surprised not all men on this planet are walking around deaf, blind, full of warts, retarded or had their penises shrivel up and fall off! How can something that feels so good, does not hurt anyone, is done in private, and as the stand-up comedians say, "you don't have to get dressed up for," be so bad?

In a survey of sexual practices reported in *Redbook* magazine (May 1997), about 94% of males and 70% of females masturbated to orgasm. In addition, 55% of men and 49% of women felt guilty after masturbating.

The simple truth remains that sexual self-pleasure is a harmless but beneficial activity to help maintain the operating integrity of the male sexual apparatus.

Think young

New books are hitting the bookstores monthly on anti-aging programs. A few that combine scientific research with practical advice are:

- *Brain Longevity,* by Darmesh Kalsa Singh, M.D.
- *Stop Aging Now,* by Jean Carper
- *The New Nutrition,* by Michael Colgan, Ph.D.
- *The Super Hormone Promise,* by William Regelson, M.D., and Carol Colman
- *Grow Young with H.G.H.,* by Ronald Klatz, M.D.

When you have finished reading these books, go to other courses, book clubs and adult education classes, in whatever areas of study interest you. Play chess, crossword puzzles, bridge and other mind-stimulating games. Above all, read, read, read.

Act young

Engage in activities that are youthful and energetic, and that require mental agility and physical dexterity. Go hiking, skiing and snowmobiling. Play tennis and piano. Plant a garden, build a deck in the backyard, or tune up your car. Go back to work, or better yet, never retire. Volunteer your expertise and life-long skills to make the world a better place. Plant a fruit tree that takes at least 10 years to bear fruit. Marry a younger woman – you'll see and feel yourself growing younger by the day.

In 1991, George Burns at 95 said, "I can't die, I'm booked to perform at the Palladium in London, England, when I'm 100." Unfortunately, Mr. Burns did not make it to the Palladium. He died in 1994 at the age of 99.

Look young

Looking in the mirror and see a younger "you" staring back helps to slow the aging process. Hair coloring and plastic surgery (facelifts, nose jobs, tummy tucks) and hair transplants may provide results to retard visual aging. Exercise and weight management to firm up and trim down your body will put a spring in your step and maybe some zip in your sex life. Finally, get some new clothes with youthful styles, fabrics and colors. Choose a youthful-looking hairstyle, and get your teeth fixed with caps, braces and bleaching.

REMEMBER THIS

We can't stop the inevitable march of time and the natural process of aging, but we sure can slow it down to a great extent. There is no disease called aging; there are many diseases associated with aging, but some (probably more than you realize) are preventable. It's true that you are only as old (or as young) as you think.

66 Think young, act young, move young, keep having sex no matter how old you are, and you will be a happy man who never has to worry about ED. 99

CLOSING JOKES

Here are a few funny ones from George Burns, who was still happy and vital at the "young" age of 95:

"At my age, I may have to cut down, but I don't stop. I still walk around my pool every day, but instead of going around it twenty times like I used to, I now go around it ten times. I still do my exercises every morning, but instead of thirty minutes, I've cut that to fifteen minutes. It's the same with sex. I only talk about it half as much as I did five years ago."

"Everything that goes up must come down. But there comes a time when not everything that's down can come up."

Q: *Was there any time in your life, Mr. Burns, when you considered yourself oversexed?*
A: *Only once. From March 3, 1914 to June 9, 1981.*

CHAPTER FIVE
Castration Complex

Boy, that guy sure has balls!

Mr. D. sat down to fill out my questionnaire. He was 52, slim, with some gray in his receding hairline. He was very quiet and looked a little sad. The question about how long his erection would last showed that Mr. D. sustained his erections for only five or so minutes. This meant either poor arterial blood supply or excessive venous leakage.

He said that intercourse was difficult and that often he was too soft for penetration. His wife was frustrated and unhappy and it was she who suggested he make this appointment to see me.

Mr. D. did not elaborate much and I had to dig with my questioning to find out the true nature of his problem. He had no diabetes or high blood pressure and was not taking any medications. Right there, I knew Mr. D. could get better erections again with exercise, a better diet and a few vitamin and herbal supplements. But something else was still missing.

I asked Mr. D. how long he had this problem and if something had triggered it. Slowly and almost in a whisper, Mr. D. began to tell me his story.

"About a year and a half ago, the company I was with for 18 years, merged with another larger company and I was offered a 'package.' The numbers were reasonable and I really had no choice, so I took it."

Mr. D. continued, "The money ran out a year later and I couldn't find a decent job. I'm still out of work. My wife had to go to work. She was lucky to get a job at a publishing company and is doing very well there. In fact she just got a promotion. Then about six months ago, it started and just got worse and worse."

I asked Mr. D. how he felt about his wife working. He said he did not feel needed at home anymore and resented his wife for being successful when he himself felt like a failure.

"At first it was okay because we needed the money. Then all of a sudden the roles reversed. I became like a househusband and my wife was the breadwinner. It was as if they cut my balls off. I didn't feel like a man anymore." Testicles are often referred to as "balls" and is a common slang word in our language:

- "They cut my balls off" means they took away your manhood or your strength.
- "I don't have the balls for it" means you are afraid of risk-taking.

Mr. D. had developed what I call the Castration Complex. In the story of Mr. D., you can see where he has lost his masculine role in the marriage and perhaps also his self-image. This type of psychological castration or emasculation is often insidious, progressing in snail-like ways. It can lead to various physical abnormalities, such as depression, chronic fatigue syndrome, chronic pain syndrome, irritable bowel syndrome, and ED.

In this case, the first part of the treatment plan was already in place because Mr. D. acknowledged his feelings. Next, he required an understanding of how feelings are translated into physical bodily responses, such as ED. Finally, Mr. D. would have to attempt some lifestyle and psychological alterations to "get his balls back" and feel like a real man again.

THE LEGACY OF THE 20TH CENTURY – THE DOWNFALL OF MASCULINITY

It has taken a century for the psychological castration of many men to occur. Men today are not acting like men did in their great-great grandfather's time. Students of history will clearly find that the roles of men and women were clearly defined up until the 20th Century. And then things started to happen; good things for women, bad things for men.

When bad situations are not corrected, don't count on them fixing themselves. When a process has begun, it feeds on itself like a spiral – either continuing up or continuing down. That is the position we are faced with in men's health today, leading to the castration complex.

There are four sociological and psychological conditions, which have accounted for the phenomenon of castration complex.

1. Overbearing mothers and ineffective fathers – a bad combination

Some of today's mothers can be overly demanding, overprotective and overbearing. Women's suffrage (in the 1920's) followed by women's liberation (in the 1970's), has given women more power in politics, at parties, at the playground, in PTA meetings and finally, with the purse strings at home. By the same token, some fathers have become weak, passive and ineffective. They are physically, emotionally and spiritually not as strong or strong-willed as Great-Great Grandfather was.

Boys require a strong and vibrant father figure to model after. In addition, with the dramatic rise in the divorce rate over the past 30 years, many boys are left without their dads on a daily basis. Many boys (and girls) must settle for visits from dad every second weekend. Finally, in some segments of society, the father is either a drunkard, in jail, at the track, running around, or never home. This is not a good role model for impressionable young boys.

2. No more risk-taking

It's not the Wild West anymore, and not the jungle either. We no longer make it or break it with our skill, strength, and cunning. Now men are told what to do, how to do it, and when to do it.

The major inventions and explorations of this planet that were done almost exclusively by men are over. Now it is the exploration of the atom or the genetic code, which are the areas equally shared by gifted men and women. The inventions and discoveries of the past that often required a "seat-of-the-pants" type of action and dramatic, life challenging risk-taking are also over.

Take a look at the past for confirmation. When Christopher Columbus sailed westward into the unknown seas of the Atlantic, he was considered either a brave explorer, a fool or even worse, a lunatic. When Galileo went against the Church dogma and claimed that the sun was the center of the solar system, he also faced ridicule, scorn and the risk of death to bring the truth out into the open. The risks today are limited to deciding into which mutual funds we want to invest our retirement savings.

3. Men do not save the day anymore

Men are no longer "knights in shining armor" and women are no longer "damsels in distress." Today's women are independent – financially, socially and sexually. Women are taking self-defense training courses, attending financial planning seminars, going out to dinner and movies with their girlfriends, taking birth control pills to control not getting pregnant or even getting artificially inseminated from a sperm bank when a pregnancy is desired. Who needs a man anymore?

Women are physically larger and taller now than they were at the beginning of this century. She is not the "little woman" anymore. You've heard the slogan, "You've come a long way, baby"? The birth control pill, sexual equality, voting equality and equal employment opportunities have all improved women's self-worth and self-esteem. Unfortunately, in some areas it has been to the detriment of men's self-esteem.

Up until this century, men were in control and in charge of this planet. At the dawn of the Third Millennium, while the roles have not reversed, they have definitely and substantially moved towards an equal footing. Some feminists will argue that the rate of change is too slow and some other feminists have gone one step further. They have become man-haters.

The fact remains that men are no longer, "master of the house," "king of the hill" or "top of the heap."

❝ Men are no longer 'knights in shining armor' and women are no longer 'damsels in distress.' ❞

4. No more guns

The days of the military as we once knew it are over. Okay, the military is not over, but the days of soldiering, infantry and front lines are really what warfare has moved away from. In the First World War, we still had many regiments of cavalry (soldiers on horseback) – not so by the Second World War. There we had a war fought with tanks, air squadrons of fighter-bombers and ending with atomic bombs.

The Vietnam War and Operation Desert Storm have further shown the progression away from combat units, towards missile-launching units. The significance of the demise of the lowly private resides in what men have been doing on this planet for the past two million years.

Since the beginning of time, men were the soldiers, the warriors and the hunters. When wild animals were domesticated, men then became both farmers and soldiers. Now modern farm equipment has decreased the need for large numbers of men to work on the farms. And the laser-guided missiles have reduced the need for large numbers of foot soldiers.

A man's fist, that special icon (do you remember the symbol for Black Power?) was the traditional tool of fighting and war. Over the centuries the fist has gradually been replaced; first by the club, then by the sword and finally, by various rifles. All these weapons, however, still could not escape from the continuous requirement of men and their hands. However, the missile technology changed all that, forever.

It is this restriction of traditional masculine outlets (which just so happens to be all violent outlets), that has become another factor contributing to the modern day castration complex.

What's happening today? Beginning in childhood, most little boys prefer to play with guns and swords. However, many of today's mothers are restricting and limiting the use of these play activities with the excuse being that exposure to violent activities and products will produce violent behavior and violent men. Numerous psychological and sociological studies, however, disprove that argument. But little boys are still denied their "gun-play" just the same.

Other typical masculine experiences where you can find restrictions are:
- Limits placed on viewing boxing matches, Monday Night Football and violent movies.
- Significantly less availability of occupations that require physical and manual labor. Machines, computers and cars and trucks can do a much better job than you can. Isn't there a 200-horsepower engine located under the hood of your car? And one single horse is stronger than you'll ever be!
- Being told it is good to cry (by women of course, not by men). The traditional stoic, "macho," non-complaining attitude is suddenly out of fashion.

Did you hear the joke about the little boy who was running around the house with a toy rifle? His mother scolded him about playing with guns.

"But mother," responded the little boy, "I'm pretending it's a stick."

THE PROMISE OF THE 21ST CENTURY – THE RESURGENCE OF MASCULINITY

Here's the good news. Men can be real men again. But there will have to be some changes *in men and in women*. Let's look at history. For the success of the women's liberation movement, there had to be changes in both women and men – sociologically, emotionally, behaviorally and culturally.

We cannot turn back the clock. We must go forward into the next century. But maybe we can correct and improve some of the detrimental processes that have negatively impacted on men's lives. Did you know that in the past fifty years there has been a progressive and significant reduction in testosterone levels and sperm counts. The future of the entire human race is as stake!

Here are five ways to help bring about this resurgence of masculinity in men's lives.

1. Tell your wife the criticism joke

Question: How do you criticize a man? Answer: You don't! It's funny because it's true. Women (especially wives) need to learn how to criticize a man without "busting his balls." A four-step formula on criticism, which was developed by Spencer Johnson and Ken Blanchard, authors of *The One Minute Manager*, is an effective way of criticizing someone. It works nine out of ten times and only takes one minute to implement.

The four steps are:

1. Be specific
2. Express your feelings
3. Praise
4. Outcome

To make sure that this system works, you must keep the steps in the proper order and perform the criticism in thirty seconds or less. It's a tall order, but practice makes perfect and you can avoid a lot of fighting if correctly done.

Most people are good at criticizing but not so good at being criticized. We call it "constructive criticism" when we criticize, but it becomes "mind your own business" when we become the victims of criticism. Here is a quick and effective four-step program that I developed to help prepare people in handling criticism:

1. Agree where you can
2. Stay calm
3. Look at the other person's point of view (listen and don't speak)
4. Look for a compromise (now give your point of view)

Men need to adapt and develop a more resilient "thicker skin" approach when it comes to being criticized. My four-step program will help. And you never know, you might just learn something about yourself from someone else's "constructive criticism."

2. Be the boss again

Look for ways to take control and be in charge again. Some examples are:

- Take charge of the garden
- Perform all the maintenance on the car (it is acceptable to go to the dealer for the repairs)
- Start a new business where you are The Boss – director, worker and secretary

It is important to realize, however, that along with the glory comes the responsibility. If you start a new business or plant a new garden and it is successful, then you win. If the business fails, then you lose. And there is no one to blame except you.

At work or at home, find some area where you can make yourself indispensable. It requires a lot of thinking and planning, and might require a little time to pass before you become truly indispensable. But you will be surprised at how quickly you take over once you get rolling. Make sure you can handle the self-imposed pressure you just placed on yourself. You might have enough stress on your plate already, so do it methodically and carefully.

3. Take some risks

Here I mean calculated risks. Don't go to the track and put everything down on a long shot. Calculated risks add stress without distress to a man's life. Some examples are skydiving, white-water rafting, mountain climbing and bungee jumping (I personally will never go on that ride, it's just too "risky" for me).

There is a lesson we can learn from seniors who are nearing the end of their days and are asked, "If you could live your life over again, would you make any changes?" In other words, did they have any regrets? All consistently report the same three words, *"Take more risks."*

"I was always cautious. Didn't get into too much trouble. But didn't have much fun either," said one elderly man.

And as one elderly woman lamented, "I wish I would have worn purple more."

4. Grow up, you're not a little boy anymore

Here we are dealing with the concept of maturity – intellectual, emotional, spiritual and marital maturity. Some areas for self-improvement that you can develop are:

- Make mistakes but learn from them
- Learn how to communicate with subordinates, as well as the higher-ups
- Learn how to nurture your family and figure out, "Why do we only hurt the ones we love?"
- Learn the concepts of delegating, compromising and delaying gratification
- Practice the ethic of working smarter, not harder

One way to begin the life-long pursuit of self-improvement is by reading books on business management, personal management, financial management and finally, relationship management.

A few excellent resource books for emotional maturity are:

- *Unlimited Power* and *Awaken the Giant Within,* by Anthony Robbins
- *Psychocybernetics,* by Maxwell Maltz, M.D.
- *Emotional Intelligence,* by Daniel Goleman, Ph.D.
- *The Psychology of Winning,* by Dennis Waitely, Ph.D.
- *Inner Management,* by Ken Blanchard
- All the books by Wayne Dyer, Ph.D., and Deepak Chopra, M.D.

5. Look like a man again, a "he-man"

Get back into sports, especially the heavy contact sports, such as hockey and football. Develop your muscles as only a man can. Pick up a muscle magazine and study the pictures of the men and women. Even though the women don't look like women with all those muscles and the men look all puffed out, it's still important to model your muscular development along the guidelines that are presented in the magazines.

You will see many pictures of fit and strong men with muscles that are defined, not way out of proportion. Muscles that you yourself can attain again. To help you get your body back into shape, the magazines always feature weight-lifting exercise routines for beginners, that everyone (even you and me!) can do.

To start you on your muscle development program, here are four exercises that can be done anywhere, either at home, at work, or even in the car at a red light.

1. **Pull and Push.** Grab your fingers together in front of your chest. Without letting go, try to pull your hands apart. Next, put both palms together and push as hard as you can. Repeat, repeat, repeat.

2. **Fist in the Hand.** Make a fist with your right hand and bring it up to your right shoulder. Now place your left hand around your right fist. Push down with your right hand, straightening your right arm. At the same time, your left hand should resist the downward pressure of your right fist. When your right arm is fully extended, use your left hand to push your right fist back up towards your right shoulder. Only this time the right fist should resist the upward pressure of the left hand.

   Now, bring your left fist to the left shoulder, place your right hand around your left fist and go up and down, alternatively pulling and resisting on your left side. Repeat, repeat, repeat.

3. **Knee bends.** This exercise (squatting up and down) is designed to stimulate blood flow into the penile arteries. Simply do it over and over again. If there is arthritis of the knees, you can lie on your back, bend your knees and lift one leg up in the air. Then put it back down and lift the other leg. Stationary bicycle riding is acceptable, provided enough time is spent on the bike.

   You realize of course that these leg exercises cannot be done in the car. If you are at a stoplight, you can simply squeeze your legs together or tighten you thigh muscles. The idea is to stimulate blood flow to the thighs. Remember, a by-product of this better blood supply to the thighs is more blood to the penile arteries.

4. **Muscle posturing.** Did you ever notice how the power lifters show off their muscles at a competition? They flex specific muscle groups, such as shoulders, biceps, upper back and legs by contracting them for maximum visual effect. The muscle is still contracting and gets a decent workout, which will become noticeable

if it is done long enough. Simply tightening certain muscle areas of the body and holding the contraction until it begins to hurt is a useful muscle strengthening program that can be done anywhere, anytime.

IF MEN WERE STILL MEN

Here's an editorial I submitted to *The Globe and Mail* newspaper in Toronto in June 1998. It was never published in *The Globe*. I think the slant was too pro-male for the women editors of that paper. However, it was quickly snapped up by *The Toronto Daily Star* newspaper and published in its entirety on July 21, 1998. The *Star's* editors changed the title to "If men were still men, they wouldn't need Viagra™." I feel strongly about the message in the editorial and I thought you could benefit from it, so here it is.

Let's Get Something Straight

By Dr. David Saul

What is being done to men these days? Up until 15 years ago, if a man was having erectile dysfunction, he was told it was a psychological problem. Now, a man's ability to achieve and maintain an erection is reduced into a simple "plumbing problem." The truth is that sexual functioning for men is not as clear-cut as "either/or." In the majority of cases, medical conditions causing vascular problems such as diabetes and high blood pressure do require specific treatments – vacuum devices, penile injections and now potent pills, Viagra™ being first off the mark. However, with all the effective treatments available, the placebo effect still achieves equal successes up to thirty per cent of the time!

If that isn't bad enough, the whole erection process itself has been emasculated, by telling men to get in touch with their feelings and to learn to enjoy the pleasures of closeness and cuddling. Wait, it gets worse. When prostate cancer rears its ugly head, the treatments can often require castration (either surgical or via medications) resulting in complete impotence, elimination of all testosterone effects and the end of "manliness" as we know it.

Men, don't listen to the "experts." They are methodically leading you by the hand to accept the conclusion that your days of youthful vigor and vitality are over, and that your time for muscles, power and strength are behind you. You are told to stop competing and stop driving yourself so hard. And to top it off, a few of the proponents of the male menopause (many of whom are women, by the way) remind you that the mentality of "Me Tarzan, you Jane" is not only gone, but good riddance to boot!

For countless generations, men have been the providers and the protectors of society. Men have been the hunters and the warriors. If it wasn't for the strong, powerful, cunning and skillful men in the community, everyone either: lived miserable lives in poverty, were taken into slavery, starved to death or finally, were killed by "the enemy" – other men, wild animals or the weather.

Want to know a secret? Men are physiologically designed to go well into senior years with a minimum decline in physical, mental and sexual capacity. It is a product of adequate testosterone production *programmed to last a lifetime* in the majority of men. Provided of course that certain conditions are met.

- Maintain active muscular development such as, working on the farm, in construction or in the military.
- Maintain the position of decision-maker – head of the household, manager or supervisor at work, elder political statesman of the community.
- Maintain a hunter-gatherer type of nutrition – lots of lean meat or fish, root vegetables and nuts, instead of breads, sugar, cheese and fast foods (french fries).
- Maintain active sexual activity, i.e. every night.

Just because all women are physiologically destined to have an abrupt cessation of fertility and hormonal production in the midlife, it does not mean that men must be forced to endure the same fate. Two things are for certain; death and taxes. To which I will add a third certainty; you cannot change biology. Men are not women. They don't look like women, act like women, think like women or have sex like women. And they should not be forced into a woman's mold at the midlife stage. Perhaps at ninety, men can slow down and release the reigns to the younger bucks. Until then, let men be the men that they were destined to be.

CLOSING JOKE

There was once an older man and his 10-year-old grandson. The grandfather was telling the boy about his erections.

"When I was 20 I had an erection as hard as steel. When I was 40, I could bend it a little. Now that I am 60, I can bend it all the way back."

The grandson thought about what the grandfather had just told him, and said, "Gee – I didn't know that when you get older, your hands get so strong!"

Here's one about a man who confided his erection problems to his friend.

The friend advised, "I've heard that eating rye bread should do the trick."

So the man went to the local baker and asked for $20 worth of rye bread.

"Twenty dollars worth of rye bread," exclaimed the baker. "Why that will make it hard!"

"In that case," said the man excitedly, "Make it $50 worth!"

CHAPTER SIX
Gender Conflict

Are you in or out of the closet?

Mr. E.A. was a 24-year-old man. He complained of intermittent ED and getting soft too soon. Mr. E.A. filled out my ED questionnaire and then I asked a few more detailed questions about his sexual relationship with his girlfriend. I was searching for problems in the relationship that could be contributing factors to Mr. E.A.'s symptoms.

Mr. E.A. sat very politely. Then Mr. E.A. said "Well doctor, my girlfriend is a guy."

Mr. E.A. appeared a little hesitant to discuss his sexual preference and his sexual practices. "I haven't told anyone. I'm quite happy with my partner and he's happy with me as well. My sexual performance difficulties do not interfere with our relationship and my friend is very supportive. In fact, he suggested that I come in here today."

Mr. E.A. continued "I don't want to be like the gay people on the TV sit-coms. I won't come out and tell the world I'm gay."

Then Mr. E.A. told me the real reason why he was having ED.

He said, "I haven't told my parents about my being gay. They don't know anything about Richard, my lover. I don't think they'll ever want to know."

Mr. E.A. was not lying to himself about his gender preferences. He was lying to his parents though, and that likely created a source of conflict for Mr. E.A. which manifested as ED.

To re-establish full sexual functioning, all this man required was the acknowledgement and acceptance, to himself, that his parents (and many other members of his social environment such as other relatives, friends and co-workers) would not be able to handle this truth about himself.

For Mr. E.A. it would have to remain "our little secret." Not all gay men want or need to shout their sexual orientation from the rooftops. And Mr. E.A. was one of those gay men.

Mr. E.B. was a 32-year-old man. He was married and had two children. He described his sex life as "adequate." He loved his wife and did not have premature ejaculation. From time to time over the years of his marriage, Mr. E.B. had some episodes of what he called impotence.

"I couldn't get it up. Nothing was happening to my penis, so we stopped. Two days later, everything was fine again."

I asked what his "real" problem was, since he did not have ED. Transient flaccid times are perfectly normal for all men. A little rest and a little fantasy can usually do the trick at that age. I was concerned that he was over-reacting unnecessarily to a few episodes of softening, like so many men often do.

Mr. E.B. wasn't listening to me. He had something else on his mind and I could see that he wanted to talk about it.

Mr. E.B. began, "When I was a teenager, I felt this attraction for a male teacher. Nothing came of it. I mean, I graduated from high school the next year and never saw him again. I never had a homosexual experience with any man."

Mr. E.B. continued, "But sometimes, I have dreams and fantasies of having sex with another man. In the fantasies, it isn't someone I know. He's kind of faceless. Do you know what I mean?" I nodded yes.

"Doctor. Am I gay?" asked Mr. E.B.

That is a tough question to answer. Many men are gay (homosexual). And many gay men are completely open about their sexual orientation. However, some are still in the closet, and married with a family. Gender conflict is not always clear-cut, as the case study of Mr. E.B. obviously reveals. How does it happen? Why does it happen? What should be done about it, if anything? Can it contribute to ED? That last question is really what is important for the purposes of this book and what this chapter will concentrate on.

66 Homosexuality does not affect the incidence of ED unless there is a gender conflict. 99

Homosexuality does not affect the incidence of ED unless there is a gender conflict. If there are concerns about sexual preference, then the ED will present as difficulties in initiating or establishing an erection. It might also present as lowered libido (sex drive). This is usually the scenario for stress related psychosexual problems.

GENDER CONFLICT – THE CAUSES

Mothers vs. fathers
Similar to the castration complex, a family environment with an ineffectual father and an overbearing mother can lead to gender conflict in the son. A non-existent father as a role model – one who is either in jail, drunk, at the track or on the road – can also contribute to confusion over sexual orientation.

Caught in the act
During early adolescence, embarrassment leading to psychosexual trauma from getting caught in a sex act involving a woman (caught with your pants down) can turn a man off traditional male-female sex – sometimes for good. Similarly with women, being raped or sexually abused can cause permanent emotional scarring affecting sexual enjoyment with a man, often forever.

Genes vs. jeans
Perhaps there is a genetic predisposition to homosexuality and it is not just an environmental or family issue. New research is uncovering genes claimed to be responsible for alcoholism, obesity and depression. These conditions were previously thought to occur solely on a "nurture" not "nature" basis. However, today the jury is still out.

GENDER CONFLICT – THE SOLUTIONS

Try the "shrink" approach
Psychotherapy with a therapist specializing in gender conflicts is definitely helpful. Often the psychotherapeutic approach used is to uncover any psychic trauma from the past. The process involves exposing the trauma; seeing the flawed thinking patterns (from the original time); and beginning the process of reconciliation and release. It is a slow and often painful process but can be very rewarding with significant personal breakthroughs.

THINKING VS. DOING
If a homosexual fantasy turns you on and enhances your heterosexual experiences, perhaps you can try it (in your mind as a fantasy

only) and see what happens. Often it can stay right there and act as a mechanism for increasing sexual fulfillment. There is a danger, however, that fantasy can lead to reality and you can turn towards homosexuality. It's a tough call.

Many women have lesbian sexual fantasies but are not themselves lesbians. Why can't this work for men in the same way? Probably because of the ingrained homophobic fear and disdain many heterosexual men have for homosexual men. Times are changing, however, with tolerance and indifference gradually replacing fear and hatred.

> **❝ In ancient Greek and Roman times, homosexuality was not only accepted but was widely practiced. ❞**

In ancient Greek and Roman times, homosexuality was not only accepted but was widely practiced. But so was the practice of burning witches at the stake in the Middle Ages. Acceptance and fear can both be used to justify or nullify certain actions. However, fear sometimes has a more powerful influence on the actions and beliefs of people.

Maybe you are gay

It might turn out that you actually are gay, and have been living a lie most of your life. It happens often enough. Who's to say what is right and what is wrong? The point to always remember is to try to be happy with your life because you only have one turn on the dance floor called your life.

SOME FINAL THOUGHTS

Suzie Bright, in her book *Suzie Bright's Sexual State of the Union*, presented some non-validated, informal data, which she collected from college students. Responses were from 351 women and 111 men attending Williams, Bryn Mawr, Vassar and Wesleyan colleges. Questionnaires asked about experiences with masturbation, orgasm and sexual attraction to men, women or both.

Concerning the section on attraction or sexual relations with the same or different genders, here are the results:

- 64% of men identified as being attracted to women
- 8% of men identified as being attracted to men
- **29% of men identified as being attracted to both**

- 45% of women identified as being attracted to men
- 12.3% of women identified as being attracted to women
- **43% of women identified as being attracted to both**

Suzie Bright comments on the results: "In their answers, they (men and women) would often say that they hadn't actually had an experience with the same sex, but that they thought about it, fantasized about it, or liked to keep an open mind." She continues, "I thought it was interesting that only 64% of the men identified themselves as straight, period. I don't think I would have gotten that result when *I* was in college – men were much more uptight about bisexuality. No men answered "not sure," but some women did, indicating again that women are less confident in general about what turns them on."

Are these statistics representative of college students in the U.S. today, or an isolated sample? Whatever the answer is, the statistics are still food for thought about potential changes in sexual behaviors and attitudes in today's society.

CLOSING JOKE

Here's one from Milton Berle:
The wife asks her husband, "Do you feel that the sex and excitement have gone out of our marriage?"
The husband replies, "I'll discuss it with you during the next commercial."

Here's one from Rita Rudner:
Why are women wearing perfumes that smell like flowers? I've been wearing a great scent - it's called New Car Interior.

CHAPTER SEVEN

Better Sex Equals A Better Marriage Equals Better Sex...

*Women—
you can't live with them;
you can't live without them!*

Mr. W.A. came in to my office after seeing me on a television interview. It was a feature interview with the subject being lowered testosterone levels in men. On the show I discussed the physiological need men have for more regular sex in order to maintain sexual desire and sexual functioning, and how women can help their men avoid or overcome ED.

Mr. W.A. told me that his wife never liked having sex. "Over the 37 years of our marriage, my wife never once asked me to have sex. I always had to ask for sex. She also refused me many times."

He continued, "When I was younger, I figured that's the way women were and I just accepted it. As long as I was getting sex and not having any trouble getting it up, it was okay. Not great, but still okay."

When I asked Mr. W.A. about his ED he responded with, "In the past couple of years I couldn't get it up. I couldn't get stimulated and I gradually lost all my desire for sex. My wife was happy that she didn't have to bother with sex anymore but I wasn't."

That's when Mr. W.A. told me, "I think I've resented my wife all these years for not being able to at least try to have a good sex life. We don't sleep in the same bed anymore. And we are just getting further and further apart."

Mr. W.B. came in to see me in a real state. He made no attempt to hide his anger. Mr. W.B. said he had just come from another fight with his wife. "All we do now is fight. At the beginning of our marriage 12 years ago, everything was fine. We were happy, we had lots of sex, we hardly fought at all. Then after a few years, she turned into a real bitch."

"Sex became something she would hold over me, like she was doing me a favor or rewarding me for something. I always hated that, then I suppose I started hating her."

Mr. W.B. was in his early forties, without the risk factors of diabetes and high blood pressure. His testosterone was on the low end of normal for his age and he was a non-smoker.

I knew that Mr. W.B. had psychological causes for his ED because he said, "When my wife and I have sex it goes soft soon, and the ejaculation is not that strong anymore. But when I masturbate, I don't have any problems."

Mr. W.C. was 55 with borderline diabetes and high blood pressure. His testosterone level was fair. Mr. W.C. complained about having ED for the past six months.

"I can get an erection all right, but I lose it after five minutes. It's not as hard as it used to be. Usually if I can get it in, we're okay but sometimes it slips out and that's it."

When I asked if he and his wife were still having sex, Mr. W.C. surprised me by saying that they hadn't had sex for almost five years.

"I have a girlfriend," said Mr. W.C. "My wife probably knows about her, but I won't bring it up. I mean, what do you expect? My wife never liked sex, and I had to get it from somewhere."

These three case histories provide graphic examples of many marriages, showing that marriage is not just about sex, communication or the differences between men and women. Marriage is about all three combined! If you can learn to enjoy sex, communicate better and integrate the knowledge of male-female differences, and have all three working for you simultaneously, then you can achieve a marriage which the experts term as one "made in heaven."

Too many couples today are unhappy in their marital and sexual relationships. A closer examination of stress and marriage and the association to sexual functioning will reveal eight sexual turn-offs and two sexual turn-ons. Unfortunately, there are four times as many turn-offs than turn-ons.

I know it doesn't make sense that something as natural as sex should have four times more inhibitors than promoters. But not all marriages are made in heaven. And since it is in the realm of marriage that the majority of adults spend their sexually active years, it behooves us all to maintain a satisfying marital relationship and a satisfying sexual relationship as well.

&&Fix the sex first and you will see the love relationship improve. &&

If you do not have a significant physical cause of your ED such as high blood pressure or diabetes, then look at the turn-offs to see if one matches your marriage. That's where some work has to be done. If you and your wife can achieve some improvement in those particular areas of the marriage, the sex will often fix itself. By the same token, if there is a turn on and you still find ED is present, then there almost certainly is a physical cause for your ED. In these cases, fix the sex first and you will see the love relationship improve.

Turn-offs

- The wife never liked sex at all, and rejected the husband most of the time when he wanted to have sex. Now that he has ED she is happy that she won't be bothered.
- The wife used to like sex, but after her menopause her desire was way down and she was happy not to do it.
- The wife used to like sex, but recently she and her husband have grown apart and she is busy in a new career, and has no time or desire for sex any more.
- The wife used to like sex, but since she was 35 she had a chronic illness (depression, migraines, irregular vaginal bleeding, fibromyalgia, etc.) and always had a physical excuse not to have sex.
- The wife does not want to engage in oral sex with her husband even though she knows that he really would like it.
- The wife never liked sex but was always willing to have it and never rejected nor refused her husband. However, she never initiated sex and acted disinterested all the time.
- The wife was unable physically or mentally to have sex due to serious life-threatening medical illnesses and/or treatments.

- The marriage is on the rocks, with constant fighting and arguing.

Turn-ons

- The new girlfriend (whether the man is married or not) wants to have sex.
- The new wife (or girlfriend) is twenty years younger than the man and wants to have sex.

HOW TO IMPROVE SEX IN MARRIAGE

There is an equation that is very applicable and appropriate for the title of this chapter: *Better sex equals a better marriage equals better sex.*

Sex and marriage go hand in hand. If you improve the marriage, the sex is better. If you enhance or repair the sex, it can also promote a better marriage. Here are some guidelines for improving sex in marriage.

Get back that lovin' feeling

Do you remember the song by the Righteous Brothers, "Bring back that lovin' feeling, wohh, that lovin' feeling"? Try to recall how good you felt at the beginning of your marriage. Get back to the state of mind when you cared only about your partner's happiness. Do you remember how you overlooked faults and mistakes or promptly forgot them? Are you doing that today or are you now a "fault finder"?

> **66 Women crave affection. Romance her more often and she will give you lots of lovin'. 99**

Are you bringing up negative memories of the past for your partner's benefit or for your benefit? Do you care if you end up hurting your partner's feelings with your words or actions? Or do you just act and react without considering the effect on your partner? In other words, are you treating your partner with the respect and consideration that you gave when you were first married?

Here are a couple more suggestions (for men) to bring back that lovin' feeling with your wife:

- Go out on a date with her

- Plan a romantic weekend getaway
- Bring home fresh-cut flowers
- Call her during the day, just to say "Hi"
- Leave a love note on her pillow

Remember, women crave affection. Romance her more often and she will give you lots of lovin'.

Just do it

If there is ED and the marriage or relationship is still good and solid (the penis isn't but the marriage is) here is something you can do to improve the ED and benefit the marriage at the same time. Plan to have sex two times per week for the next two weeks. Schedule the date and the time in advance. Make an appointment with your partner and keep it. Pretend it's like an appointment at work or a lunch date with a friend. Precise scheduling is important to make sure you will be there on time and ready to go.

Of course, by doing this you are eliminating all spontaneity. However, you are also eliminating all potential surprises, misunderstandings and rejections as well. Both you and your partner will be there ready and willing, in mind and body (even though not fully able). *The only rule to observe is that of no intercourse.* You are allowed to do whatever you and your partner feel comfortable with, but under no circumstances should you attempt intercourse.

Also, put all of your attention onto *your* arousal and stimulation, not your wife's. Just for these four times, not forever. Arousal can be in the form of mental fantasies, magazines and videos. Stimulation involves getting back into a focused awareness of your own bodily responses referred to as sensate focusing. Learn what physical actions (by you and your wife) turn you on, turn you off or don't do anything either way.

In this way you will become fully aware of the specific arousal and stimulation techniques which are the necessary prerequisites for good erections – just for you. Then, if and when it gets softer next time, you only have to perform the arousal or stimulation strategies that are guaranteed to get you hard again. And *voila*, you are back in business. There is one more important benefit of practicing sex without intercourse. The anxiety of performance pressure is temporarily removed from your brain. Your sympathetic nervous system is turned off and your parasympathetic nervous system is turned on, resulting in better erections.

Go to the library

Read marriage books. Read sex books. Read, read, read. The information is out there for you to do something right now. Here are a few good books to help you get started:

- *Super Sexual Orgasm,* by Barbara Keesling Ph.D.
- *Sex Tips for Straight Women, from a Gay Guy,* by Dan Anderson and Maggie Berman
- *What You Can Do For Your Marriage, By Yourself,* by Susan Page Ph.D.
- *Light His Fire, Light Her Fire* and *The 10 Second Kiss,* all by Ellen Kriedman Ph.D.
- *The New Male Sexuality,* by Bernard Zilbergeld Ph.D.
- *Why Men Don't Get Enough Sex and Women Don't Get Enough Love,* by Jonathan Kramer and Diane Dunaway
- *Dr. Ruth's Guide to Erotic and Sensuous Pleasures,* by Ruth Westheimer Ph.D. and Louis Lieberman Ph.D.
- *Hot Monogamy,* by Patricia Love Ph.D. and Jo Robinson.
- *How to Stay Lovers For Life,* by Sharyn Wolf.

In the book *What You Can Do For Your Marriage, By Yourself,* Susan Page presents a model for marital therapy which she has found to be extremely effective. I have not run across such a concept in all my research on marital therapies, and you likely will not either. Here goes: stop pointing the finger at your partner to improve or change. Instead, point the finger only at yourself to look at what *you* can do to improve or change (leave your partner out of the equation for now) and thereby help your marital relationship.

Isolated introspection is generally quite difficult to accomplish because of a reflexive action we have to point the finger away from ourselves whenever assigning blame and responsibility for the troubles in our lives. We blame the boss, the teacher, the parent and even the "system" for our misfortunes. In marriage we blame our partners. Dr. Page suggests that you look at specific ways of improving your particular style of communication with your partner; personal perceptions and beliefs about your partner; and patterns of behavior towards your partner.

The difference between this form of marital therapy and traditional therapies is that it only involves one partner – *you*. It is strictly a one-sided form of therapy. But guess what? It sometimes works faster and more effectively than with both parties present. I have used the suggestions from, *What You Can Do For Your Marriage, By Yourself* with many of my patients who had one foot in divorce court. They have since been able to reconcile and recoup their marriages.

The recommendations for marital therapy in Page's book are no different than those found in all the other marital self-help books. The only difference is not saying "If I do this for you, what will you do for me?" Once you get over your finger pointing habit and just examine your role in your predicament, you will change and your marriage will change – both for the better. Remember, a better marriage equals better sex equals better erections equals better sex equals better *erections*... Get the picture?

Creative writing

I have developed a creative writing workbook which I use in my clinic to help patients suffering from chronic fatigue syndrome and fibromyalgia. I designed the writing workbook to act as a catalyst for self-discovery. The program provides specific questions and the patient writes down their personal answers in a confidential manner (not ever to be shared with anyone).

The writing process elicits information from the subconscious mind. The answers are often precisely what the patient needs to work on to improve his/her physical or mental state. Often it seems to my patients as if the tip of the pen has a magical power to provide just the right answer at just the right time.

Here are two variants of the creative writing exercise, which I have adapted to potentially improve any marital discord:

1. Take a piece of full-sized lined paper. Draw a line down the middle of the page. On the left side write the heading "WHAT DO I LIKE ABOUT MY PARTNER?" On the right side write the heading "WHAT DO I DISLIKE ABOUT MY PARTNER?" Now proceed to fill up the page. Begin with either side, it doesn't matter. However, you must try to fill up both columns.

For creative writing to be effective, do not stop to think. Just write. Forget about spelling or grammar. Do not let the pen leave the page. Just write. When you are finished, you might be surprised by a few revelations such as:

- You are carrying around grudges from long ago that are irrelevant today.
- You have been taking your partner for granted regarding certain marital issues.

- You have been overlooking the good or positive qualities of your partner and you have instead been dwelling on the bad or negative qualities.
- *You really do love your partner.*
- You really do not dislike your partner as much as you thought you did.
- Things are not as bad as you thought they were.

Not bad for ten minutes of work, don't you think? Just make sure no one sees your writing page. Never share the information with anyone. I mean it! Otherwise, even before you start, you will enlist and produce your built-in censor and only get the information from your subconscious that you feel is acceptable to share and read to someone. If you share your written work you will miss out on the true purpose of this creative writing exercise, which is self-discovery.

2. Another creative writing exercise you can do if you are finding that your marriage is on the rocks is to get another full-sized sheet of lined paper. At the top of the page, write the heading: MY LIFE WITHOUT MY WIFE (or husband if you are the wife). Now proceed to write and fill up the page. Again, ignore spelling and grammar. Just write. Imagine what your life would be like without your spouse. Are you happy, sad, secure, lonely, sick, healthy, troubled, or bankrupt?

I mentioned this exercise to a woman last year and she told me, after some careful thought, "If I would have done this creative writing before I split up with my husband, I never would have gotten a divorce. I never fully comprehended what was in store for me. I never looked at the big picture because I didn't want to."

She went on, "I'm not any happier now that I am divorced, in fact I'm very unhappy. And my prospects for a better relationship are worse than they were with my ex-husband."

Sometimes the truth does hurt, but it is still important to know it and accept it. And by using this medium of creative writing, you will be able to deal with these truths before any damage occurs. Of course, it is always much easier to fix something before it occurs than to fix it afterwards.

BRING OUT THE WEDDING ALBUM

When you bring out the wedding pictures, what feelings do you tend to have? Most people remember the happy, loving, positive and hopeful times, strictly because all the pictures are happy and loving and positive. You might be feeling negative and resentful towards your spouse at the present time, however, your brain cannot hold onto two images at the same time. Positive or negative, your brain does not care which thoughts it dwells upon.

You cannot physically go forwards and backwards at the same time. Your brain does not care which way you go or which thoughts you have either. It will proceed in the direction of the established thought or action pattern, without judging, just following through.

Looking at the wedding album is a guaranteed way to align the brain into a positive state toward your spouse. Troubles won't seem as bad and achievements will be perceived as much better. You'll be surprised at how fast this exercise can work to bring marital partners closer together and *improve erections* as well. So do yourself a favor, feed your brain with positive images instead of negative ones.

LEARN HOW TO STOP A FIGHT

While it is important to know how to stop a fight (before it turns into a war) of course it is much better to know how to avoid starting a fight in the first place. However, for the majority of marital couples today, fighting (not physical, just verbal) is an inevitable fact of life. Since marriages can be destroyed, not only by the frequency of fighting, but more often by the intensity and the duration of disagreements, here are two sure-fire ways of stopping a fight on a dime, *whenever you choose.*

1. **Hug and Kiss.** The next time you are fighting, both of you, stop right in the middle, give each other a big hug and a kiss, and then get right back into the thick of it. (I know that no one will do it, but let's assume that both of you could stop for an impromptu hug and kiss. What will happen?)

I hope that you will ask yourself, "Since this is the person I love, then why am I saying things that will hurt her? I would never be using words like this to a boss, a customer or a friend."

The answer is, because *you only hurt the one you love*. And sometimes we become accustomed to having a little too much freedom in our speech and behavior when it comes to our spouses. In many marriages, the partners have forgotten that they actually are allowed to say and do anything they want to their partner, provided they follow one rule: *you are **not** allowed to purposely hurt your partner or yourself with your words or actions, at any time*. Following this one rule will go a long way to stopping fights from getting out of hand.

2. **Let Women Cry and Let Men Walk.** What do the majority of women do when a fight has escalated and/or gone on too long and they want it to stop right away? Women cry. The tears start to flow and cannot be contained.

Have you ever wondered why women always feel better after a good cry? It turns out that women have a physiological reflex built into the act of crying which stabilizes their brain chemicals. That's why the tears cannot be stopped once they start to flow, and make women feel much better afterwards.

What do men do when the woman is crying? The majority of men don't know what to do. Should they support their mate, say something, hug her, leave her alone or leave the room? Whatever they do, it always seems to be the wrong thing.

❝ It is going against biology to expect men to cry like women can in the middle of a dispute. ❞

What about the act of crying for men? Crying does not correct the man's neurochemical brain imbalance produced during an argument. Rather, the activities of walking, pacing or sometimes even more aggressive actions, such as throwing or breaking the furniture allows the re-setting of the neurochemical levels in his brain.

When men feel the need to leave (similar to women feeling the need to cry) they usually just get up and go. But what do women say at that point? Often there are angry or sarcastic remarks about him *always* running away from his problems. This just fuels the fire.

Instead, a more appropriate choice of words for a woman to say to her man when he gets up to leave in the middle of a fight would be, "I know you have to go out for a walk to stabilize the neurochemical imbalance in your brain. But when you get back, then we'll talk and work this problem out."

It sounds funny, doesn't it? But without this appreciation of the different physiological responses that men and women have to their frustrations and hurt feelings, a woman could never say those words to her man. However, it is going against biology to expect men to cry like women can in the middle of a dispute.

Men require the freedom to leave when they feel overwhelmed. Upon their return, "cooler heads will prevail" and men are much more willing and able to resolve any differences at that time. And you never know, men might come back from their walk, admit they were wrong and even apologize.

Sex and housework

In a recently published self-help book on improving marriage, called *How to Stay Lovers for Life*, by Sharyn Wolf, the author presents a unique and original program designed to improve your marriage. I had to pinch myself to make sure she was for real, when she unveiled the combined chapter, "Sex life and housework."

Wolf claimed that women's biggest concern in the marriage was the huge amount of housework they were doing and the miniscule amount that hubbies were doing. Women were upset, fights were rampant, marriage counselors were doing a brisk business, and men were not getting enough sex! All because men were not doing enough housework.

The chapter then expands into various solutions for the sex/housework dilemma, which I won't go into detail about here. What I will mention though, and what was discussed in the book are all the things that men do around the house that are often not recognized, recorded or rewarded by women. When Wolf reversed roles with her husband for one week and she did his chores while he did hers, she realized that men were doing many things and simply not talking about them (and not getting any credit for them either). Therefore, it might appear that men are not pulling their weight, when in fact, the opposite is true.

Here are some examples from everyday life and marriage to show how men and women can perhaps stop resenting each other regarding the sex/housework conundrum:

- Men take responsibility for the majority of car maintenance without being asked or thanked.
- Men do almost all the heavy work around the house, garden and garage.

- Men would do more lighter housecleaning and food preparation if they were praised and not criticized for the way they did those things. Too many wives resort to saying, "I may as well do it myself" but then proceed to berate hubby for not doing it after she just finished doing it.

- Men are not mind readers and don't see or smell the mess as readily as women do. If a woman wants her man to do something around the house, all she has to do is ask, and not get upset if he doesn't jump the minute she asks. He will do it, maybe after the ball game is over on television, but he will do it.

- Next time the housework needs to be done, try doing it with both of you dressed only in your underwear, or better still…? If there are kids around, then plan an entertaining activity for them, which will allow you to have a special sexual encounter right after the housework is completed. It's the carrot on the stick principle, but it works just the same. And it tends to produce a pretty stiff carrot.

Marital counseling

Find a good marriage counselor, and /or a sexologist. Make sure the therapy focuses on bringing back that lovin' feeling, and doesn't just give you a forum to criticize and complain. Don't focus solely on what is wrong with the marriage or sex life. Instead, focus on what is right (or was right at one time).

> **66 Forget the bad times and remember why the two of you got married in the first place. 99**

Too many times in marital counseling, the therapist concentrates on getting feelings out on the table, helping couples to develop fair fighting techniques and finally, repetitive discussions of the past difficulties. While improvements of these issues are useful for many couples, in my experience with marital counseling, I have found that it is much easier and often more effective to just start new and fresh. Forget the bad times and remember why the two of you got married in the first place.

Another proven technique used by many marital therapists involves switching roles. In a typical counseling session, the husband and wife would literally exchange chairs and continue their dialogue, only now from the other's point of view. This way a couple can quickly realize and appreciate where he or she might be wrong and where the partner might be right. It is a difficult mechanism to enact properly, as it does require creative playacting, commitment and honesty. However, if it is performed well, it is very effective in improving marriages and sex.

Bring on the massage oil and candlelight

Use massage oil as part of your foreplay rituals. Make sure it is enhanced with "scentual" aromatic oils such as lavender, ylang ylang, sandalwood, citrus and frankincense. You will be amazed at how you feel. These scents may contain chemicals similar to pheromones which go directly through your nostrils into the pleasure centers of your brain. Pheromones are chemicals that appear to act through the sense of smell and have the power to turn you on or turn you off sexually.

Find out which scents turn you on and stick with them. Finding a trustworthy aromatherapist is a good idea to help you get started. In addition, you can use scented candles to set the mood for sex. Try dimming the lights, lighting candles or using a red light bulb. Put some romantic music on the stereo. In other words, you set the stage and your brain gets in gear. This leads to bigger and better things.

Sexy Tidbits

Here are a few additional tidbits that will improve your sex life and marriage:

- *Touchy, feely.* Touch each other frequently. And it does not necessarily have to be in a sexual manner. Simply extending a hand to the lower back or to the shoulder is sufficient. Of course, a quick touch or caress of a buttock or breast, playing "footsie" or some nuzzling behind an ear is nice for both partners.
- *"Are my seams straight?"* The clothes may be different, but the effect is timeless. Taking a queue from the old days of seamed stockings, an updated version can be an amateur, in home strip-tease show or, trying on different brassieres, boxer shorts, etc.

- *Clean up your act.* Enhance what nature gave you. How? Primping by women, via hair styling or coloring, leg and bikini waxing, finger and toenail painting are all ways of reaffirming femininity. And for him, a close shave (especially before sex) and other attentive grooming techniques work as sexual turn-ons for women.

- *Happy birthday to you.* It's easy to be attentive to your partner on his/her birthday. However, you can solidify and enhance your love relationship when you make a day for no special reason, where you treat your partner to the benefits of being "king of the castle" or "queen for a day." On that day, you can go far out of your way for your marital. Remember, more love and more good feelings lead to more sex and better erections.

- *Never go to bed mad.* It's an old rule for successful marriages that you probably heard from grandma – and it works. If you have to stay up very late to talk things through or even to fight it out, just do it. You will likely end up with kissing and making up. And that will lead to you-know-what. As an added benefit, you'll always sleep better after sex.

- *Talk it up.* What do you talk about in bed? Studies on language styles of men and women reveal that men want to hear how big they are and how good they are (penis size and sexual performance). Women want to hear how beautiful they are and how nice their breasts are. And both men and women want to hear it frequently and with passion.

- *Sexy talk.* Talking dirty is not necessarily profane, and can be done within a loving relationship. Sexual talk can be loving talk. And remember, where there is smoke there is fire, and talk can lead to action (sex).

- *Sweet talk.* Bring back your pet names for each other. You know, those endearing names you both used for each other when you were courting or during the early years of your marriage. Just try to feel negative or resentful to someone you are calling "honey bun," "sweetheart," "snookums," or "lover boy" – you can't, your brain won't let you.

- *Listen, listen.* Men and women sometimes speak different languages regarding sex. Wouldn't it be nice to have an interpreter to avoid sexual misunderstandings? In the July 1998 issue of *Cosmopolitan* magazine there is just such an article: "How to use guy-speak to get what you want in bed." She says, "Touch my breasts." He hears, "Grab my nipples as hard as you can and hold on for dear life!" She says, "That's right, keep doing that." He hears, "Keep doing just that (and *only* that) until your tongue/hand/pelvis/mind begins to go numb." She says, "Harder!" He hears, "Faster!" You get the picture?

- *Passionate sounds.* There is one phrase women can use that requires no interpretation: "Put it in real deep!" Most men are relatively quiet during sex, but women often are very vocal in the throes of passion, which just turns men on even more, so women, don't hold back from uttering what you're feeling–it will enhance the experience for both of you.

REMEMBER THIS

We all want a good love relationship and good sex. Some of us want a great love relationship and great sex. You can have whatever level you desire. Just plan a course of action and follow it. Be proactive in making your *whole* life better – not just your sex life. You'll be surprised at how fast your sex life will improve.

❝ You can fix the relationship and you will have better sex… or you can fix the sex and you will have a better relationship. ❞

CLOSING JOKES

Here are two jokes, one is a poke at women and the other takes a swipe at men, just to be fair!

A husband and his wife were celebrating their 40th wedding anniversary. The wife asked where her present was. The husband presented her with an envelope. Inside was a certificate for two burial plots.

The wife asked, "What's this? And for our wedding anniversary no less."

The husband replied that the two of them were not getting any younger and he thought it would be good idea to be prepared. The wife thought about the gesture and accepted it in good faith. The next year at their anniversary, the same thing happened – no present.

"Where's my present?" asked the wife, a little indignant now.

"Why should I get you a present?" replied the husband, "You didn't use the one I gave you last year!"

Here is a true story from Dr. Bernie Siegel, a surgeon in the U.S. who deals with a lot of cancer patients, using mind body approaches. He was talking to a woman with breast cancer after her mastectomy (removal of the breast).

"How are you feeling?" asked Dr. Siegel.

"I feel great," replied the woman. "In fact I've never felt better. And I also divorced my husband."

"What do you mean, you never felt better?" asked the doctor.

"Well," said the woman. "I got rid of a tit and an ass!"

CHAPTER EIGHT

Psychosexual Connections

Thinking about women can turn me on and turn me off.

Mr. T.A. was 27 years old. He was responding to an ad I placed in a new magazine catering to a younger population in downtown Toronto. He was a tall, well-built and handsome young man. I naturally assumed his problem was premature ejaculation (PE), since that was what usually brought younger men in to see me. However, when he filled out my standard question sheet, I was surprised to see that his complaint was severe ED.

Further questioning revealed that he did not have diabetes, a serious illness, medication side-effects or any other physical cause for his ED. Masturbation was fine for Mr. T.A. It was frequent, reliable, and always pleasurable. He did not have any gender conflicts and was never without eligible women.

"The first time we have sex, it always fails me and doesn't get hard enough for intercourse. It's been like this since day one." He continued, "There was one woman I was going out with where it did improve after a few times of lovemaking, but I need an erection that I can count on, first time and every time."

Mr. T.B. was identical in every way to Mr. T.A. except that he was 43 years old. Mr. T.B. had never married, but had many relationships with women over the years. His history and initial testing did not provide any physical causes for his ED. In addition, Mr. T.B.'s reliance on masturbation was not only sufficient for his needs, but his erections while masturbating had been reliable for 30 years.

Mr. T.B. told me "I have all the control I want while I'm masturbating. Two minutes, 10 or 20, whatever I decide. I have no problems with erections when I'm alone. It's with women where I have the problem. It doesn't work. And it's been that way for almost 25 years."

Both Mr. T.B. and Mr. T.A. wanted erections that they could count on to perform on a consistent basis.

Mr. T.B. continued, "I saw a urologist last year. I was offered injections into my penis, and that's not what I want. I heard about the new pill in the magazine that can guarantee erections. Is it available?" he asked. "I'd like to try it."

I knew that Mr. T.B. was referring to the new kid on the block, Viagra™ (sildenafil), which was not available on the market at that particular time (neither was Vasomax™). I also knew that Viagra™ would help this man, but that he might require the pill for erections on a permanent basis, much like the effect sleeping pills have on patients with insomnia.

After a little more time questioning both Mr. T.A. and Mr. T.B. on their sexual histories, I uncovered psychosexual traumatic episodes from their pasts which I felt were contributing to their ED. Some targeted sexual counseling would be necessary to correct these difficulties.

WHAT IS PSYCHOSEXUAL TRAUMA?

Both men and women can suffer from this psychological disorder. In essence, it is identical to any other psychological event that leaves a permanent impact on attitudes or behaviors. A common example is the post-traumatic stress disorder after a car accident. The shock and fear resulting from the accident can cause some people to temporarily avoid driving. Sometimes the effect can be permanent.

Similarly, if you had contact with a dog when you were a young child and you were bitten, almost bitten, or even deathly afraid that you *could* be bitten, then it is possible that psycho-trauma can permanently become embedded in your brain.

**66 *An event that occurred in the past,
even one single time, can be enough
to influence your sex life.* 99**

This can cause you to fear or dislike dogs for the rest of your life. And it only has to happen once to cause a permanent behavior pattern. It can even generalize to cats and other pets!

When it comes to sex and psychosexual trauma, an event that occurred in the past, even one single time, can be enough to influence your sex life to a minor or major degree. For women, this is especially true if there has been any sexual abuse such as incest or rape. Some studies in the U.S. estimate that 35% of all women were sexually abused as little girls. And here is another startling fact: 7% of all little boys suffered sexual abuse.

Sexual abuse is usually in the form of forced sex such as rape. It also encompasses any inappropriate touching or hugging, often from a relative or other family member. Sometimes sexual abuse can be a part of innocent childhood games, such as spin the bottle and other sexual explorative play. Finally, wolf whistles, excessive staring at bosoms and even inappropriate joking can be construed as sexual abuse.

It is a well-recognized fact that the vast majority of all sexual abuse was done by men to girls and women. Often the men were relatives such as fathers or grandfathers. Sometimes, it was a teacher or a coach. There are many acts of sexual impropriety against boys both by women and men (mostly by men), but not nearly to the extent as performed on girls and women.

THE LOVE/SEX DICHOTOMY

Here we have to acknowledge that there are differences between men and women regarding sex and sexual practices. In general, women prefer love and romance with sex. Women tend to bring a lover inside of them and feel as if they are opening themselves up to a man. They feel more vulnerable, passive and accommodating when it comes to sex.

Men, on the other hand, do not necessarily require love when they are having sex. They put themselves into a lover and feel as if they are "doing it" to a woman. Men cannot equate passivity with sex. In fact, they feel in command and in control most of the time they are having sex. Men take the active role in sex. They always have.

The slang phrase "screw you" comes from a sexual connotation of someone actively doing something (unfortunately bad) to someone else. Men want to hear, "You were wonderful (because of your performance during sex)."

When men are teenagers and young adults, the concepts of love, closeness and caring (called a relationship) are not fully developed. The desire for sex, however, is well established long before the commitment of love. To younger men, the sex act itself and not the surroundings of love and romance are far more important and often all-encompassing.

❝ Love/sex immaturity can continue into middle-age for a few men and lead to a mid-life crisis. ❞

As a result, certain sexual practices and attitudes can be established in this formative time and unfortunately, for some men, never mature and evolve properly. This can sometimes lead to sexual troubles early on in life. Two examples are the need for promiscuous sex, or the avoidance of girls that are known not to "put out" or to get involved in sex.

This love/sex immaturity can continue into middle-age for a few men and lead to a mid-life crisis. It has been known that a man around the age of 50 can suddenly divorce his wife of 20 or 30 years in favor of a much younger woman. He can even begin to father another family with this woman. I personally know of two men in this age group who suddenly went out and purchased a big, powerful motorcycle to boot!

SEX AND FANTASY

Men grew up with the understanding that they were making love "to" a woman, more than "with" a woman. In addition, men could make love "without" a woman as frequently as they desired. All they had to do was masturbate.

The sexual arousal and stimulation systems for men are different than for women. Sometimes they are dramatically different. In general, men have a much richer and fuller sexual fantasy life than women do. The early and frequent exposure to masturbation with its prerequisite fantasies helped to establish a solid connection between erections, ejaculations and fantasies.

Take a look at the results of a survey published in *Men's Fitness* magazine in March 1998, from almost 1,400 responses, in answer to the question, "Towards whom do you most often feel sexual attractions?"

- Someone seen but never met   42%
- Regular partner   27%

- Casual acquaintance 27%
- Close friend 25%
- Celebrity 4%

(Many respondents selected more than one answer.)

Women generally do not have a deeply ingrained sexual fantasy repertoire compared to men. They are catching up fast, however, as Nancy Friday proved in her book, *My Secret Garden*, published way back in 1973. It is still a popular book encompassing the entire spectrum of women's sexual fantasies.

Dr. Ruth's Guide to Erotic & Sensuous Pleasures, by the famous Dr. Ruth Westheimer and her co-author Dr. Louis Lieberman, devotes an entire chapter strictly for women on how to develop fantasies. Many studies conducted on University students in the mid-1980's revealed that both men and women of young adult age had similar sexual arousal abilities from the use of sexual fantasies.

In the "Sex is the theme" issue of *Cosmopolitan* magazine (August 1998), 1,000 *Cosmo* readers (mostly younger women) responded to the *Cosmopolitan* sex survey. Here are the results to the question, "Have you *ever* fantasized about having sex with...?"

- A best friend who's a guy 56%
- A professor or teacher 47%
- Your boss 38%
- Someone inappropriately younger 36%
- Someone inappropriately older 36%
- A best friend's boyfriend 34%
- A best friend who's a girl 32%
- A friend's father 23%
- Your work subordinate 22%
- A family member 14%
- A clergy member 10%
- The president 6%

When the use of sexual fantasies are for enhancing arousal, blocking out distractions, intensifying desire and adding variety, as they are for the majority of men (and many women), then the system works just fine. However, troubles can arise in the psychosexual realm when the following occurs:

- The fantasy leads to guilty feelings instead of enhanced sexual arousal.

- The fantasy cannot be contained any longer just in the mind, and is acted out.
- The fantasy leads to sexual obsession.
- The fantasy leads to other mental disturbances such as depression, panic attacks, obsessive-compulsive disorders, etc.
- The fantasy leads to self-destructive or high-risk behaviors.
- The fantasy becomes a coping strategy for alleviating personality problems or other life stresses.

ACTING OUT SEXUAL FANTASIES

The great majority of men keep their fantasies where they belong, *in their heads*. They don't talk about them to other men and certainly not to their female sexual partners. These sexually explicit fantasies are private and are designed to do one job only – maintain sexual arousal for proper sexual functioning. For men, this simply means to: initiate an erection, keep an erection, get an erection back (should it falter) and ejaculate on demand.

When men see an attractive woman walking down the street wearing a short skirt, and yes, with her breasts bouncing, what thoughts are going through their minds?

- Ignore her?
- Fantasize about having a romantic sexual encounter with her?
- Fantasize about having a forced sexual encounter with her against her will?
- Fantasize about having a sexual encounter with their wives or girlfriends?
- Feel the need to masturbate as soon as they are alone?
- Forget the fantasizing and get right down to business by asking her to get together on a date?
- Forget the fantasizing and get right down to business by forcing her to have sex (raping her)?

Surprisingly many men, will often *think* about a forced sexual encounter with the woman, not a romantic interlude. Is this wrong? Well, yes and no.

It is wrong only if thinking leads to actions, since we know that the rate of violent crimes against women and the number of sexual assaults is far too high (one is too many). However, does a sexual thought necessarily lead to an action? The answer for almost all men is an unequivocal *no*.

Therefore, men should not be blamed for their sexual fantasies and thoughts, whatever form they take. The process of thinking is part of brain functioning, and sexual fantasizing is part of normal brain functioning for most men.

When women see a good-looking man walking down the street, do they have similar thoughts? I don't know. I'm not a woman. But, psychological research studies show that most women would size up the man as a potential mate *only if the woman was single*. If she was married, she would usually ignore him and go on her way.

Another question from *Cosmopolitan* (August 1998 issue, 1,000-reader survey) shows this aspect about women quite clearly. Here's how women answered the question, "Do you accept your man for who he is, or while making love, do you occasionally pretend he's somebody else?"

- 50% – Never fantasized about another person while having sex with my partner
- 35% – Occasional wandering mind
- 11% – At least half the time
- 2% – Always think about someone else while in the arms of my lover

Most women would not fantasize about a strange man to the same extent that men are fantasizing about strange women. That's one of the differences between men and women when it comes to sexual arousal. Men are always in a state of arousal, whether they know it or not. It starts during puberty as a direct effect of testosterone on a boy's brain. The sexual arousal system via fantasizing is working continuously (sometimes on over-drive) and can become an ingrained pattern of brain functioning.

66 *Men are always in a state of arousal, whether they know it or not.* 99

What most teenage boys do with this onslaught of sexually arousing thoughts is to tune out the vast majority of them so they can sit still in class at school or throw a ball properly on the field. They also practice while masturbating to fine-tune their fantasies in order to gain control of their erections and ejaculations. In a short time, they have matured from boys with sexual thoughts bombarding their brains all the time into young men with the ability to turn these thoughts on and off at will.

But sometimes things can go wrong. Some men become obsessed with their fantasies. Some act out their fantasies. Some develop more significant mental problems because of their fantasies. Some men feel so guilty about their sexual thoughts or about masturbation that they learn to completely turn off their ability to become sexually aroused through the use of fantasy.

SEX AND GUILT

With Mr. T.A., his first sexual experience at the age of 18 with a young woman was a disaster. He was so nervous and fearful about his performance (from lack of knowledge and experience) that his sympathetic nervous system was working overtime and he could not achieve an erection. However, the episode was so traumatic that his brain had deeply ingrained that first negative experience (like the child being bitten by a dog). Every time he was with a woman after that initial disaster, his normal sexual response was conditioned to be one of ED.

With Mr. T.B., he was caught in some innocent sex exploration with his younger female cousin when he was 12 years old, "You show me yours and I'll show you mine." He was severely reprimanded and punished by his mother for the incident. The ensuing guilt was sufficient enough for him to completely turn off his natural fantasy arousal system.

As an adult when he was sexually involved with a woman, he had no visual arousal ability and felt guilty every time he saw the woman naked. During masturbation, Mr. T.B. did not use a girlie magazine or fantasies. He simply closed his eyes, rubbed his penis and became aware of the pleasurable physical sensations only. It worked every time he was alone but not with a woman.

Another patient of mine, Mr. T.C. became involved with religious fundamentalism in his thirties and willed himself to consciously stop his sexual fantasies because of a newfound guilt. He was very successful with his ability to control his mind and his "evil" thoughts. Unfortunately, he totally turned off his sex drive and developed ED instead.

One more patient of mine was Mr. T.D., who was raised by extremely religious parents. They constantly indoctrinated him to believe that sex was dirty and evil. They were also extremely strict with him and used buttock spanking quite liberally when he was young. When Mr. T.D. grew up and tried to make a life for himself, here is what happened. His marriage failed. He lost his job and went bankrupt. And finally, he became a sexual addict, frequenting prostitutes for sexual gratification. But here's the worst part for Mr. T.D. – he could only achieve an erection and an ejaculation (orgasm), while he was being spanked by the prostitute.

66 *The 'naughty' or 'dirty' thought can be a real spark to light the sexual fire and initiate erections.* 99

These four case histories are examples of some of the troubles that result from psychosexual trauma. Fortunately for men and their erections, psychosexually related difficulties are uncommon. It is also important to note that while there can be ED from psychosexual trauma, the erection system is a very resilient system and not as vulnerable as some of the examples might have portrayed.

Many men (and women) use a little of their own particular sexual prohibition to begin their own personal process of sexual arousal. The 'naughty' or 'dirty' thought can be a real spark to light the sexual fire and initiate erections.

For the vast majority of men (and women) the "naughty" thought never ever leads to sexual problems, emotional dysfunctions or personality disorders. And, for those few but unfortunate men who are severely affected by psychosexual trauma, the intervention of sexual psychotherapy can improve and sometimes reverse the detrimental effects of the traumatic episodes or troubled upbringing.

IS IT EROTICA, ART OR TRASH?

There are some self-help sexology books which refer to the erotic content in some stories and pictures as "trashy." There is no question that much erotic material is done in poor taste. However, many erotic movies, photos and novels can be perceived as sensitive and tasteful. Yet both varieties can still be "erotic."

My questions about the "art" and "trash" dichotomy are:

- Where did the "cheap, trashy" pornography come from?

- Who is looking at and buying this type of pornography?
- Why is there such an abundance of this type of pornography?
- Should we ban it, severely censor it or leave it alone?

Hang in for the answers, they're coming up.

What about other "experts" in the field of sexology? Dr. Patricia Love in her book, *Hot Monogamy*, presents many different ways of increasing the variety in your sex life. According to her, "When you create your own sex games, you can make them as X-rated, R-rated, or "politically correct" as you wish. What's important is that you both agree on the nature of the adventure and the outline of the plot. The goal is to create scenarios that excite both of you."

66 *Isn't it the underlying crudeness, restriction and restraint that charges the sexual fantasy with electricity?* 99

After more discussion on the quality and content of sexual fantasies for both men and women, Dr. Love then provides what she calls "some classic scenarios." They include sexual encounters between:

- Captain on a sailing ship and high-class passenger
- Maid and demanding master
- Strict schoolteacher and naughty student
- School principal and seductive student
- Patient in traction and horny nurse or doctor
- Gardener and rich employer
- Older woman and younger man
- Older man and younger woman

Do you think men might have different, more trashy, fantasies for the above titles than their female partners do? Most would, but you might be surprised to learn that many women's fantasies would not be so far removed from their man's. And don't the titles require some variant of "trash and cheapness"? Isn't it the underlying crudeness, restriction and restraint that charge the sexual fantasy with electricity? Isn't it precisely because the fantasy is "cheap" that it is so appealing and titillating?

Suzie Bright's Sexual State of the Union, by Suzie Bright, is an extremely eye-opening and sometimes eye-popping book about sex, politics, sex, female sexuality, sex, the author's lesbian experiences and did I forget to mention it was about sex?

Here is what Suzie has to say about pornography: "What I perceived was the Pink Elephant of the pornography discussion: what turns you on may not match your artistic values, but it is just as much a part of you, just as real and substantial, as any other aspect. It's not a defect or a weakness, it's your intuitive ability to take all that's unbearable and crazy and unspeakable about life and turn it into juice – eroticism."

She continues, "Don't you dare go around with your nose in the air pretending that anybody's fantasies are low-class or despicable, because without that juice you wouldn't be alive, wouldn't be able to discriminate; you'd be a stranger both to your capacities and your limits. Here's your world without porn – a world without sex, without creation."

In another superb book on men titled *Cracking the Armor*, the author Michael Kaufman poses his riddle of pornography. "Pornography expresses the distorted ways we experience power because it can be, at once, a celebration of eroticism and a statement of men's sexual alienation and loneliness. It is a depiction of sexual energy and of men's domination of others, especially of women."

Kaufman continues, "We should not be surprised that penises are symbols of power in porn, nor that men are portrayed as having the capacity to dominate women, and that women have their own, seductive ways to control men. Nor, that women should be prized for their bodies before their minds, hearts and souls. All these things and more are examples of the very same values and beliefs that permeate patriarchal societies."

In an excellent book about men titled *About Men, Reflections on the Male Experience: from the Column in The New York Times,* edited by Edward Klein and Don Erickson, you will find a powerful essay by Paul Theroux, which he called "The Male Myth." in which he writes, "There is a pathetic sentence in the chapter "Fetishism" in Dr. Norman Cameron's book *Personality Development and Psychopathology*. It goes: 'Fetishists are nearly always men; and their commonest fetish is a woman's shoe.' I cannot read that sentence without thinking that it is just one more awful thing about being a man – and perhaps it is the most important thing to know about us."

There is often a fine line between eroticism and pornography. You must achieve a personal balance that you and your partner find stimulating but not psychologically damaging.

More sexology books that will help you find your own answers regarding the dichotomy between pornography and eroticism are:

- *With Pleasure, Thoughts on the Nature of Human Sexuality,* by Paul Abramson and Steven Pinkerton.

- *The Sexuality of Men,* by Andy Metcalf and Martin Humphries.
- *Sex, Power and Pleasure,* by Mariana Valverde.
- *Slow Motion,* by Lynne Segal.
- *Pleasure and Danger: Exploring Female Sexuality,* by Carol Vance.
- *Secrets of Seduction for Women,* by Brenda Venus.
- *Secrets of Sizzling Sex,* by Cricket Richmond.
- *Mindblowing Sex in the Real World,* by Sari Locker.

PSYCHOSEXUAL RESEARCH

The scientific research on erections and sexual fantasies shows that the use of fantasies for men results in faster, longer-lasting and – possibly more important – larger and firmer erections. Even when penile injections were used for men with severe ED (which usually guarantees an erection), the studies showed bigger erections with the additional use of fantasies.

Two sexology research facilities, one in Rotterdam, the Netherlands and the other in Lisbon, Portugal, both advocate combining visual erotic stimulation plus diagnostic intracavernosal injections (ICI) when evaluating men for ED.

At the Male Reproductive Medicine and Impotency Program in New York, in 1993, after the addition of audio-visual sexual stimulation to ICI, 56.5% of patients experienced significant improvement in their erections. Even more important to the researchers were the 13% of men who showed the attainment of adequate erections when ICI alone failed!

In a study done in Australia in 1991, 66 men were assessed for their level of penile firmness (tumescence) while they engaged in fantasies containing the following: sensual, genital, public sex, sexual dominance-submission, and sexual aggression. The results showed that sexual responses (erections) to any of the sexual fantasies did not correlate to standard tests of non-sexual visual imagery and daydreaming.

The researchers concluded that sexual fantasy may be mediated by processes different from those involved in non-sexual imagery. In other words, a man's personal sexual fantasies do not depict what type of a person he is. Very nice men can have very naughty fantasies.

In another study, also done in Australia in 1990, men who in earlier experiments had been unable to enhance penile tumescence (firmness) to any substantial degree by engaging in erotic fantasy were given two sessions of either sexual imagery training or general imagery training. Only participants in the sexual imagery training program and not in the general imagery program subsequently demonstrated increased physiological and subjective sexual arousal during sexual fantasy. The gains were undiminished at follow-up one month later.

&&Very nice men can have very naughty fantasies. &&

In a meta-analysis review from Kent State University in 1993, nine different studies of subjects were evaluated for penile responsiveness to rape stimuli. The results suggested that the men who were the most sexually aggressive toward women exhibited only *slightly* more rape arousal than control or comparison subjects did. In other words, the "rapists" did not show substantially more arousal and responsiveness (erections) than "normal" men, only slightly more.

Finally, from the University of Georgia (1997) comes further information about sexual arousal to erotic and aggressive stimuli with sexually coercive (sex offenders in prison) and non-coercive (college) men. Using instruments to measure erections, both groups of men viewed audio-visual presentations of sexually explicit material varying in degree of force. The results indicated that the sexually coercive group exhibited more erections than non-coercive controls to scenes involving verbal pressure and verbal threats.

Detailed evaluation of the results, however, revealed that the control (normal) participants were able to inhibit their sexual arousal with the introduction of force cues, but the sex offenders could not. This study further confirms the position that the vast majority of men can turn themselves on or off to varying forms of sexual fantasies, at will.

WHERE DO WE GO FROM HERE?

We've covered a lot of ground in this chapter. I might have opened up a can of worms with the examination of sexual fantasies, pornography and the exploitation of women. The important issues to consider for maintaining erections and male sexual desire are:

- Almost all men have an active sexual fantasy system in place.
- Sexual fantasies can enhance sexual performance.

- Disturbances in fantasies can in turn lead to disturbances in sexual functioning.
- Sexual psychotherapy can improve ED resulting from psychosexual trauma.
- Find out what turns you on, lock onto it in whatever form you need for quick and effective arousal (magazines, videos, garter belts, six-inch high heels?) and develop mental mechanisms to keep the fantasy strictly in your mind. Unless you and your partner decide together to act out any or all of your special fantasies, **never** use them in reality.

CLOSING JOKE

There's the story about the man who went to his Rabbi.
"Rabbi, you have to help me. I don't know what to do."
The Rabbi asked, "What's wrong?"
"It's my wife, all we ever do is fight. Our marriage is a mess."
The Rabbi thought about the problem and said, "I think you should get a divorce."
"But Rabbi," said the man, "I love my wife so much. We've had many wonderful years together."
The Rabbi now said, "So stay together."
"But Rabbi," said the man, "all my wife does is criticize me. I can't stand living with her."
"So get a divorce," said the Rabbi.
"But Rabbi," said the man, "What about my kids? I can't leave my kids."
"So stay together."
"But Rabbi," said the man, "My wife's mother lives with us and she constantly puts me down. It's horrible."
"You know what I think you should do?" asked the Rabbi, "I think you should become a Christian."
"But Rabbi," said the man, "how will that help?"
"It won't," replied the Rabbi, "but you can drive the minister crazy instead of me."

PART TWO
MEN AND SEX:
THE BODY

*Physical and medical
ways to"keep it up"*

CHAPTER ONE

Diabetes And Cholesterol

Partners in crime.

Mr. L.A. was 54 years old. He was a little overweight, but only around the stomach (typical for middle-aged men). The form that Mr. L.A. filled out revealed that for over two years, he had completely lost his erections. His sex life was non-existent, but that was not his worst problem.

Mr. L.A. knew that his ED was due to his diabetes. He was diagnosed with diabetes in his mid-forties.

Mr. L.A. elaborated, "I went on a diet for about a year. It didn't help. Then I went on pills for a couple of years. The diabetes was still not controlled, and I've been on insulin needles for the last five years." He continued, "The sugars are pretty good, but last year the doctor had to split my needles to two times a day."

I knew at that point that Mr. L.A. would require either penile injections, urethral insertions, a vacuum device, surgical implants or the new drug, Viagra™. The other oral preparations, Vasomax™ and apomorphine, were not approved yet.

Mr. L.B. was 47 years old. He had had diabetes for three years.

Mr. L.B. told me, "I've only had to take one pill a day since my diabetes began. The doctor says I'm doing fine. My problem is, I lose the erection in five minutes. It's usually long enough for sex and orgasm, but not always, and many times my erection slips out during intercourse. I think I've developed a habit of purposely coming too fast while I still have my erection. And anyway, five minutes is not enough for my wife."

I knew that Mr. L.B. could be helped (in the long run) with a change in diet, which would likely eliminate his dependence on a diabetes pill, improve his diabetic condition, and possibly eliminate his ED.

Diabetes is responsible for almost 50% of all cases of ED. That's a major chunk! From the recently completed Massachusetts Male Aging Study (MMAS), men with diabetes had an eight-fold increased risk of developing ED. The reverse also held true. Men with ED had a greater chance of developing diabetes.

BLOOD SUGAR AND INSULIN

How is diabetes the "big bad wolf"? The answer lies in two words, sugar and insulin. Let me explain.

The body requires the calories it gets from sugar to provide energy. The body can also metabolize fat for the same purpose. The brain, however, can only utilize sugar (glucose molecules). That is why if the blood sugar drops too low, as with hypoglycemia, it can result in a lightheaded or dizzy feeling. Sometimes it can lead to fainting (syncope).

When you eat a meal, usually more than half the calories are derived from carbohydrates. These carbohydrate foods are classified as starches such as bread, rice, pasta, potatoes and cereal. In addition, all fruits, some vegetables and most beans are largely composed of carbohydrates. All carbohydrates are broken down in the stomach by special enzymes into sugar molecules called glucose.

White bread, white rice, and simple sugars such as table sugar, honey, molasses and maple syrup are all converted into glucose within minutes. The vast majority of vegetables have a high fiber content, extending carbohydrate breakdown and absorption into hours. Fruits have fiber too, but the fiber is not as dense as in vegetables and with their higher water and sugar content, the glucose in fruit is extracted much faster.

Since the brain requires sugar for its proper metabolic functioning, the blood level for sugar must be strictly maintained. Blood sugar control is accomplished by a hormone called insulin. Insulin is manufactured in the pancreas and responds immediately to any glucose rise in the bloodstream. As the sugar rises, the insulin rises accordingly. What insulin does with the glucose essentially is to bring it out of the bloodstream and deposit it into the cells. There the glucose can be utilized and burned for energy or stored for later use as a compound called glycogen.

Glycogen storage sites are found in the liver and in the muscles. The total body storage of glycogen is approximately 450 grams, or one pound. When the storage areas are full (as they usually are), the excess glucose is reconverted and stored as fat (triglycerides) inside the fat cells. There, the cells can burn the fat for heat or for energy. Otherwise the fat is stored for later use, such as missing a meal (fasting) or as in previous centuries during famines from droughts and crop failures.

BLOOD SUGAR, INSULIN AND DIABETES

Are you with me so far? Let's continue. It will get a little more complicated, so please hang in – it's important.

Two problems have arisen in this century:

1. The almost epidemic proportions of Type II Diabetes, also referred to as Maturity Onset Diabetes
2. The rise of Syndrome X, with one major contributing factor being insulin resistance

Let's now examine these two conditions. Over the past 100 years there has been an enormous increase in sugar production and corresponding sugar consumption. Sugar cane and sugar beets have been grown, refined and marketed for use in candies, cakes and coffee at an exponential rate.

This excessive consumption of sugar and sugar-containing foods has led to an increased demand for insulin production from the pancreas. Many people are genetically programmed to handle this high sugar intake with no ill effects. But just as many people are not.

If the islet cells of the pancreas, where insulin is manufactured, become overwhelmed and fall behind in the demand for more insulin, then the blood sugar rises and diabetes can be the consequence. When starchy type foods (starch = carbohydrate = glucose = sugar) are eaten, they are absorbed from the digestive tract into the bloodstream. A little is burned as energy, but without sufficient insulin the vast majority cannot enter the cells, either for metabolism or storage in the form of fat.

In addition, without the proper amount of insulin, the sugar level in the blood cannot be brought down into the normal range, other than to dump it into the urine via the kidneys. In that way, any food that is eaten goes right through the body into the urine and rapid weight loss ensues. That was the process by which thousands of unfortunate diabetics died, up until the first part of this century. In 1921, Banting and Best from Toronto first isolated insulin from a dog's pancreas and a treatment for diabetes was discovered.

ANOTHER PLAYER IN THE BLOOD SUGAR DRAMA

I have spent a considerable amount of time going over the background physiology of glucose and insulin. I will now add one more player to this drama, the hormone glucagon. Also manufactured in the pancreas, glucagon is a hormone that works in an opposite way to insulin. It is designed to raise blood sugar levels should they fall below the minimum level of normal. Glucagon can release glycogen from storage sites in the muscles and the liver. In addition, glucagon has the ability to initiate gluconeogenesis, which means making glucose by breaking down protein (muscle tissue).

When blood sugar levels fall to a point where the brain has an insufficient supply, the production of glucagon is triggered. It also turns off the production of insulin to avoid driving the blood sugar level even lower. Therefore, insulin and glucagon are reciprocal in nature, like a teeter-totter. When one is up the other is down, and vice versa.

WHAT IS SYNDROME X?

Insulin resistance is a sign of modern times. It is a way in which diabetic disease processes are hastened and the destructive effects of diabetes are manifested. Essentially, insulin resistance means that when glucose rises, the corresponding insulin rise is sluggish. This is often due to insulin antibodies preventing the fast action of insulin bringing the sugar level back down to the normal range.

When the blood sugar rises even higher, the pancreas finally responds with an excessive amount of insulin and the high insulin will overshoot the target. While this brings the blood sugar level back down, it suddenly drops too low and a transient hypoglycemia occurs. You end up feeling tired and dizzy with fuzzy, clouded thinking.

Insulin resistance is a hallmark of Syndrome X. Syndrome X is the medical term for a collection of signs and symptoms including:

- High blood sugar levels
- High insulin levels
- Insulin resistance
- High blood cholesterol and triglycerides (fats)
- High LDL (bad cholesterol)
- Low HDL (good cholesterol)
- High blood pressure
- Increased heart attacks and strokes
- Increased maturity-onset diabetes

ERECTION PHYSIOLOGY AND SYNDROME X

What does all this have to do with you, ED and men's health? *Everything*. And all because of Syndrome X. The insulin resistance, high cholesterol and high blood pressure (just to name a few of the major aspects of Syndrome X) all combine to promote ED. They also tend to advance the progression of cardiovascular disease, heart attacks, strokes and poor blood flow to the legs (claudication).

Since this book is mainly concerned with ED, I will not elaborate on heart disease or strokes. However, the cellular and physiological mechanisms for a heart attack and ED are very similar, but not identical.

High cholesterol in the blood causes plaque to build up along the walls of the arteries, narrowing them to the point of complete obstruction. High blood pressure further constricts and narrows the lumen (diameter) of the arteries, reducing blood flow and perfusion.

❝The cellular and physiological mechanisms for a heart attack and ED are very similar, but not identical. ❞

The penile arteries are very small (don't look at the size of your penile veins!) You cannot see the arteries; they are deep within the penis. These arteries have lumens just a little bigger than a pinhead.

If the arteries are tiny to start with, it won't take much cholesterol to block them with plaque build-up. That's the first part of the ED problem. Another problem has to do with the veins draining the blood from the penis. Still a third part involves the muscles and vasodilator (blood vessel expanding) and vasoconstrictor (blood vessel narrowing) chemicals that actually make the erection.

In the flaccid state (soft penis) the veins are wide open and the arteries are almost completely closed. The blood therefore bypasses most of the muscular portion of the penis, allowing only a trickle of blood to enter. During sexual arousal, the arteries open with a rush of blood into the penile muscle bed. This sudden influx of blood squeezes the veins shut, allowing only a minimal amount to escape. The result is a firm erection. (More physiology of erections will be coming. Let's just talk about blood here.)

If the blood is not surging in fast enough, the veins won't close, and the blood simply leaks out. This results in the condition referred to as inadequate vein valves. It feels like a semi-erect penis that is not hard enough for penetration or loses firmness in just a few minutes.

Diabetes, Syndrome X and cholesterol all combine to prevent a sufficient inflow of blood, which results in too rapid a drainage out. The culprits of this leakage are those two words used at the beginning of this chapter, insulin and sugar.

ANATOMY OF AN ERECTION

Here is the detailed version of the anatomy and physiology of an erection. I will explain it in a step by step manner, so that you will clearly understand the entire process.

The penis is composed of three cylinders that run from the head (glans penis) to the base. The base is attached to the pelvic bones for support. Otherwise, the penis would flop around wildly when erect.

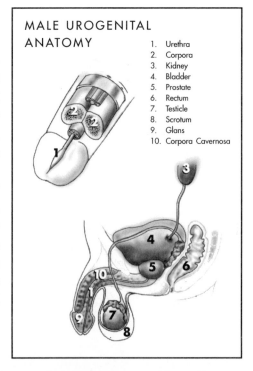

MALE UROGENITAL ANATOMY

1. Urethra
2. Corpora
3. Kidney
4. Bladder
5. Prostate
6. Rectum
7. Testicle
8. Scrotum
9. Glans
10. Corpora Cavernosa

There are two large cylinders called corpora cavernosa on each side and one smaller one called corpora spongiosum on the bottom, with the urethra (the urine tube) running through it. The corpora spongiosum does not get as rigid as the corpora cavernosa. This prevents total obstruction of the urethra and allows for proper ejaculation. Also, the spongiosum continues into the head (glans) of the penis, which is required to remain softer than the shaft of the penis.

Each cylinder has a meshwork or latticework of smooth muscle cells. These cells are different from skeletal muscles in the arms and legs because they are not under voluntary control like arms and legs are. They are innervated (powered up) by involuntary nerve impulses from the spinal chord.

Inside the muscle framework are small sacs called sinusoids lined with special endothelium cells. These cells are very elastic and stretchable. They also secret many chemicals, the main one being nitric oxide, which causes a relaxation of the smooth muscle cells. The endothelial cells can also secrete other substances such as endothelin, which works opposite to nitric oxide to contract the smooth muscle cells.

When the smooth muscles are tight, the sinusoids are shriveled and the penis is flaccid (soft). When the smooth muscles are relaxed, the blood rushes in. The sinusoids will then literally balloon out and fill with blood. They keep on filling, encouraged by nitric oxide and the other vasodilatory (allowing more blood flow) chemicals, until two things happen:

1. The outer covering of the cylinders called the tunica albuginea begins to stretch. This tunica is a tough but elastic fibrous cover. When it is fully stretched it becomes taut like canvas.

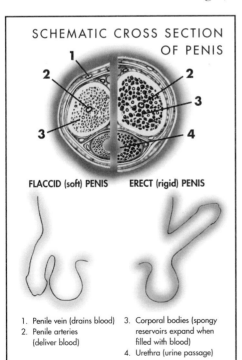

SCHEMATIC CROSS SECTION OF PENIS

1
2
3

2
3
4

FLACCID (soft) PENIS   ERECT (rigid) PENIS

1. Penile vein (drains blood)
2. Penile arteries (deliver blood)
3. Corporal bodies (spongy reservoirs expand when filled with blood)
4. Urethra (urine passage)

2. The full sinusoids now compress the veins against the tunica albuginea by squeezing them in an oblique manner. This effectively cuts out blood loss from the sinusoids.

At this point, there is a trickle of blood in and a trickle out. A firm, long and sustained erection is the end result. The tunica is very important to the erection process, because without it, the sinusoids would over-fill and burst. In addition, if the tunica lost its ability to stretch and tighten, either a small erection would result or just a soft erection due to excessive venous leakage. Finally, scars or damage to the tunica can cause angular or bent erections (Pyronie's disease).

Let me tell you the funny story of the first erection. We have to go back to the time of Adam and Eve in the Garden of Eden for this.

Adam was getting his first ever erection, and he said to Eve, "You better stand back, Eve. Get back. I don't know how big this thing is going to get!!" You can stop laughing now. Let's continue. With detumescence (softening after ejaculation) the nerves send specific signals to contract the smooth muscle cells. This causes tightening and closing of the sinusoids. Also, numerous chemicals are released to further constrict the muscles and sinusoids. As a result the veins no longer have adequate compression and the blood drains out.

The penis can get hard or soft quickly and repeatedly, provided ejaculation has not occurred. After ejaculation, the penis enters a refractory period for 10 minutes to one hour to one day (in older men) before another erection can be achieved.

MORE BAD NEWS

Before I get to the good news describing corrective and preventive strategies, I must conclude this section with more information that might upset you. Please hang in, the good news is on the way.

Blood sugar vs. damage

All therapeutic programs for diabetes have the mandatory prerequisite of stabilizing blood sugar levels. While it is not always easy to achieve, lower and stabilized blood sugar will help to limit the future heart and ED damage caused by a prolongation of Syndrome X. However, getting blood sugar levels down to normal might be too little, too late. Some studies show that the damage is done even before blood sugar goes out of balance.

Don't rely just on insulin

Injections of insulin can be lifesaving and are preferred by most endocrinologists when the pills, called oral hypoglycemics, do not provide sufficient blood sugar control. However, being on insulin or diabetic pills is like driving a car with the shock absorbers set in a middle position all the time. The delicate balance of your natural insulin production is lost forever.

Pills vs. pills

Some pills such as glyburide actually squeeze out any remaining pancreatic insulin, thereby hastening the need for insulin by injection. Other pills such as glucophage help to lower insulin resistance, thereby saving your own insulin and allowing it to work more efficiently. Unfortunately, most doctors prescribe glyburide instead of glucophage.

Diets vs. Syndrome X

High complex carbohydrate diets, advocated by many national food guides, heart programs and even diabetic programs, all perpetuate the problem of Syndrome X and insulin burnout. While times are changing, the information on Syndrome X and its relationship to ED is slow to disseminate among doctors.

More nerve damage

Diabetes also causes severe nerve degeneration. This is seen in fingertips and toes, and also in the nerve endings responsible for the sensitivity of the penis. There are reports that the vagus nerve, a major nerve controlling many automatic heart and stomach functions, can be damaged from diabetes and Syndrome X. Vagus nerve damage has also been implicated in ED.

Don't forget about oxygen

The smooth muscle cells of the sinusoids, which also produce the chemicals driving the relaxation of the sinusoidal blood vessels require a lot of oxygen for proper functioning. With less blood flow, there is less oxygen. With less oxygen, much of the smooth muscle of the sinusoids degenerates and is permanently replaced by scar tissue. These fibrous tissues are unable to contract or relax like the intact smooth muscles can. Therefore, no further erections.

And finally, without blood and oxygen, the endothelial cells also lose their ability to produce enough nitric oxide and other chemicals necessary for proper sustained vasodilatation. Therefore, again no erection.

With repeated daily and nightly erections over the years (men can't help that!) there is oxidative free-radical damage to the lining of the penile arteries. This free-radical damage is just like the damage that occurs with plaque build-up in the arteries of the heart. All the more reason to invest in some antioxidant vitamins and supplements.

ALL IS NOT LOST – HERE'S THE GOOD NEWS

For diabetics like Mr. L.A., who have lost their erections because of permanent damage to the arteries, nerves and sinusoidal smooth muscles, they can at least regain erections by artificial means. The use of penile injections, urethral pellets, vacuum devices, nitric oxide-enhancing pills and other vasodilating pills and surgical implants provide effective, temporary erections. These erections look and feel natural, but are produced by artificial means. Here are seven examples:

1. Viagra™

Viagra™ (sildenafil) was approved for sale in the United States on March 27, 1998. This drug is taken orally and works by blocking the enzyme that breaks down the active metabolite of nitric oxide. More nitric oxide allows more blood flow into the penis and that means better erections. Side effects from Viagra™ include headaches, facial flushing, nausea and some color vision changes, all of which are generally mild and not significant. Viagra™ cannot be used in conjunction with nitrate medications (used in angina therapy), as it can result in severe low blood pressure and a potential heart attack.

Viagra™ by itself will not produce an erection. However, with adequate stimulation (physical and mental), it will allow a normal erection to occur and most importantly, to be maintained. The pill is swallowed an hour or so before sex is planned. But remember, nothing will happen unless you get started (in a physical way).

The benefit of Viagra™ over previous herbal preparations such as Yocon™ (yohimbine) is the high percentage of successful erections (70%) for multiple causes of ED. Viagra™ has been shown to be effective as first–line treatment for ED caused by diabetes, high blood pressure, and neurogenic and psychogenic conditions.

66 Viagra™ has been shown to be effective as first–line treatment for ED caused by diabetes, high blood pressure, and neurogenic and psychogenic conditions. 99

2. Penile injections

Hormones such as prostaglandin E1 (alprostadil) and chemicals such as phentolamine and papavarine cause an immediate surge of blood flow (vasodilatation) into the sinusoids. This compresses the venous outflow and a sustained erection is the result.

These medications can be injected singly, such as Caverject™ (alprostadil), a mixture of two, or all three together. After proper dosing is established, the medication is injected (by the man, not the doctor) directly into the penis halfway down the shaft. Within minutes, a firm erection results which can last for up to one hour or more. Most men with diabetes, prostate cancer, nerve damage or mixed physical and psychological ED find a very good response to injection therapy.

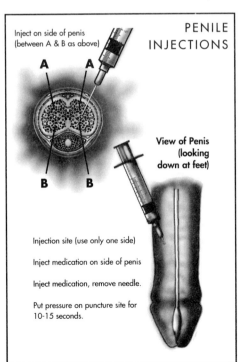

Inject on side of penis
(between A & B as above)

PENILE INJECTIONS

A   A

View of Penis
(looking
down at feet)

B   B

Injection site (use only one side)

Inject medication on side of penis

Inject medication, remove needle.

Put pressure on puncture site for
10-15 seconds.

Studies show high satisfaction rates for penile injections such as with Caverject™, and a high percentage of men stay with the product long-term. Acceptance by the female partners is also very good due to consistency of the erections for intercourse.

Some female partners have become quite adept at injecting their men with the Caverject™ kit for home use.

There is one side effect with this procedure and it is not the pain of the injection, which is hardly noticeable. The side effect to be concerned about is a prolonged erection (priapism) lasting more than four hours. Priapism is a rare occurrence but is treated as a medical emergency to prevent any permanent scarring in the penis.

By the way, the injections have been in use as a standard treatment for profound ED for the past 15 years. Men generally do not feel any pain with the syringe, as the needle has the smallest gauge available.

3. Intraurethral pellets

The product for this procedure is called MUSE™, which stands for Medicated Urethral System for Erections. MUSE™ has been available in the United States (under the trade name Vivus™) for almost one year and has recently been approved for use in Canada. A tiny pellet containing a specific amount of alprostadil, the same vasodilating medication, which is in the penile injections, Caverject™, is inserted by applicator about one and a half inches down the urethra (urine tube) in the penis. After a little massage of the penis, the medication then permeates through the urethra into the sinusoids causing an erection very similar to the type achieved from the injections.

The pellet system can be effective in psychogenic ED but is often used by diabetics, older men, or men with severe heart and circulation problems. These men have a significant plumbing problem but do not relish the injection, vacuum pump or surgical implant route to erections. MUSE™ can be helpful for those men who find Viagra™ ineffective, or for those who have difficulty coordinating the preparation of a syringe and the injection itself, such as those with poor eyesight or Parkinson's disease.

Side effects are mostly similar to the injections, because the active ingredients are the same. They include minor fibrosis or scarring inside the penis, local pain and rarely, priapism. Some men have reported slightly more pain with MUSE™ than Caverject™. This has been attributed to the action of the drug alprostadil migrating through the urethra into the sinusoids.

The likely place for the pellet system will be as second line treatment between Viagra™ (and other oral agents such as Vasomax™) and Caverject™.

4. Vasomax™ (Phentolamine)

Upon completing investigational clinical trials, Vasomax™ (phento-lamine) is likely to soon be approved by the U.S. Federal Drug Administration. This drug acts as a generalized vasodilator allowing for an increase in penile blood flow.

Chemically, Vasomax™ works by blocking a specific receptor of the sympathetic nervous system called the alpha-1 receptor. Blocking the SNS drive promotes a corresponding increase in the parasympathetic nervous system influence. The net effect is better erections.

Initial studies of the drug showed a rapid onset of action and fairly good erection success in the majority of cases assessed. The side effects of dizziness and lower blood pressure were generally mild and rarely resulted in discontinuation of the drug in the clinical trial programs.

Vasomax™ should prove to be a viable alternative to Viagra™ for men who do not respond to it, cannot tolerate some of its side effects or are taking nitrate medications for angina.

5. Apomorphine

As the demand for oral agents such as Viagra™ and Vasomax™ continues to increase, we will probably see an oral form of apomor-phine for ED within one to two years in the U.S. and Canada.

This drug is a derivative of morphine and works directly on the brain by modifying one of the brain's neurochemicals – dopamine. Apomorphine causes an adjustment of dopamine receptors, which in turn increases the sensitivity in special brain neurons to dopamine. This sets the stage for a "promotion" or "initiation" of sexual response.

Early clinical studies showed a steady linear improvement in erec-tion ability and rates of successful intercourse by using increasing dosages of apomorphine. Unfortunately, as the dose of the drug increased so did the major side effect of nausea, which was caused from a central brain effect, not from a stomach problem.

6. Vacuum devices

This is how vacuum devices are used: a large plastic tube is placed over the penis and connected to a hand, battery or electrically oper-ated vacuum pump. The vacuum created in the tube, with the penis inside, draws the penis up into an erect state. Blood rushes into the penis to create a fairly firm erection.

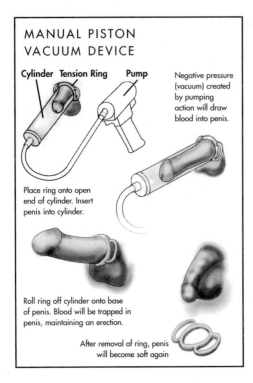

MANUAL PISTON VACUUM DEVICE

Cylinder   Tension Ring   Pump

Negative pressure (vacuum) created by pumping action will draw blood into penis.

Place ring onto open end of cylinder. Insert penis into cylinder.

Roll ring off cylinder onto base of penis. Blood will be trapped in penis, maintaining an erection.

After removal of ring, penis will become soft again

When the tube is removed, an elastic constricting ring is immediately placed at the base of the penis. This acts in place of good vein valves holding the blood within the penis. Intercourse is usually attempted right away, otherwise there is discomfort or bruising from prolonged use of the ring.

7. Surgical implants

These are often used as a final resort, usually by men who have not had success with injections or vacuums. The surgical procedures are costly and have a high rate of complications. But, when all else fails, they can be helpful.

Two kinds of implants are used. One is a silicone-filled cylinder inserted into the penis to create a permanent but shorter erection. The other implant is a two-stage system, beginning with a small sac (acting like a reservoir of fluid) which is inserted into the scrotum. Then, via an implanted tube that runs under the skin from the scrotum to the penis, the fluid is pumped into an awaiting vacant cylinder implanted into the penis. It sounds a little complicated, but when all the parts are properly inserted, the system functions quite well.

What's on the horizon?

For obvious reasons, doctors and patients prefer oral agents as the routes for administering drugs to enhance erections and sexual desire. In addition to pills, nasal sprays and pastes applied in the mouth are being investigated.

Vasoactive (causing increased blood flow) substances are being mixed with special creams and gels which can be rubbed on the penis.

The vasodilating chemical (similar to alprostodil found in Caverject™ and MUSE™) then diffuses through the skin of the penis into the cavernosa and the sinusoids and bingo – a good erection.

One of these chemicals presently being tested in controlled studies is called VIP (Vasoactive Intestinal Peptide). At the August 1998 meeting of the International Society for Impotence Research held in Amsterdam, there were positive reports for erections using the injection route of a combination of VIP and phentolamine mesylate (Invicorp™).

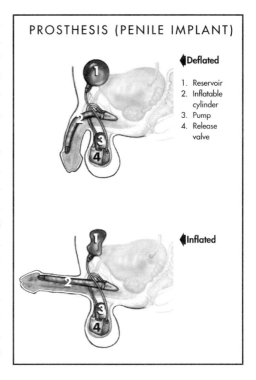

PROSTHESIS (PENILE IMPLANT)

Deflated

1. Reservoir
2. Inflatable cylinder
3. Pump
4. Release valve

Inflated

Also at the meeting, a consensus was circulating about the future use of combination therapies for male erection difficulties. Specialists in the field of male sexuality were envisioning the investigational studies of combining an oral agent with an injection (Caverject™) or with MUSE™. The treatment arsenal for doctors at the conference appeared to be expanding very rapidly. This was acknowledged to be a result of the early success of Viagra™.

From my perspective and from many others who attended the conference, ED is viewed as a multi-factorial medical condition, which must be treated in a holistic, multi-disciplined manner. The effective use of prescription medications (applied through a variety of means) along with natural remedies (vitamins, supplements, nutrition, etc.) also requires a psychological understanding of the patient and his partner in the treatment of ED.

My approach to ED will always be about a man and his penis and not a penis with a man attached to it.

IF IT'S NOT THAT FAR GONE...

Not everyone requires or desires artificial systems to initiate and maintain erections. Just because pills or injections work the vast majority of the time for plumbing-related ED, psychologically related ED or mixed ED, many men tell me they would prefer the "natural" way if possible. *And it is more than possible.*

For patients like Mr. L.B., I have found great success with modification of the diet, an exercise program, vitamin and mineral supplements and some herbal products.

THE DIET

As you might have surmised from the previous introduction on glucose metabolism, the high carbohydrate diets are responsible for the perpetuation of much of diabetes and diabetic related ED.

You might also at this point, be wondering why I am advocating a diet and nutritional program that contradicts the food guides of the low fat diet advocates. The answers come from basic science and physiology. Remember the physiology: increased glucose = increased insulin = fat accumulation = insulin burnout = diabetes = heart disease = ED.

The library is full of books on nutrition written in the past three years that detail the benefits of lower carbohydrate diets. Here is a sample of recent books that are almost all written by M.D.'s and popularized on radio and television:

- *Protein Power,* by Michael Eades, M..D.
- *Enter the Zone,* and *Mastering the Zone,* by Barry Sears, Ph.D.
- *Endocrine Control Diet,* by Calvin Ezrin, M.D.
- *G-Index Diet,* by Richard Poddel, Ph.D.
- *Carbohydrates Addicts Diet,* by Richard Heller, M.D. and Rachel Heller, M.D.
- *Diabetes Solution,* by Richard Bernstein, M.D.

Medical research

Numerous medical studies are confirming the *failure* of the low fat diets in reducing cholesterol levels. In addition, newer medical studies are confirming the *success* of lower carbohydrate diets in reducing cholesterol levels.

Don't take just my word for it

Endocrinologists and other diabetic specialists in increasing numbers are advocating lower carbohydrate diets to their patients with excellent results. Here is an example from a Canadian medical journal, *Parkhurst Exchange* (July/August 1996).

Dr. J.L. Robichoud, a family doctor from Toronto, Ontario, Canada, asks Dr. Gregory Curnew, a cardiologist from McMaster University, this question, "What dietary advice would you offer a 50-year-old male who exercises regularly but can't get his triglycerides down to normal limits?"

Dr. Curnew responds, "In most cases, hypertriglyceridemia responds well to diet and lifestyle changes. Generally, cutting down on the intake of simple sugars, eliminating alcohol, and exercising to maintain an ideal body weight will all help. Make sure to rule out the possibility of subclinical hypothyroidism. If diabetes is present, controlling the blood sugar will help to improve the lipid profile. For an optimal individualized diet program, a consultation with a dietitian can be very helpful. Also, there are many excellent books available to help patients find the most beneficial foods. If necessary, drug therapy to help lower lipids can be added."

Did you see anywhere in the answer, these words: fat, low-fat diet, or saturated fats? I didn't. But I did see the words sugar and diabetes.

Want a little more proof? Here are the endorsements on the book cover for Dr. Bernstein's *Diabetes Solution*:

"Dr. Bernstein has developed a method for the highest control of blood glucose yet achieved, yielding extremely promising results...A major contribution to the field of diabetes treatment."

– Joseph Larner, M.D., Ph.D., Head of the Diabetes-Endocrinology Research Center and Chairman of Pharmacology, University of Virginia.

"Dr. Bernstein's book is written from the unique perspective of someone who has not only lived with Type 1 diabetes for 50 years, but who has expertly translated insights gained from this experience into his medical practice as a diabetes specialist. Please read this book if you really want to be proactive in the lifelong battle against diabetes and its complications."

– John A. Colwell, M.D., Ph.D., past president of The American Diabetes Association.

DIET DO'S AND DONT'S

The meal plan is quite simple. Here are the basic principles:

- Eat a meal three times a day.
- Every meal consists of identical food portions (not identical foods).
- Lower the calories for each meal to around 500 instead of 700 – 1,000.
- Lower the carbohydrate calories from 60% to 40%.
- Raise the protein calories from 20% to 30%.
- Raise the fat calories from 20% to 30% or lower the fat calories from 40% to 30%.

And that's it. Provided of course, you are not diabetic. But if you already are, I would suggest reading Dr. Bernstein's book and following his diet closely. These are some of his guidelines:

- Eliminate all starches: bread, rice, pasta, cereals, potatoes
- Eliminate all fruit and fruit juices
- Eliminate tomatoes and tomato products
- Eliminate all dairy products
- Eliminate all beans and bean products
- Acceptable are proteins from meat, fish, tofu, egg whites
- Acceptable are all vegetables except carrots and corn

As you can see, Dr. Bernstein is much stricter on all carbohydrate containing foods for diabetics. If you have borderline diabetes or a family history of diabetes, I would suggest following the meal plan from Dr. Barry Sears, found in his book *Enter the Zone*: 30% calories from protein, 40% calories from carbohydrate, 30% calories from fat.

A SHORTCUT VERSION OF THE DIET

Here is a handy way I developed of always balancing meals, regardless of the meal or the location. **Eat lunch three times a day.** That's right; lunch for breakfast, lunch for lunch, and lunch for supper. It means the same proportions and the same amounts of foods. But don't worry, there is still adequate variety in your choice of foods comprising carbohydrates, fats and proteins.

Lunch (a meal) consists of:
- A big salad or raw vegetables with olive oil-based dressing
- A scoop of egg, tuna, salmon, chicken, cottage cheese or tofu
- One piece of bread (or half a bagel)
- One fruit
- Four almonds (unless you had the olive oil dressing)

Eat that meal three times a day and you will:
- Lose excess storage fat
- Have more energy
- Eliminate hypoglycemia
- Lower insulin resistance
- Lower total cholesterol
- Raise HDL (good cholesterol)
- Lower LDL (bad cholesterol)

WHY IS PROTEIN IMPORTANT FOR ERECTIONS?

Proteins are composed of 22 amino acid building blocks. Nine of these are essential and must be obtained daily from the diet. The body can manufacture the other 13 amino acids from the nine essential ones.

One amino acid called arginine is not an essential one, but it is the precursor (building block) for nitric oxide. Nitric oxide, as you will recall, is a major chemical along with other prostaglandins responsible for the vasodilatation in the penis, allowing it to fill with blood. Intact endothelium cells of the sinusoids and properly functioning smooth muscle cells can together produce nitric oxide to sustain an erection.

Do you see the problem? Without nitric oxide, there is a poor erection. Without arginine there is insufficient production of nitric oxide. With a low-protein, high-carbohydrate diet, there is a direct lack of arginine and the other amino acids necessary for its synthesis. All the more reason for a good scoop of a protein food with every meal.

VITAMINS, MINERALS AND HERBAL SUPPLEMENTS

What I am about to say requires some qualifications:

First, check with your family doctor before taking *any* supplements or products. There can be drug-to-nutrient/herb interactions and it is important that your family doctor is aware of all the medications you are taking, including vitamins and supplements.

Second, your family doctor might not be up to date with the latest information on nutritional and herbal supplements. You might have to educate yourself and your doctor or provide your doctor with sources of current information on nutritional, supplemental and complementary medical advice.

My suggestion is to read recently published books on the subject. A few books you can get started on includes:

- *Antioxidants, the Real Story* and *The New Nutrition,* both by Michael Colgan, Ph.D.
- *Stop Aging Now,* by Jean Carper
- *The Antioxidant Revolution,* by Kenneth Cooper, M.D.
- *Herbal Prescriptions For Better Health,* by Donald Brown, N.D.
- *Prescription for Nutritional Healing,* by James Balch, M.D.
- *The Complete Medicinal Herbal,* by Penelope Ody
- *The Encyclopedia of Nutritional Supplements,* by Michael Murray, N.D.
- *The Male Herbal,* by James Green

Third, follow your own "gut" feelings about the benefits or risks of supplementation. If it doesn't feel right or you don't experience benefits, re-evaluate your supplement program and do some more research. You do not need *every* vitamin sitting on the shelves of the health food store, *but you will require some.*

Antioxidants

Diabetes causes nerve degeneration. It also promotes clogging of the arteries, reducing blood flow. The antioxidants vitamin C, vitamin E, beta-carotene (provitamin A) and selenium are the main antioxidants that help the blood vessels to resist continuous narrowing and damage caused from free-radical oxidation processes.

Also remember that poor oxygen availability (from poor blood supply) can result in damage to the smooth muscle cells and the endothelial cells in the framework of the sinusoids. The cells can be destroyed and replaced with fibrous tissue. Fibrous tissue cannot stretch or contract and cannot produce nitric oxide. When that happens, it's goodbye erections, hello ED.

Chromium

This trace mineral, which has been reformulated into its compounded form chromium GTF (Glucose Tolerance Factor), has been shown to decrease insulin resistance and allow insulin to work more efficiently. Less insulin fluctuations, lower body fat storage and stable, lowered blood sugar are the result of chromium supplementation.

Medical studies reveal that it is impossible to consume enough food in a day to obtain the required amount of 200 micrograms found in a single pill. Remember, lowered insulin and lowered blood sugar equals bigger erections.

Other herbal products for ED

Two herbal products that I have found to work moderately well for ED with a limited but proven track record in medical studies are Ginkgo biloba and Panax ginseng. Patients requesting an alternative approach (vitamins and herbal products) to ED may want to consider ginkgo if the problem is physically related, and ginseng if the problem is psychologically related.

Ginkgo biloba is made from the leaves of the ginkgo tree. Ginkgo has been shown to be an effective vasodilator for the arteries in the brain. But it can in addition, increase the blood supply to the penile arteries.

Ginseng is made from the roots of the ginseng plant and acts as a stimulant and adaptogen. Ancient Vedic texts from India claim ginseng will "bestow the power of a bull on men both young and old" and "cause an aroused man to exhale fire-like heat."

The specific ginkgo preparations which have been tested in medical studies and have been shown to improve ED are available under the trademarked names Ginkoba™ and Ginkgold™. These patented, standardized extracts of ginkgo biloba contain the most extensively studied ginkgo extract called EGB761.

Ginsana™ is another herbal product that may improve ED. This patented Panax ginseng extract contains the highly concentrated substance G115™ and has an impressive number of clinical studies behind it. There is also a combination preparation of Ginsana™ and Ginkoba™, which uses a standardized extract GK501 under the brand name Gincosan™.

"Ginsana™ *is another herbal product that may improve ED."*

Yet another herbal product, available by prescription, is Yocon™ (yohimbine). It is made from the bark of a tree in Africa and has a long history of effectiveness as an aphrodisiac which can stimulate erections and sexual desire. Medical studies evaluating the effectiveness of yohimbine are mixed, however, with some studies showing quite good responses and others showing no benefit over placebo. The major side effects are nausea, headache and insomnia.

CHOLESTEROL

Diabetes usually goes hand in hand with elevated cholesterol levels. On the other hand, sometimes the two are not in sync. Not yet. My advice is this: don't wait for the two to join forces to give you Syndrome X and a heart attack, ED or all three. Here is what you can do to reduce cholesterol and its potential for ED.

Cholesterol and medication
In the past 10 to 15 years, the pharmaceutical companies have developed effective medications with little or no side effects that reduce elevated cholesterol levels. Many patients and doctors are very happy with the lowered numbers (cholesterol and triglyceride blood levels) resulting from the pills.

However, if low-fat, high-carbohydrate diets are still enforced, then the dosages of the pills will sometimes have to be increased. And Syndrome X will still progress, although slightly delayed. It might be wise to consider switching to a low-carbohydrate diet to considerably lower the risk of Syndrome X and reduce the need for medications.

Cholesterol and diet
Pills for lowering cholesterol levels work by inhibiting an enzyme called HMG CO A Reductase, which is important in controlling the production of cholesterol. This enzyme is stimulated by insulin (related to high-carbohydrate diets) and results in the production of more cholesterol. HMG CO A Reductase is also inhibited by glucagon (related to low-carbohydrate diets), which has the effect of lowering cholesterol.

Eighty percent of the cholesterol in your body is manufactured in the liver and later released into the bloodstream. In all other cells it is made via HMG CO A Reductase. Cholesterol is a major building block for all cell membranes and the majority of hormones produced by the body. Therefore, if the cells cannot synthesize their own cholesterol, they will take it from the bloodstream and reduce blood cholesterol levels in the process.

In addition, if the liver's HMG CO A Reductase activity is reduced, it's the same slowdown for every cell. When that happens from the use of the cholesterol-lowering medications or low-carbohydrate diets (both block HMG CO A Reductase), the cells of the body become more inclined to extract the cholesterol from the bloodstream. This process lowers the blood cholesterol levels very effectively.

On the other hand, if HMG CO A Reductase is stimulated (from a high-carbohydrate diet), then more cholesterol is produced by the liver and also by every cell. Since the cells have now easily made their quota of cholesterol, the excess that is produced by the liver simply stays in the blood vessels. That is, until a portion of it gets deposited along the walls of the arteries as cholesterol plaque.

Finally, when the cells of the body need cholesterol, the active extraction of cholesterol from the blood also helps to lower LDL cholesterol (the bad cholesterol fraction) and raise HDL cholesterol (the good cholesterol fraction).

Lowered carbohydrate diets have been shown to favorably adjust cholesterol levels via the HMG CO A Reductase pathways just the same as the medications. Both pills and diet will work to improve blood flow in the penis, allowing for better erections. One way is free (the diet) and the other is not (the pills). Your choice.

Cholesterol and nutritional supplements

Lecithin, garlic and niacin (Vitamin B3) have all been shown in medical studies to help reduce blood cholesterol when taken in supplement form. Often the use of these supplements, when combined with the dietary changes I have outlined, is sufficient to lower the cholesterol level into the optimal ranges.

66 Lecithin, garlic and niacin (Vitamin B3) have all been shown in medical studies to help reduce blood cholesterol when taken in supplement form. 99

The recommended dose of lecithin is 1,200 mg twice a day. For vitamin B3 it is 50 to 100 mg per day, but be prepared to experience the niacin (B3) "flush" until your body becomes accustomed to its vasodilating effects. Much of the cholesterol-lowering research on garlic was done using an aged garlic extract called Kyolic™ taken in capsule or tablet form.

REMEMBER THIS

Nowhere in the practice of medicine does Benjamin Franklin's wise old saying, "an ounce of prevention is worth a pound of cure" ring more true than for diabetes and cholesterol. These two partners in crime wreak havoc on the vascular system and the damage they cause often results in ED. There are medications and physical treatments presently available to produce an erection. Even nutritional supplements and herbal remedies can help improve male sexual functioning. But more than anything, a healthy diet with a moderate carbohydrate intake is the best way to prevent the damage from diabetes and high cholesterol.

66** Remember when all it took was the smell of her perfume or the look in her eye to get you hard as a rock? You can have that again. **99

CLOSING JOKE

There's the story about the elderly man who is having dinner in an elegant restaurant with a beautiful young woman.

The man secretly tells the waiter to put some herbal sexual stimulant pills (yohimbine) into the soup. When the dinner is delayed for 30 minutes the man complains to the waiter.

The waiter leans down close to the elderly man and whispers to him, "I'm sorry sir, but we are still waiting for the noodles to lie down."

CHAPTER TWO

High Blood Pressure

Keep it stable to keep it up.

I will begin by presenting two case histories for high blood pressure, like I did for diabetes and cholesterol. That is because high blood pressure (hypertension or HPT, the abbreviated medical term) accounts for another large majority of ED problems, at least 25% – 35%. To use a boxing analogy, a one-two punch combination can often result in a knockout. Diabetes and high blood pressure (HPT) together form the medical one-two punch combination, causing up to 75% of all ED cases!

Mr. P.A. was a 68-year-old man with ED. Here is his story.

"I've had high blood pressure for over 10 years now, treated with pills. I go to my doctor regularly for checkups and the pressure is stable," said Mr. P.A.

Mr. P.A. did not have diabetes or cholesterol trouble. He and his wife still had an eager desire for sex and attempted it on a regular basis. Mr. P.A. elaborated, "I can get an erection but it only lasts a couple of minutes, not enough for effective intercourse. It goes soft even after penetration."

Mr. P.A. went on, "A few years ago, I purchased a vacuum pump. It works okay, but I have to hurry up because the ring is painful after about five or six minutes. The whole sex act is too brief for me and my wife."

When I inquired what medications Mr. P.A. was taking to control his HPT, he told me the trade name of a class of drugs referred to as beta blockers. These medications are very effective in controlling and lowering HPT. They also are high on the list of medications that cause ED as a side effect.

I knew right away that by switching Mr. P.A.'s HPT prescription I could alleviate at least 50% of his problem. And did, within only three weeks!

Mr. P.B. was a 50-year-old black man. He gave me a history of HPT and high cholesterol but no diabetes. Mr. P.B. was taking an HPT drug of a different class, called angiotensin-converting enzyme inhibitors (ACE for short), plus an effective cholesterol-lowering pill.

As I expected, Mr. P.B. had normal blood pressure and normal blood lipids (fats). His ED complaint was similar to Mr. P.A.'s.

"It doesn't last long, Doc.," he told me.

Mr. P.B. was embarrassed to discuss his ED problem, but he did not feel good as a man to have ED.

"Can you help me, Doc?" he pleaded.

Mr. P.B. was suffering from poor arterial blood inflow, and excessive venous outflow. As I presented in the previous section on diabetes and cholesterol, damage to the artery system from cholesterol plaque deposition can lead to permanent narrowing of the penile arteries. With less oxygen getting to the smooth muscles of the sinusoids, damage and fibrosis results, and hence ED

While Mr. P.B. had normal blood pressure and cholesterol now, a lot of damage had already been done. I realized he might end up requiring the use of hardware, like Mr. P.A. was doing with the vacuum pump.

"We could also use an injection system for improvement of your ED," I explained to Mr. P.B. (Neither Viagra™ or the other oral preparation Vasomax™ was available at the time I saw Mr. P.B.) "But I would also recommend changing your diet, doing more exercise and taking some vitamins. These changes can sometimes be helpful, but they will not work as fast as the hardware, like the injections for your erections."

I then asked Mr. P.B. if he was prepared to stop smoking. Like all smokers, he wanted to stop, but felt powerless to overcome his nicotine urge. He had a surprised and skeptical look on his face when I told him I could give him a guaranteed strategy to allow him to stop smoking in only two minutes. Guess what? You will be getting that same strategy later on in this chapter.

HPT – THE PROBLEM

In the chapter on psychological problems causing stress and then leading to ED, I presented the model of the sympathetic nervous system (SNS), and the parasympathetic nervous system (PSNS). During the flaccid state of the penis, the SNS is predominating, with tight smooth muscles and closed sinusoids. During the erect state, the PSNS is predominating, with relaxed smooth muscles, opening up the sinusoids and filling with blood. Ejaculation requires the SNS to come into play and the flaccid state returns soon after.

Hypertension (HPT) can be a consequence of prolonged SNS drive and insufficient PSNS response. The hormone adrenaline is responsible for keeping the arteries leading into the penis tightly clamped. In addition, adrenaline is responsible for the contraction of the smooth muscles in the sinusoids.

The other problem whereby HPT causes ED was detailed in the previous chapter on diabetes – clogged, narrow arteries from Syndrome X can cause HPT. Less blood flow from continuous or chronic HPT leads to less oxygenation of the smooth muscles and endothelium of the sinusoids. This promotes their damage, deterioration and replacement with non-functioning fibrous tissue.

And let's not forget smoking. This by itself can cause HPT, although from as yet unknown mechanisms. The end result of diminished blood supply to the heart, brain, legs and penis is nevertheless a dire and often life-threatening condition directly related to smoking.

HPT – THE UNKNOWN

Some studies show that up to 80% of the time the cause of HPT is unknown – not diabetes, cholesterol, obesity, smoking or stress. It is medically termed essential HPT (naturally occurring). Most likely, essential HPT has a genetic component associated with it. It might also turn out to be an adaptive physiological response which is programmed into most humans as part of the aging process. I personally feel that the stress response and the lack of regular heavy exercise are very significant factors contributing to HPT.

HPT – THE CURE

Until we have the definitive answer for the cause of HPT, we must rely on the most effective treatments available. These are in the form of prescription medications, lifestyle modifications, and non-traditional or complementary vitamin, mineral and herbal supplements.

Diet

The nutritional advice for diabetes, cholesterol and Syndrome X is the same advice for HPT. The emphasis for HPT, however, is on weight loss. The loss of excess storage fat (not muscle) will be easily and effortlessly achieved by following the previously outlined dietary formula. Here are two simple facts – lower body fat equals lower blood volume and lower blood volume equals lower blood pressure.

The statistics on middle-aged Baby Boomers reveal that as a group, they are more obese than previous generations were at this time in their lives. A report published in the Journal of the American Medical Association (1997) presented the following disturbing observations: despite a substantial lowering of total fat consumed, in addition to a modest lowering of total calories in the diets of American adults over the past 15 years, average weight gain had increased, not decreased.

The authors of the study concluded that it was the lack of consistent exercise that could be the cause of the resulting net weight gain. I personally feel that it is the emphasis on the higher carbohydrate, lower protein diets that is responsible.

Pills

The use of anti-hypertensive medications will reduce HPT. That is good news for the erections. However, the use of *certain* anti-hypertensive medications, while lowering blood pressure can also directly promote ED. Check the list in the chapter titled "Medication Side Effects" with your doctor to ensure your HPT medications do not interfere with your sex life.

Here is one more fact about HPT pills that can contribute to ED. From my own clinical experience and also confirmed in the medical journals on HPT, there is a significant percentage of patients on HPT medications that have what we call poor compliance – they don't take the pills regularly as prescribed.

HPT commonly does not manifest with any symptoms. Sometimes there are headaches and for many men there is ED, both as a direct effect of HPT. But for the most part HPT is asymptomatic (no symptoms). Many patients end up simply not taking the pills as regularly as they should because they do not feel any difference. The important point to appreciate about HPT and medications is that often the only symptoms your may experience are a heart attack, stroke or ED – after it is too late.

Exercise

There are two kinds of exercise:
1. Aerobic – with oxygen, such as jogging, biking, stair-climbing, swimming, skipping rope and aerobic dancing
2. Anaerobic – without oxygen, such as weight training and isometric resistance exercises

Aerobic exercises help to lower insulin resistance thereby decreasing all the negative aspects of Syndrome X. Aerobic exercises also promote the loss of excess storage fat, lower blood pressure and stronger erections.

My recommendations might sound more demanding than other exercise advocates. I won't apologize. From my clinical experience, substantially more exercise is required for HPT control and ED benefits. I recommend 30 minutes of jogging, biking, swimming, etc., or 60 minutes of continuous walking on a daily basis. That is the key point – on a daily basis.

❝My recommendations for exercise might sound more demanding than other exercise advocates. I won't apologize. ❞

I also recommend doubling that amount on the weekends or one day per week of your choosing, as a bonus exercise. I do not recommend any rest days. If you are sick, you can have a day off. Otherwise, lace up those sneakers!

The secret of a regular aerobic exercise program is in the scheduling. When the time for the exercise is fixed in your mind in advance and you organize your day with aerobic exercise as a priority, it will get done.

Exercise will not be accomplished if you say, "I'll see how I feel," or "Only if I have time available," or "I have to finish everything else first."

There is never enough time in the day to exercise and do all the other activities you have to do, so make the time. Postpone something else if you have to, but not the exercise. Make exercise a mandatory part of your day, like you do for some things such as brushing your teeth and using dental floss. You mean you don't floss or exercise on a regular basis? Well, start today!

One final point to help you. You will rarely feel excited and energized at the beginning of your daily exercise time. Instead, you will likely discomfort and fatigue *during* the exercise. However, you will always feel energized and have a sense of accomplishment <u>after</u> the exercise has been completed.

It has been quoted so often that it has become part of our vocabulary. It's the Nike slogan, "Just do it." I'm sorry for quoting an overused slogan, but nothing says it better.

Smoking

The Massachusetts Male Aging Study (MMAS) revealed data that linked smoking with a two times increased risk of developing ED. MMAS research did not show greater ED incidence with high cholesterol levels, lack of exercise or alcohol use. Smoking leads to many more medical conditions besides ED – lung cancer, emphysema, duodenal ulcers, poor circulation in the legs, and above all coronary artery disease. Stopping smoking (and second-hand exposure as well) is probably the number-one health improvement you can make.

To help you achieve the benefits of smoking cessation, here is my two-minute strategy for stopping smoking. It is guaranteed to work every time, and it never works! Did you hear what I said? It is guaranteed to work every time and it never works. Sounds strange doesn't it? I will explain this smoking paradox, at the end of this section (unless you figure it out yourself before the closing joke).

Say the following two sentences without believing them:
1. "I do not smoke."
2. "I am a non-smoker."

Say them 500 times today, 200 times tomorrow, 100 times the next day, 50 times the fourth day, 25 times the fifth day, and none the sixth day. By the sixth day, you do not have to repeat the two sentences any longer. You now *believe* them.

Here is how the brain's neuro-linguistic mechanism works – your brain cannot say one thing and do something else. Your brain does not like it if you say, "Yes" and shake your head from side to side at the same time. It cannot tolerate you saying, "No" and nodding your head up and down. Try either, and you will find your head going around and around in circles and you don't know what you're saying anymore.

If your brain gets mixed signals, it cannot perform effectively and your body begins to shake. The brain must be in sync with its words and actions. Regarding smoking, if you say, "I do not smoke" and you have a cigarette in one hand and a lighter in the other, one of two things will happen. You will either put the cigarette and lighter away, or you will change your words to "I'll just smoke this one," and proceed to smoke it.

In both cases, your brain said and did the same thing. The brain, however, did not care which behavior; smoking or not smoking, you did, just as long as both the words and the actions were congruent. It's analogous to the soil of a farm producing corn or marijuana. The soil does not care what is planted. If the seeds, water, sun and fertilizer are all present, the soil will produce whatever is planted, without judgement of right or wrong. Your brain is the soil in which you plant the seeds of thought.

And now for the smoking paradox: how does this plan work every time and yet never work? Here's the answer: if you don't do it, it doesn't work, but if you do do it, it works every time. Your choice.

Vitamins, minerals and herbal supplements

Similar to the section on diabetes, cholesterol and ED there is also a little bit of an overlap for the beneficial effects of supplements with both HPT and ED. Once again, I advise checking with your doctor before using any supplements. Here are a few of my nutritional recommendations:

- Antioxidants, the same dose and frequency as for diabetes.
- B-complex vitamins, 50 mg once a day. This supplement has been shown to lower homocysteine blood levels thereby lowering the risk of heart attacks.
- Aged garlic extract (Kyolic™) in capsule or tablet form, two or three a day. Garlic can lower blood pressure as well as cholesterol.
- Calcium and magnesium, in a ratio of 2:1, twice a day lowers blood pressure.

- Salmon oil capsules, 1,000 mg twice a day. Salmon oil, which is rich in omega-3 fatty acids, lowers cholesterol and blood pressure and reduces the likelihood of developing Syndrome X.
- Coenzyme Q10, 50mg, twice a day. This nutrient is especially effective if you suffer from coronary heart disease.

Stress management

Aspects of stress management were presented in earlier chapters. In this section on HPT, I will focus on the reduction of anger. Anger has been strongly correlated with HPT in numerous medical studies over of period of more than 25 years. Some excellent books on the medical problems resulting from anger are:

- *Anger Kills,* and *The Trusting Heart,* by Redford Williams M.D.
- *Treating Type A Behavior – And Your Heart,* by Meyer Friedman, M.D. and Diane Ulmer, R.N., M.S.
- *Type A Behavior and Your Heart,* by Meyer Friedman, M.D. and Ray Rosenman, M.D.

Anger by itself is not a bad thing. It is a necessary emotion built into all human beings as part of our psychological makeup. The main benefit of anger is in the part it plays in the human survival process. Only the *prolonged expression* of anger without sufficient modification or modulation can contribute to HPT, and indirectly result in ED.

> **❝Only the prolonged expression of anger without sufficient modification or modulation can contribute to HPT, and indirectly result in ED. ❞**

Anger is part of the "Type A" personality triad, first identified and described over 25 years ago by two San Francisco cardiologists, Ray Rosenman and Meyer Friedman. "Type A" personality portrays the following personality characteristics:

- Always in a rush, referred to as "Hurry Sickness"
- Extremely competitive and self-centered
- Overt expression of anger, especially hostility

Certain psychologically based therapies have been designed, which can specifically and effectively deal with the hostility component of anger, thereby decreasing HPT and improving ED A few very helpful books dealing exclusively with anger management are:

- *The Dance of Anger,* by Harriet Lerner, Ph.D.
- *Celebrating Anger,* by Angela Jackson
- *Facing the Fire,* by John Lee

The following sections will serve as a condensed version of the anger management skills I teach in my stress management groups.

Anger management strategy #1 – look for the opposite

Anger simply means something is wrong. As described in a previous chapter, making a wrong into a right by looking for a positive but opposite outcome will immediately eliminate anger. In addition, reframing, seeing a different perspective of the problem is another way of reversing what is wrong into something that is right.

Anger management strategy #2 – acceptance

Use the power of acceptance. But be careful. Too often, you may have equated acceptance with agreement. Here is my tried and true formula for acceptance:

- Acceptance does not equal agreement.
- Acceptance does equal awareness.
- Awareness means looking at your point of view *in addition to* another's viewpoint.

Once that is done, the next step is to ask yourself the following two questions:

1. "Do I fully understand what this means to me and to them?"
2. Then ask, "What do I do now?"

And that's it. Just ask the questions and wait for your brain to respond. The correct answers will become clear to you. You might not like what you will find, but remember, your brain does not care if a thought is good for you or bad for you, uplifting or upsetting. A thought is just a thought to your brain. Sometimes the truth will hurt, as when your brain shows you where you went wrong or where you were not so right. Remember, acceptance does not equal agreement, it equals awareness.

Anger management strategy #3 – affirmations

The use of affirmations trains the brain to move into a positive, relaxed and resourceful state. The brain can think either in a positive way or in a negative way. Whichever way you direct your brain, it will follow along. The glass is either half full or half empty. But it's the same glass! If you do not consciously direct your brain, it will proceed with subconscious pathways that are often habitual and negative. The soil on the farm does not decide on its own to grow corn or marijuana. It just grows whatever was planted.

The use of affirmations is simply a way of synchronizing your conscious and subconscious thought processes. Whether you believe in the affirmation or not makes no difference to your brain. Just saying the words, repeatedly will provide you with the benefit you require.

Try saying the following affirmations to yourself the next time you are angry. You might find that very quickly you will be believing and experiencing them.

- "Take it easy."
- "Calm down."
- "It's not so bad."
- "I'll handle it."
- "Everything will work out for the good in the end."

Anger management strategy #4 – finger-pointing

Whenever you are angry with someone for what they said or did, don't point your finger at them and say "You made me angry!" Instead, point your finger at yourself first and say, "I am allowing myself to be angry..." Now point your finger at them and continue "...with what you said (or did)." By using this particular choice of words and order of finger-pointing, you are confirming five things:

1. You decided to be angry in the first place.
2. You decided to continue to stay angry.
3. You are <u>not</u> handing over responsibility for your emotional and behavioral states to another person. Instead, you are telling the other person that you are not their puppet on a string.
4. You are demanding acknowledgement from the other person that they are <u>also</u> involved in this dispute, but confirming that they are not exclusively the culprit.
5. You have the option to discontinue your anger at any time, whenever you wish.

Use this technique the next time you are angry with someone and you will find yourself calming down *right in mid-sentence!* Just like smoking, it works every time and it never works. It works if you do it, but it doesn't work if you don't.

REMEMBER THIS

Some medications are very effective in controlling and lowering high blood pressure, but they are also high on the list of medications that can cause ED as a side effect. You would be surprised at the number of men who regain their erection abilities when I simply switch their HPT medications. Learn to control HPT through diet, exercise and stress management. Be aware of your stress response, especially when it comes to anger. The next time your anger button is pushed, instead of flying off the handle, practice the anger management strategies I have suggested. The rewards will be worth the effort.

66 When you lower your stress response, you increase your ability to produce bigger and better erections. 99

CLOSING JOKES

There's the story about a young bride who fed her husband oysters on their wedding night because she heard they could stimulate sexual functioning.

When her mother asked her the next morning about the oysters' effects, the girl was disappointed and replied, "Well, I fed him a dozen but only nine of them worked."

Then there was the story about the young couple whose relationship had progressed to the stage where they contemplated having sex. The man was concerned that his penis was too small and whether he could satisfy his girlfriend. As a test, when they were alone together and in the dark, he quietly opened his pants, pulled out his penis and put it in her hand.

The girlfriend said, "No thank you darling, you know I don't smoke."

CHAPTER THREE

POST-MI

Getting it back up after your heart attack.

The abbreviation "MI" means myocardial infarction. The common expressions for MI are heart attack or coronary. The predisposing risk factors contributing to heart attacks are Syndrome X, diabetes, HPT, cholesterol, smoking, inadequate exercise and high stress, as discussed in previous chapters. Here, I will describe what happens to men in relation to ED after the heart attack, or post-MI.

Mr. M. came into the office. He was a 49-year-old accountant. He looked 60, with completely gray hair and a hunched back. There was also a sad and fearful expression on his face. Mr. M. told me during the interview, "It's been just over a year since I had my heart attack. They told me it was a massive heart attack and I was lucky to be alive."

Mr. M. continued, "Because I was having continuous chest pain, I had an angioplasty procedure performed. It helped for a while, but the pain continued and now my cardiologist is scheduling me for coronary bypass surgery."

Mr. M. complained of six months of severe ED. "I can't count on it getting up, and it usually goes soft in a few minutes. Anyway, I also lost my desire for sex, and we've only done it maybe a half-dozen times in the past six months."

Then Mr. M. delivered the clincher "To tell you the truth, I'm afraid of getting another heart attack during sex. What a way to go, eh?"

POST-MI - THE BAD NEWS

A weak heart

A heart attack always results in permanent damage to the heart muscle and/or the heart's electrical conduction system. The dead muscle is replaced with scar tissue, but scar tissue can no longer help the healthy heart muscle to pump blood. The larger the area of the MI, the greater the amount of scar tissue.

This weakness in heart action results in less pump pressure. Blood cannot be effectively propelled out from the heart or drawn back through the veins to be pumped out again. Heart failure, with fluid backing up in the lungs and ankles is a common complication of MI. So is ED. The equation is simple – less pump pressure equals more ED.

Medications

Medications referred to as beta blockers are commonly used in the post-MI period. These medications have been conclusively shown to protect the heart from further damage or from a recurrent MI. However, as was previously mentioned, beta blocking medications are notorious for causing ED. A risk/reward assessment for beta blockers must be done by the cardiologist when considering pre-scribing these medications. It is important to note that there are alter-native medications available with no ED side effects.

Hormone changes

Excessive adrenaline production can be a complication of the post-MI experience. This of course results in ED by keeping the smooth muscles of the penile sinusoids tight and constricted. Also, the pro-found stress from an MI can tax the adrenal glands' production of cor-tisone. This can result in a detrimental shift in the adrenaline/corti-sone ratio. ED then becomes another by-product of this hormonal fluctuation. Adrenaline is the main player in the sympathetic nervous system while acetylcholine drives the parasympathetic nervous sys-tem. Too much adrenaline caused by the stress of an MI will lower the PSNS potential – and down go the erections. As described earlier in the book, cortisone is the main player of the parasympathetic ner-vous system, allowing for proper erections.

The stress of the MI itself can also lower blood testosterone levels. Just like gasoline for a car's engine, without enough testosterone the sexual system can also stall and lead to ED. And the physical inactivity often associated with MI further lowers testosterone levels.

Beware of the diet

Like a slow boat to China, the medical dogma continues to advocate high-carbohydrate, low-protein, and very-low-fat diets to MI patients. As I have explained in detail, this diet can exacerbate Syndrome X and cause further ED as well as heart disease.

To reiterate, lower-protein diets have less of the amino acid arginine, which is the precursor to nitric oxide. Without enough nitric oxide, erections are difficult to maintain.

Stress, stress and more stress

We can't get away from this word, can we? Numerous medical studies clearly show that stress is associated with causing primary MI's, recurrent MI's and is also a direct result of the MI. Stress, stress and more stress is always involved in ED (cause and effect) and concurrently in post-MI's in the following ways:

- *$$$*. Many men never fully recover from their MI. Many must retire or accept alternative, lower-paying positions. The concern of the money supply is a significant source of stress to men. An honest dollar for an honest day's work is a motto many men grew up with and receiving reduced financial benefits because of an MI is tough on men, and tough on erections.
- *Fear of next MI.* Like a diagnosis of cancer, fear of the recurrence of a heart attack always haunts the patient. The fear is inescapable. Sleep is disturbed, social life suffers and anxiety becomes a constant companion as the potential for a recurrent MI hangs like a black cloud over men's heads, not to mention interfering with erections.
- *Fear of next MI during sex.* Many men (and women) express this concern, as did Mr. M. in the case example. Although MI's during sexual encounters do occur, the actual incidence rate is far less than patients expect. In truth, medical studies do report a slightly higher recurrence of MI's while engaged in sexual relations. But only with a girlfriend, not with a wife!

Closeness, caressing and the pleasures of intercourse and orgasm for a man are all health-promoting aspects enhancing his chances of recovery from the MI. Sex is also beneficial for prevention of ED as well. It is sad and ironic that so many men abstain from a potentially healing experience because of unfounded fears.

POST-MI – THE GOOD NEWS

Fix each one

Here's the good news. Medical science has advanced very rapidly during my 22 years of practicing family medicine. Post-MI death rates have been substantially reduced due to the discovery of many cardiac medications and treatments. Your cardiologist is well aware of the necessary follow up for post-MI conditions, so I suggest that you consider your cardiologist's advice very carefully. If coronary bypass is suggested, then plan on it. If you are advised to stop smoking, stop. If you are prescribed medications, take them, but if you develop ED while on the pills, ask your doctor for other medications.

Attend cardiac support groups to deal with stress issues and to develop coping skills. Sometimes antidepressant medications or psychiatric intervention or both are required. Get involved in an exercise program, preferably one linked to a cardiac rehabilitation program. This helps stabilize the hormones adrenaline, cortisone and testosterone. Consider a lower-carbohydrate diet (previously described in detail) to maintain lower blood sugar and cholesterol levels.

Vitamin, mineral and herbal supplements

Under your doctor's supervision, consider taking antioxidants, calcium, magnesium, and possibly chromium. CoQ10 is widely used in Japan and Europe for heart and coronary artery disease. Calcium and magnesium supplements have been shown to be beneficial for high blood pressure. Make sure your potassium levels are checked frequently.

Vitamin E at a dose of 400 IU once or twice a day is commonly prescribed now by cardiologists for the prevention of MI and the treatment of post-MI.

Ginkgo biloba in double-blind, randomized medical studies shows benefits for memory loss and Alzheimer's disease due to its vasodilatory effects (better blood flow). While it is not contraindicated for post-MI, it does not have complete endorsement from the cardiologists as yet, but since the side-effect profile is so favorable it is worth taking on a regular basis in the post-MI period. Standardized extracts of Ginkgo biloba, EGB761 (available as Ginkoba™ and Ginkgold™) are recognized as the most effective sources of Ginkgo biloba.

Ginsana™ has also been the subject of several medical studies which have verified its ability to increase energy often lacking in the post-MI period. Like Ginkoba™ and Ginkgold™, Ginsana™ is not specific for heart problems but could be a source of extra energy, especially since the medications can cause extreme fatigue as a side effect. Discuss the possible use of these two herbal supplements with your doctor. Your local health food store can provide you with information to take with you on your next doctor's appointment.

REMEMBER THIS

It's extremely important to get yourself *and* your penis back up after a heart attack. I know that your life will be changed forever after your MI. Maybe that's not such a bad thing. It may just be what you needed to turn your life around and start to take better care of yourself and pay attention to those things that impact on your heart's health, such as nutrition, exercise, smoking and stress management. In this way, you can start to heal the damage caused by your heart attack and begin a new life.

"Embrace a lifestyle that prevents the recurrence of a heart attack."

CLOSING JOKE

A psychologist was showing a male patient some inkblots to help assess his state of mind.
"What do you see in this one?" asked the doctor.
"I see a naked woman," replied the patient.
The doctor showed him another inkblot and asked what he saw in it.
"Here I see a man and a women having sex," replied the man.
The doctor showed the patient one more inkblot.
"This one, let me see, I would say that I see an orgy going on."
The doctor gave the man his diagnosis. "Your problem is that you have sex on your mind all the time."
"But doctor," said the patient, "you're the one showing me all the dirty pictures."

Thomas Szasz, the American psychiatrist said this about masturbation:
"Masturbation is a primary sexual activity of mankind. In the nineteenth century, it was a disease; in the twentieth century, it's a cure."

Ann Landers had this observation:
"Women complain about sex more than men. Their gripes fall into two major categories - not enough, or too much."

Zsa Zsa Gabor said:
"I want a man who's kind and understanding. Is that too much to ask of a millionaire?"

CHAPTER FOUR

Male Menopause

It's real and it's preventable.

Mr. I.A. was actually my very first case of ED, and it was because of him that I began to research male sexual dysfunctions and subsequently developed my interest in men's health and the treatment of ED. Mr. I.A. was 47 years old. His initial complaint was a lack of sex drive. Medically this is termed loss of libido.

"I just lost my interest in sex. I could do without it, if you know what I mean. Fantasies didn't do anything for me anymore. Looking at beautiful women was not exciting. It was as if I was turned into a eunuch."

After I researched the medical journals and textbooks on male menopause (the media term) or lowered testosterone levels (the medical term), I was able to get a much clearer and detailed history from Mr. I.A.

"Now that you ask, doctor, I have been extremely fatigued in the past year. I have no energy or stamina. I have so much trouble getting through a tennis match that I just don't play it anymore. And yes, my wife and I have been getting into more fights and arguments lately. I seem to be very irritable with my kids, too."

Mr. I.A.'s blood tests revealed a borderline diabetic tendency, also indicative of lowered testosterone. His blood pressure was normal, as was his thyroid level. Two blood tests for testosterone came back very low and confirmed a likely diagnosis of male menopause – testosterone deficiency.

Mr. I.B. presented with another interesting case of ED. Mr. I.B. was a 51-year-old man with a three-year history of depression which was unresponsive to the standard dosage of antidepressant medications. His psychiatrist tried different types of drugs to help alleviate this severe depression. An increased amount of antidepressant medications still did not produce the desired lift in mood and well-being, but instead resulted in loss of sex drive, ED and difficulty ejaculating. The attending psychiatrist then referred Mr. I.B. to me for a consultation.

Mr. I.B. did not have the usual risk factors for ED, such as diabetes or high blood pressure. He did, however, have a low testosterone blood level. He also was suffering from medication-induced ED Within three weeks, I was able to gradually taper Mr. I.B.'s antidepressant medications down to nil and substituted testosterone undecanoate (Andriol™) oral tablets in their place.

What happened to Mr. I.B.? Not only was his depression gone, but his sexual functioning had returned to normal without any difficulties. And I am not joking – three weeks was all it took to eliminate the depression and reverse the medication's ED side effect.

These are exciting times in medicine today. Study after study is outlining the benefit of testosterone replacement, instead of or sometimes in addition to, antidepressant medications for middle-aged and elderly men who have symptoms of depression. Results are often dramatic as the case of Mr. I.B. clearly pointed out.

Mr. I.C. was a special case, which I considered to be a real diagnostic challenge and one that required a full history to help establish the diagnosis. He was 26 years old with a story of ED that was typical for a diabetic or an elderly man.

Mr. I.C. told me that he went to another men's ED clinic prior to seeing me and was offered injection therapy or vacuum devices. He declined both of these hardware items and came in to my clinic after watching me on a television interview.

First, his erections took a few minutes to react instead of the normal few seconds for other men his age. Second, he would lose the rigidity after five minutes and would often be unable to complete an act of sexual intercourse because his penis would slip out of his partner's vagina. It was very unusual for a man as young as Mr. I.C. to have such significant ED complaints.

More questioning revealed the following important information: "I was married at age 22 but divorced last year. The erection problem was very rare at the beginning of the marriage but it occurred more frequently about a year before our divorce."

I assumed that Mr. I.C. was having marital troubles and that stress was likely the cause of his ED. But I was wrong.

Mr. I.C. elaborated, "My wife had an affair and one day came home to tell me she wanted out of our marriage. As far as I was concerned, I thought our marriage was fine. I was shocked and hurt and soon after that we got a divorce. But I was having erection trouble from time to time before my wife told me that she'd had an affair. Since the divorce I have had two girl friends and the erections were still not good."

Again I assumed the ED was related to the psychosexual traumatic stress from the affair and the divorce, but once more I was wrong.

Two and two did not add up to four because Mr. I.C. had ED *before* the knowledge of the affair or the divorce. Something was missing. Then I asked Mr. I.C. about his work.

"I'm a policeman and my wife is also a cop. We worked shift work but because we were also on different police forces, it meant our schedules always conflicted. It was almost impossible to find a time for sex that coincided with our shift work schedules."

That's when Mr. I.C. gave me the missing piece of the puzzle.

"And anyway, with our shift work I was always too tired to have sex. Sometimes I only get four hours of sleep because my body has trouble adjusting to the changing shift times of the police force."

The puzzle piece of course, was sleep deprivation. It was causing a lowering of Mr. I.C.'s testosterone level below the minimum requirement of testosterone necessary for his sexual functioning.

Blood tests confirmed my suspicion of a significant lowering of testosterone during times of sleep deprivation for Mr. I.C. Some guidance on sleep-inducing techniques: relaxation and meditation, blackout window blinds, and certain foods before retiring, all helped Mr. I.C. to bring up his testosterone *naturally* to levels that allowed for consistent sexual functioning.

MENOPAUSE – A MISNOMER

Technically, there really is no such thing as "male menopause." Men don't have monthly menses or periods like women do, so they cannot have a menopause. But there is a condition that does affect men, scientifically termed *hypogonadotrophic hypogonadism*. Other descriptive terms used are: andropause, viropause or testosterone deficiency syndrome. These different labels essentially mean a loss off androgens, which are the most dominant sex hormones in men.

Some excellent books on this subject of male menopause are:
- *The Male Sexual Machine,* by Kenneth Purvis, M.D., Ph.D.
- *Hormonal Health,* by Michael Colgan, Ph.D.
- *Male Menopause,* by Jed Diamond, Ph.D.
- *The Alchemy of Love and Lust,* by Theresa Crenshaw, M.D.
- *The Superhormone Promise,* by William Regelson, M.D. and Carol Colman
- *Maximizing Manhood,* by Malcolm Carruthers, M.D.
- *Viropause/Andropause,* by Aubrey M. Hill, M.D.
- *Look 10 Years Younger, Live 10 Years Longer,* by David Ryback.
- *The Testosterone Syndrome,* by Eugene Shippen, M.D. and William Fryer
- *Understanding Men's Passages,* by Gail Sheehy

In many areas of medicine (and life in general) we are faced with the common dilemma – which came first, the chicken or the egg? Andropause is either a brain phenomenon or a testicular phenomenon, but the end result is the same. Here's what happens:

- The hormone from the brain (called LH or leutenizing hormone), designed to stimulate testosterone production in the testicles, is operating at a low level. Since 95% of a man's testosterone production comes from his testicles, this results in testicular shrinkage or atrophy. The brain's LH levels have been shown to decline in an isolated way, without other precipitating factors. Or we could simply call it aging.

- The specialized Leydig cells of the testicles can decrease their production of testosterone independent of and in spite of high levels of the stimulating hormone from the brain. This can begin because of a primary genetic predisposition towards decreasing fertility. Or again we could simply call it aging.

By the time a man has a definite and permanent decline in his testosterone blood levels, his testicles have shrunk significantly and the brain has given up trying to flog a dead horse. In other words, the stimulating hormones are usually low and the end product, testosterone, is also low. It really does not matter which came first, the chicken or the egg because the damage to the body and sexual functioning is the same. It is the recognition of male menopause which has to be addressed and treated.

TESTOSTERONE THROUGHOUT YOUR DAY
AND THROUGHOUT YOUR LIFE

Testosterone production in little boys and little girls is very low. Then at puberty, the stimulation from the brain's sexual precursor (stimulating) hormones leads to a rise in blood levels of estrogen and progesterone in girls and testosterone for boys. The higher testosterone in boys accounts for muscular development, enlargement of the penis and testicles, frequent erections, deepening of the voice, facial and body hair and odiferous perspiration.

The highest lifetime level of testosterone both for men and women is between the ages of 15 and 35. Most of the testosterone in the bloodstream is tightly bound to proteins and cannot be used. Only 2% of the total circulating testosterone, referred to as the free testosterone, is not in a bound form. This tiny amount is considered to be the most active form.

New research is showing that there can be 40% to 50% of the blood testosterone in a unique form referred to as bio-available. This bio-available fraction of testosterone is reported to be loosely bound to proteins in the bloodstream and can be readily used by testosterone-dependent tissues and organs of the body. New diagnostic blood testing kits for bio-available testosterone are being developed to replace the existing total and free testosterone analyses.

❝Testosterone fluctuates throughout the day by as much as 25%. The highest level is from six to eight a.m. The lowest levels occur between two and four p.m. ❞

Declines in testosterone can begin at age 30. The reports show declines of up to 1% per year for total testosterone and 2% per year for the free or unbound testosterone fraction. There are many factors involved in this decline, which will follow shortly in this chapter. Please hang in.

Also, the decline is not consistent in all men, with some men well into their nineties having youthfully high levels. Still other men can have significant fluctuations (downwards) in their levels in just a few short years. Nothing is static and nothing is written in stone when it comes to testosterone levels.

Testosterone fluctuates throughout the day by as much as 25%. Women, on the other hand, have estrogen and progesterone modulations on a monthly not hourly basis. The highest 24-hour level of testosterone for essentially all younger and middle-aged men is from six to eight a.m. The lowest levels occur between two and four p.m. When testosterone begins to decline, the first thing to go is this diurnal (daily) variation. The testosterone levels for andropausal men become blunted and remain consistently low during both daytime and nighttime.

One final point on the variations of testosterone levels – this causes men to have sexual urges and erections anywhere, any time, day or night. In addition, because testosterone can fluctuate to such an extent and with so much frequency, the sexual urges for men can disappear just as fast as they are initiated.

THE DECLINE AND FALL OF THE TESTOSTERONE EMPIRE

Testosterone can be thought of as a car's gas tank. A full tank of gas or a quarter tank will both allow the vehicle to perform in the same way. The car will run just fine as long as you maintain at least a quarter of a tank of gas at all times. Running out of gas in your car can be compared to running out of testosterone.

There appears to be a minimum level of testosterone that is necessary for certain physiological processes to occur. These include muscle, bone, brain and sexual functions. However, with testosterone there is a wide range of "normal" values. Likely this is because at the younger ages (20 – 35), there is more than enough testosterone to maintain fertility and male sexual functioning. When men age *(and I am not joking – the testosterone levels begin to decline at age 30)* their testosterone can reach below this minimum level.

66 Running out of gas in your car can be compared to running out of testosterone. 99

In comparing men and automobiles (a common comparison when speaking with and about men), there are certain similarities and differences for various men and their bodies, just as there are for various men and their cars:

- Some men take good care of their bodies and as a result get good lifetime performance from their bodies.
- Some men do not take good care of their bodies but nevertheless are still blessed with good health and longevity.
- Some men take good care of their bodies but their bodies break down or "rust out" prematurely (early andropause).
- Some men will often take much better care of their cars than their bodies.
- Some cars are lemons, no matter how much maintenance is done or money spent.
- The body, if given a chance can repair and replace almost all cells, tissues and whole systems. The car of course, is another matter, i.e. gas guzzlers, rust heaps and money pits.

What would be ideal, but I realize not very practical, is to have a few blood tests performed at age 20 for testosterone. Then put the results in a safety-deposit box and open it 25 years later. In this way, you will have a record of what *your* ideal testosterone level is to maintain youthful performance. That figure is your ideal number, which might be higher or lower than your neighbor's. Also, the ideal number is usually well above the minimum level for your body.

The problem that many doctors who deal with andropause are faced with is deciding just how high or how low the level of testosterone should be for middle-aged and elderly men. The consensus so far is to maintain a level at least above the lowest level of normal for young men. The normal range for men ages 20 to 35 is 40 to 80 nml/l of free testosterone. This minimum figure, 40 nml/l, often becomes a mid-range figure for middle-aged men and a high-end result for elderly men.

One final point to understand regarding replacement of testosterone (which is coming up later in this chapter) is that it must be individualized to be of maximum benefit. Too often doctors are solely looking at numbers and not at the patient as a total man.

WHAT TO LOOK FOR
IF YOU SUSPECT ANDROPAUSE

There are specific physiological signs and symptoms associated with male menopause, or andropause. They do not all have to be present in order to establish a diagnosis and initiate treatment. In

addition, some men have certain symptoms that are more pro-
nounced than others. Many signs and symptoms are specific to middle-aged men, such as mood changes and sexual dysfunctions,
while others are specific to elderly men, such as balance problems
and osteoporosis.

What follows is a list of 10 signs and symptoms of testosterone decline.

1. Increased fatigue, decreased stamina
2. Decreased muscle strength
3. Increased abdominal fat
4. Sexual dysfunctions, especially decreased libido and often ED
5. Coronary artery disease, heart attacks, strokes
6. Osteoporosis, loss in height
7. Anemia
8. Alzheimer's disease, memory loss, depression, irritability
9. Balance problems, decreased visual-motor skills
10. Decreased hearing, decreased vision

As I said previously, not all of these conditions have to be present
to make a diagnosis of male menopause. If you or your doctor begin
to evaluate some of these particular symptoms, a clearer picture will
emerge. Many doctors are not aware of some of the examples in the
list, such as the increased incidence of heart attacks in many patients
with male menopause. The reason why lowered testosterone is associated with a greater number of heart attacks is due to an increase in
blood-clotting factors that can plug up the coronary arteries.

❝Testosterone is critical for libido, but not as critical for actual erections. ❞

An important consideration for this book, however, is the relationship
that testosterone and male menopause have on ED. The medical
research studies tend to show that testosterone is critical for libido, but
not as critical for actual erections. While it is necessary for overall erection functioning, extra testosterone does not turn men into super-studs.

Remember the analogy to your car. If you have a full tank of gas or
a quarter tank of gas, there will be no difference in your car's performance. That is the way it appears to be with testosterone. There
must be a minimum amount for adequate erections. Any more does
not confer any advantage.

THE DECLINE IN TESTOSTERONE PRODUCTION AND AVAILABILITY

Now let's examine the phenomenon of testosterone decline from the perspectives of how and why. Some of these factors are timeless and affect all the men on this planet. Others are specific to geographic locations. Still other factors are related to the continuous exposure of precipitating circumstances. Even one isolated circumstance or event can cause a decline in testosterone.

Here's why testosterone is so susceptible to a decline:

Age

The older you get, the lower your testosterone levels tend to be. This might be related to age itself as an independent factor or to the type of lifestyle that many elderly men lead. We cannot stop the aging process, but as I mentioned in the preceding section, as long as a minimum amount of testosterone can be maintained, sexual functioning can continue uninterrupted.

One mechanism that has been shown to lower sperm count and sperm morphology (composition and appearance) is the raising of the temperature in the testicles. The scrotum is the sac that houses the testicles and is designed to hang downwards and away from the body to keep the cargo (testicles) 1° F cooler than body temperature.

Tight underwear, tight jeans or pants or sitting for long periods of time (driving taxi or long-distance bike riding) can bring the scrotum up and more towards the body. This keeps the testicles warmer than they should be for proper functioning of sperm. It might also affect the testicular ability to produce testosterone in the long run.

As boys grow into men and then into older men, they sit more on and off the job. Cavemen never sat very long. For one thing, chairs weren't invented yet. Neither were jockey shorts. Cave men were always on the go. However, once they stood upright on two legs instead of swinging through the trees like their primate ancestors, walking and running for miles and miles every day became the norm. How much walking and running do older men do today? Learning a lesson from our caveman ancestors to keep physically active would help to improve our testosterone production.

Genetics

Some men have a genetic predisposition for a more rapid decline in their testosterone levels. This can be due to a biological program built into all men designed to decrease fertility with aging. It is well known that sperm count and corresponding sperm motility decline with aging, which directly affects the ability to father a child.

Perhaps, similar to women, it was not meant for elderly humans to be the parents of young children. Perhaps being grandparents is the mechanism of choice for taking care of small children when we become middle-aged or older.

Some things in life are irreversible and three things you cannot change are your two parents or your genetic code. (You thought I was going to say the obvious death and taxes. Fooled you.) All you can do is try to maintain your personal minimum testosterone level once you figure out what that number is. Blood testing at an early age will help to determine it.

Exercise

Exercise stimulates testosterone production, but not for all men and not by all exercises. Studies show that intensive aerobic exercise, i.e. running a marathon, can cause a testosterone decline in 30% of men, including athletes. Weight resistance exercises, however, tend to promote higher levels of testosterone.

> **66 Weight-resistance exercises tend to promote higher levels of testosterone. 99**

The heavier exercises involving the larger muscles of the back, arms and shoulders require testosterone to promote muscle mass and muscle strength. In turn, the greater the muscle mass, the higher the level of circulating testosterone. It becomes either an uphill spiral: more testosterone = more muscle mass; or a downhill spiral: less testosterone = less muscle mass.

Aerobic exercises (running, biking, etc.) require very little muscle mass. This is especially true for upper-body muscles. Leg muscles are the muscles of choice for aerobic exercise but do not increase substantially in mass from aerobic exercises. Weight resistance exercises can be done at a gym or fitness club, in your home or with specific isometric exercises described in Part One, Chapter Five. As previously mentioned, weight training exercises must be done at least three times a week to be beneficial for raising testosterone, building muscle mass and improving erections.

Obesity

As we age, we tend to accumulate more fat due to a decrease in physical activity and testosterone production. Research shows that overweight men have lower levels of testosterone than physically fit men. One theory suggests that this is due to the higher insulin levels associated with obesity. Another theory involves a protein in the blood called sex hormone-binding globulin (SHBG), which increases as we age. SHBG binds and inactivates over 60% of the free active testosterone from the bloodstream.

To make matters worse and cause a further reduction in testosterone levels, HGH (human growth hormone) levels tend to decline with aging, and as HGH decreases, SHBG levels increase. HGH production is stimulated by protein and inhibited by carbohydrates – reason enough to begin a lower carbohydrate diet and lose excess storage fat.

Another hormone which has been the subject of a lot of recent research is the hormone called leptin. Higher leptin levels have been associated with increased storage fat. There could be a genetic predisposition to this phenomenon, but in addition, higher leptin levels and lower testosterone levels are correlated. So far, all we have is an association with lowered testosterone, and not a causal effect.

Sexual activity

More sexual interactions stimulate more testosterone production. Conversely, lower testosterone levels are related with less sex. Remember, the highest daytime level of testosterone is at 6 a.m. to 8 a.m., which is why many men wake up with an erection. That also helps to explain why many men have a strong sexual urge first thing in the morning. Women, however, have a higher sexual urge last thing at night. Go figure.

Men require more regular sexual episodes, with or without a partner, to maintain adequate levels of testosterone. As with exercise, testosterone and sexual frequency are either an upward spiral or a downward spiral. (Sorry, no penis pun intended.)

In the first section of this book, I went into many psychological and marital conditions that often contribute to less sex drive and less sex.

These usually are insidious in that they occur slowly over time, yet suddenly present with infrequent sex and the resulting ED. The physiological process accounting for the decreasing libido and the ED from marital disharmony is often a lowered testosterone level.

66More sex stimulates more testosterone production. 99

Sleep deprivation

Since most of the testosterone production occurs during your sleep, if there happens to be sleep deprivation on a regular basis, your levels can be affected. Therefore, it is important to get the required amount of total sleep and REM (rapid eye movement or dream sleep) every night. For most people, seven to eight hours should be the minimum daily requirement. Catching up on Sunday mornings by sleeping in until noon won't do it, for testosterone or health in general.

To improve restful therapeutic sleep there are prescription medications available. But instead, I recommend natural sleep inducers and techniques. Two very good books which not only detail the importance of sleep but also provide ways for achieving and maintaining sleep on a natural basis are:

- *Sleep Thieves,* by Stanley Coran, M.D.
- *Power Sleep,* by James Maas, M.D.

Here is some specific advice from these books to help you improve your sleep routines: take a hot bath before bed; avoid alcohol before bed and try warm milk instead (for the increased tryptophan to possibly increase your melatonin); avoid exercise before bed; have sex before going to sleep; and finally, when all else fails, counting sheep is not too bad.

Chronic illness

Chronic illnesses, such as cancer, cirrhosis (liver damage usually from alcoholism), multiple sclerosis and emphysema all result in lowered levels of testosterone. This is likely due to the stress of the illness. And the longer the illness prevails, the lower the testosterone. Remission or resolution of the illness as soon as possible is desirable, not just to recover from the disease itself, but to counteract the negative effects on testosterone levels.

One condition that is seen very infrequently but still seen enough to cause trouble in regards to testosterone is malnutrition. Medically, this is referred to as the Tea and Toast Syndrome, where the diet is deficient in nutrients and vitamins found in fresh fruits and vegetables and protein containing foods. This can happen in elderly, independent men who live alone.

I already discussed the mandatory need for more protein, to help limit the detrimental effects of Syndrome X and also to make more nitric oxide for better erections. Remember, the proper balance of proteins, carbohydrates and fats is important for maintaining health, and has also been shown in medical studies to ensure adequate testosterone production.

Hormone imbalance

Lowered testosterone is correlated with higher insulin levels and, of course, diabetes. Also, if HGH levels are lower, so is the testosterone level. An excellent book on growth hormone, is *Grow Young with HGH,* by Ronald Klatz, M.D.

There is considerable research going on today in the field of andrology, showing the mutual declines of growth hormone and testosterone. The medical studies clearly point out that both these hormones often decline together in the aging male. Growth hormone replacement therapy is not advocated at the present time for aging symptoms in men or for ED due to insufficient research.

However, men with higher levels of growth hormone have benefits similar to men with higher levels of testosterone, especially better erections. In addition, the mechanisms that you can initiate yourself (coming up soon in this chapter) to improve your testosterone levels will also raise your growth hormone levels.

Medications

The following medications are related to ED or the lowering of testosterone:

- Prednisone
- Digoxin
- Beta blockers (blood pressure pills)
- Thiazides (water pills)
- H2 antagonists (stomach acid blockers)
- Selective serotonin reuptake inhibitors (SSRIs)
- Antidepressants (e.g., Prozac™)

Many doctors are not aware of the ED and testosterone depletion that occurs with these medications. There are many other excellent medications available that your doctor can substitute for the offending pills which lower testosterone. Ask your doctor to check the potential side effects of your medications, as well as your testosterone levels.

Stress

Physical stress from a major injury, a car accident or from an operation depletes testosterone. Sometimes the decline is dramatic and leads to emotional, physical and sexual complications. However, the decline in testosterone does not necessarily translate into further troubles – physiologically or sexually.

Those patients with higher testosterone levels to start with (before the accident) usually have a faster recovery and develop fewer complications as long as their bodies are able to maintain an adequate level of the hormone after the injury.

“Continuous rejections, failures and criticisms all take their toll on men by lowering testosterone. ”

Emotional stress is another way that testosterone is depleted. Continuous rejections, failures and criticisms all take their toll on men by lowering testosterone. At work, at home and even self-directed, put-downs abound. Constant exposure to negativity in the man's environment can really drive down testosterone levels. Learning stress management and relaxation skills will go a long way in improving your resilience to any testosterone decline.

Psychological states

The concepts of competition, winning and losing have a strong relationship with testosterone. Right before an athletic competition, testosterone runs high. For the winners, it stays high. For the losers, it goes down with them. The same holds true in business affairs and other personal pursuits. Everyone knows that winning feels better than losing, but you probably never realized that testosterone was responsible for those feelings – even for women.

With subsequent contests in sports and business, the testosterone level will always rise again, but if you previously won, you will start at an even higher level. If you previously lost, you will start at only a moderately high level. Testosterone sampling done on athletes provides an explanation for winning streaks and losing streaks in sports. The same studies were done on courtroom lawyers, both men and women, and the winners had higher testosterone levels than the losers.

Competition drives testosterone production, but it becomes a double-edged sword. Just like being nervous before performing in a sports or business event, a little competition is good, while a lot is bad when it comes to testosterone levels. Want one way to maintain proper testosterone levels? Find the right balance of competitive goal direction vs. competitive "win at all costs" drive. This proper balance will help avoid any diminishing returns in sports and business, which are the two dominant areas in men's lives.

Environmental changes

Only in the last few years have many chemicals, by-products and toxins in the environment been suspected of potentially being disease-promoting. The quality of the air, water and soil has deteriorated to dangerous levels in many places of North America – and everything in the air, water and soil contributes to our food supply. Some of the toxic products of modern industry and inadequate disposal or storage of these compounds has led to various chemical sensitivity syndromes. These can result in both lowered sperm counts and testosterone levels.

In addition, allergic reactions to some foods such as dairy and wheat products can cause specific immune changes, such as abnormal antibody responses at certain target organs. One of these organs can be the testicles, the main suppliers of testosterone. An overactive inflammatory response to allergic food sensitivities has been linked to the deterioration in testosterone production.

Here is one final point about environmental factors and testosterone: the meat industry which produces beef and chicken specifically has had good success over the past 20 or more years in making animals fatter and therefore heavier through the use of estrogen supplementation. The estrogen in the form of injections or supplements in the animal's feed has been approved by health and drug safety boards around the world.

However, there are reports in scientific journals that the extra estrogen found in the animals can disturb the human estrogen/testosterone balance in men and women who eat meat. This has been associated with increased breast cancer rates in women. The higher estrogen has also been associated with lowered sperm counts and sperm swimming impairment. Finally, a skewed testosterone/estrogen ratio weighted with excess estrogen can interfere with testosterone physiology without dramatically lowering total testosterone levels.

For all of the above reasons, many farmers and livestock ranchers are switching to organic farming methods, natural pasture and free-range grazing. Also, many consumers (myself included) are eating substantially more organically grown vegetarian foods and obtaining high quality protein from tofu instead of from meat.

This has been a particularly depressing section. However, on an uplifting note, it is good to know that the human body is a very resilient machine and has built-in mechanisms to counteract and detoxify negative environmental conditions. Otherwise we would all be eunuchs.

Iatrogenic effect

Iatrogenic effect refers to a condition specifically and directly caused by medical treatments or diagnostic procedures. Side effects of medications and complications after surgery or medical tests are common iatrogenic conditions. *Statistics reveal 5% of all illnesses are iatrogenic in origin.* It is part of the price to pay for the progress of modern medicine. And remember, *the good (in medicine) has far outweighed the bad (iatrogenic effect).*

With this in mind, there is a controversy going on in the urological community today about potential iatrogenic effects from vasectomies. A vasectomy is the male sterilization procedure. It requires a minor operation to permanently tie off both sperm tubes (epididymi). Sperm production continues uninterrupted in the testicle but sperm never leaves the epididymi.

Some reports showed lower testosterone levels and higher prostate cancer rates after vasectomy. Other reports showed no short term or long-term problems with vasectomy. The little guys (sperm) arrive at a dead end. However, it is presumed that they are resorbed by the body. One theory which offers an explanation to the lowered testosterone levels following vasectomy is the increase in antibody immune changes directed against the testicles that is sometimes observed. This can damage the Leydig cell production of testosterone, lowering hormone levels.

There likely will not be a definitive answer on vasectomy and its association with lowered testosterone levels for a while. Urological Associations around the world endorse the vasectomy procedure for male sterilization as safe and effective.

Since a vasectomy is essentially a procedure that cannot be reversed, if it turns out to be a cause of your lowered testosterone, then you likely will require supplementation of testosterone (pills, patches or potent injections). A more important issue is not *if* vasectomies cause testosterone depletion, but in *recognizing* the depletion and *treating* it effectively and appropriately.

One final area related to testosterone lowering via an iatrogenic cause has to do with diagnostic procedures or testing that can cause damage to the hormone-producing cells in the testicles. Two special tests are X-ray tests of the abdomen (upper and lower stomach). These are called an upper GI (barium swallow) and a lower GI (barium enema). Performing these tests results in a substantial amount of radiation directed towards the abdomen. There is a possibility that the testicles can be affected by this radiation. This is especially true for a barium enema.

I do not mean to alarm any readers with this section on iatrogenic mechanisms for lowering testosterone. I am merely stating scientific facts and possibilities, the majority of which are not relayed by the medical profession to the public. A frank discussion with your physician should be the first step if you have any concerns about iatrogenic problems in your medical care.

ARE WE DOOMED?

No! In many men, testosterone can be produced once again to near youthful levels by the testicles. You cannot get any younger, but many times you can turn on and improve your growth hormone levels, your testosterone stimulating hormone (LH) levels and finally your testosterone producing cells in your testicles. If the brain's systems for releasing the stimulating hormones are still functioning, then the entire system can fire up again.

Here's what you can get started on:
- First, you can begin a weight-training program on a regular basis.

- Second, better nutrition will help you lower your tendency towards diabetes and help you lose weight.
- Third, you can ensure that you get more restful sleep.
- Fourth, having regular sexual relations with or without a partner is essential – use it or lose it.
- Fifth, check with your doctor to see if some of your medications need to be adjusted or changed.
- Sixth, begin to tackle your stressful triggers and minimize the effects that stress has on your body. Practice meditation on a regular basis.

These are all important factors which will potentially improve your present testosterone levels and prevent any further declines.

What if those particular lifestyle changes do not work? They sometimes don't because in some men the testicles have simply reached their capacity for any extra production in response to stimulation. The testicular capacity to manufacture testosterone can be permanently turned way down to idle speed. In those cases, testosterone supplementation is an important consideration. There are three methods for testosterone augmentation, which I call the three P's: potent injections, patches and pills.

> ❝ *There are three methods for testosterone augmentation: potent injections, patches and pills.* ❞

1. Potent injections

The injections are given in the hip either once a month or sometimes every two to three weeks. They work well, but do not duplicate the diurnal testosterone rhythm of being higher in the early morning hours and lower in the evenings. For most men on these injections, testosterone levels during the first two weeks are slightly to significantly higher than normal. During the second two weeks testosterone levels are slightly or substantially lower than normal.

When taking injections, many men feel really good for the first two weeks, but not up to par during the second two weeks. Hence, the shots are given every three or sometimes even two weeks apart. However, with more frequent injections (every two weeks) the level of testosterone might be slightly higher than desirable and may cause problems with the prostate.

2. Patches

The patches are applied to the skin with a special adhesive and provide daily dosing of testosterone. They are readily absorbed but have demonstrated a moderate risk for skin rash. Some manufacturers advocate application of the patch on a shaved scrotum for better absorption. For many men who are involved in sports, a shaved scrotum with a patch on it might provoke too many questions in the locker room and can be a limiting factor in the successful use of the patches. The patches are available in the U.S. but not in Canada.

3. Pills

The newer pills which are presently available in Canada (not yet in the U.S.) have demonstrated good absorption, excellent tolerance and very reliable results. Taken two or sometimes three times a day, the daily variation of testosterone is well maintained. In addition, the specific oral preparation of testosterone undecanoate, bypasses absorption by the liver and therefore has no potential for liver cancer. This was a serious side effect (iatrogeny) seen in the earlier oral testosterone medications.

Testosterone replacement studies conclusively show marked improvement in bone density and muscle mass as well as less fat storage. In addition to increased energy reported by the men, sexual functioning also improved significantly.

For many men whose ED has been proven to be associated with lowered testosterone levels, oral replacement therapy and monitoring of the blood levels will often show improvement. Some studies show complete recovery of ED. Replacement almost always guarantees more libido and desire. Sometimes that is enough to start the ball rolling. Sorry about the pun.

In a recent study presented at the First World Congress on the Aging Male in Geneva, Switzerland in February 1998, the use of oral testosterone undecanoate resulted in an increase in sexual activity in 85% of the patient group treated. In that particular study, the percentage of patients with ED engaging in sexual intercourse jumped from 0% before testosterone supplementation to 55% after treatment!

There are side effects (iatrogenic) to consider with all the replacement methods. If the patches cause a rash, they have to be discontinued. There is a slight increased risk of prostatic enlargement with testosterone replacement in some men but not in the majority of men.

The medical studies are quite clear though, in showing that there is no significant change in the incidence of prostate cancer with testosterone supplementation.

THE COOLIDGE EFFECT

I will end this section on andropause with a story I found in the book, Love and Lust, written by Theresa Crenshaw, M.D. It has become known as the Coolidge effect.

President Coolidge and his wife were touring a chicken farm. Mrs. Coolidge asked the farmer why the hens laid so many eggs.

"Well," replied the farmer, "the rooster, he does his job every night."

"Oh," said Mrs. Coolidge, "perhaps you should tell that to Mr. Coolidge."

Then President Coolidge asked the farmer, "Tell me, does the rooster perform his duty with the same hen every night?"

"Oh no," said the farmer, " the rooster does his business with all the hens."

To that statement President Coolidge replied, "Perhaps you should tell that to Mrs. Coolidge."

The Coolidge effect – the potential of new sexual conquests – occurs in men by stimulating their testosterone production. Since adultery leads to marital disruptions and polygamy is illegal in North America and Europe, having multiple female sexual partners for men is not a viable option. Even for single men, the potential for contracting sexually transmitted diseases and AIDS is prohibitive to putting more notches on your gun belt!

What can be done then to take advantage of the Coolidge effect, achieve higher testosterone levels and still have loving relationships? My advice is to employ the techniques outlined in Part One, Chapters Seven and Eight.

Improving love will improve sex and improving sex will improve love. While women desire more love and men desire more sex (in general), a compromise and a balance can still be achieved. In this way, men can maintain good testosterone levels, have better, more frequent sex and stable loving relationships, all at the same time.

CHAPTER FIVE

Alcoholism

Drinking and sex don't mix.

M r. F. was a 60-year-old man with ED. He had been an alcoholic from age 25 to age 40. He had only a handful of alcoholic episodes from age 40 to 50 because he was going to AA (Alcoholics Anonymous) meetings during those years. Since age 50 Mr. F. had been completely sober, and was attending AA every week. For the past 15 years Mr. F. had not had an erection. No nocturnal erections, no weak erections, nothing.

Mr. F. was not all that sad or upset about losing his erections. He told me, " By rights, I should be dead, Doctor. I drank way too much, and didn't eat. I went on two-week drunks at a time. Like I said, with all the abuse I gave my body, I should be dead. No erections, not the end of the world."

Mr. F. then added, 'The reason I came to see you, Doc, is I started going out with this very nice lady, and she's been hinting about carrying the relationship into the bedroom. I didn't tell her about my trouble. But this fella at the AA meeting was telling me the other night that he can't get it up either. This fella told me he uses these injections right into his penis. Is that true, Doc? Can I use them? Will they work on a guy like me?"

ALCOHOL IN MODERATION IS FINE

Unless you are an alcoholic, taking alcohol in moderation – one to two drinks per day or night – is harmless. One drink can even relax a man enough to enhance the parasympathetic nervous system for better erections. Some studies report beneficial effects from alcohol on lipid (fat) metabolism.

When alcohol is consumed in excessive amounts, however, permanent damage can occur. Liver damage, namely cirrhosis, is the big killer. High blood pressure is common, as is high cholesterol. Finally, there can be hormonal changes of lowered testosterone and elevated estrogen. These hormonal changes are usually due to liver damage as the liver's ability to metabolize estrogen becomes impaired.

> **66 *In addition to the vascular and hormonal effects, alcoholism also causes permanent nerve damage similar to that caused by severe diabetes.* 99**

In addition to the vascular and hormonal effects, alcoholism also causes permanent nerve damage similar to that caused by severe diabetes. This will affect the nerves to the penis, prostate and testicles which are very plentiful and very sensitive.

ALCOHOL-INDUCED ED

Most of the time, in cases of ED caused by alcohol damage, we have to resort to the hardware: penile injections, vacuum devices and surgical implants. The results tend to be quite satisfactory. The decision as to which system is used depends upon the cost, ease of use, personal preference and recommendations from a friend or doctor.

Viagra™, the nitric oxide-enhancing drug in tablet form, might prove to be a boon in the treatment of alcohol-induced ED. The drug was approved for sale by prescription in March 1998 in the U.S. and should be available in Canada by the end of 1998.

Sometimes it is possible to achieve some slight improvement in alcohol-induced ED through natural means. Clean living, with no smoking, a vegetarian-style low-carbohydrate diet, exercise, vitamins, minerals, prayer and meditation, have all been shown to make at least a subtle difference.

REMEMBER THIS

Men and alcohol often go together –often to excess. While alcohol in moderation does not generally endanger a man's ability to have strong, dependable erections, a chronic drinking problem can lead to alcoholism, which in turn leads to numerous medical illnesses. Severe (and often irreversible) ED is the price a man pays for the damage caused by alcohol.

❝ What do you want most – your next drink or your next erection? ❞

CLOSING JOKES

Here are four jokes, compliments of Rodney Dangerfield:

"We sleep in separate rooms, we have dinner apart, we take separate vacations – we're doing everything we can think of to keep our marriage together."

"I'm at the age where food has taken the place of sex in my life. In fact, I've just had a mirror installed over my kitchen table."

"Last time I made love to my wife nothing was happening, so I said to her, "What's the matter? You can't think of anybody either?"

"If it weren't for pickpockets, I'd have no sex life at all."

CHAPTER SIX

Medication Side Effects

Big side effects that make it small.

When I first saw Mr. G., he was already 73 years old. He walked very slowly due to severe arthritis in his legs. Mr. G. told me that he had had progressive osteoarthritis for over 10 years. His knees, shoulders and hands were affected the most. Medications for pain and inflammation helped just a little.

Then Mr. G. related his story of ED. "After I retired, I started to have trouble keeping my erections. I would go soft very quickly after only a few minutes. My wife never refused having sex, although she never really got too much from sex in all the years of our marriage."

"I would wake up with a fair erection, and we would attempt it right away, before it went soft. Sometimes, it would work."

Mr. G. had no diabetes, his blood pressure was normal and he did not smoke. His testosterone level was on the low end for younger men, but in the middle for older men. That meant that a trial of testosterone would probably not be of much help.

Mr. G. continued, "My doctor tells me that I will need knee transplants within one to two years, but I have to be on two canes first. I'm not that bad, yet."

While Mr. G. likely did not have the best blood supply to his penis at his age, he did not have the other risk factors contributing to poor arterial flow. On the other hand, Mr. G. was not able to walk or do specific exercises with his legs that could help in promoting better blood flow to the penis.

There was one area, however, where Mr. G. did have trouble and which could be the probable cause of his particular brand of ED. Due to the long-standing arthritic condition of his knees, Mr. G. was regularly taking large doses of non-steroidal anti-inflammatory drugs (NSAIDs). These particular drugs have a potential for ED side effects.

The first recommendation for Mr. G. was to encourage him in beginning an aqua-fitness program. I wanted Mr. G. to gain the benefits of exercise for improving blood flow in his heart as well as his penis without putting a strain on his knees.

Next, I advised taking the supplement, glucosamine sulfate for his arthritis. There have been some recently published studies on the use of glucosamine sulfate showing good results in many arthritic patients by improving the cartilage surface of the joints. Mr. G. was able to taper down his NSAID medications and eventually discontinued them.

Some excellent resource books on the benefits of glucosamine sulfate are:

- *Beat Arthritis,* by Michael Colgan, Ph.D.
- *The Arthritis Cure,* by Jason Theodosakis, M.D., M.S., M.P.H., Brenda Adderly, M.H.A. and Barry Fox, Ph.D.

After three months on the new complementary treatments, Mr. G. had a significant improvement in his arthritis <u>and</u> in his ED. He was able to take a daily half-hour walk with his wife, and most important, Mr. G. was able to have intercourse once every week.

THE LIST OF DRUGS

It's a long list. A very long list! Which does *not* mean that every man taking any of the medications on the list will have ED as a side effect. Many of these medications are commonly used in medical practice today and fortunately cause no trouble whatsoever the majority of the time.

However, it *does* mean that doctors and patients (male patients in this case) need to be aware of and maybe even anticipate the potential for ED side effects from a whole host of drugs. To help in achieving this, a more concerted effort by physicians towards prevention is really in order, thereby eliminating any potential grief from ED.

One method available for your doctor is the use of substitute medications, especially earlier on in treatment. Your doctor should know of these substitutes or can readily find out about them. In addition, a medication "holiday," a break for a short time if possible, can slow down any potential side effects.

I will not go through the entire list of medication culprits for ED. I will instead provide a list of the few medications which seem to cause the *most* difficulty on a consistent basis:

- Blood pressure pills – thiazides, beta blockers
- Heart pills – digoxin
- Stomach pills – cimetidine, ranitidine
- Tranquilizers – benzodiazepines, phenothiazines
- Antidepressants – serotonin-specific reuptake inhibitors (SSRIs), lithium, MAO inhibitors
- Hormones – estrogen, cortisone, finasteride, anti-testosterone agents
- Miscellaneous – nonsteroidal anti-inflammatory drugs (NSAIDs), anti-histamines

REMEMBER THIS

Erectile dysfunction is a potential side effect of many drugs. I suggest you openly discuss your concerns with your doctor. The explosive growth over the past few years in the number of available prescription medications makes it all the more critical for all patients to take an active role in knowing everything they can about the drugs they take and their side effects.

❝ Ask for alternatives to medications that have been shown to have a risk of causing ED. ❞

CLOSING JOKES

Groucho Marx once said, "Marriage is a wonderful institution, but who wants to live in an institution?"
He also said, "Whoever called it necking was a poor judge of anatomy."

And did you hear about the man who got a vasectomy at Sears? Every time he gets an erection, his garage door goes up.

A FEW STATISTICS, ANYONE?

- Average duration of sexual intercourse for humans in minutes: 10
- Average duration for chimpanzees, in seconds: 10
- Average number of times per day chimpanzees have sex: 50
- Number of orgasms witnessed at the Masters & Johnson Institute in its first nine years of research: 14,000
- Number of condoms used every second in the U.S. (1990): 14
- Average length of an erect penis, according to U.S. men, in inches: 10
- Average length, according to U.S. women, in inches: 4

CHAPTER SEVEN

The Prostate Gland

*That's prostate,
not prostrate.*

The prostate gland is a unique structure, specific to the male anatomy. It is also poorly understood in medical circles and has many unknowns attached to it.

The prostate gland is about the size and shape of a walnut (complete with its shell) and is positioned at the bottom of the urinary bladder. It is half gland and half muscle. The urethra, the tube emptying the urine from the bladder, runs right through the middle, mostly muscular, portion of the prostate. Sperm and seminal gland fluids are mixed with prostatic fluids which are made in the glandular portion more towards the perimeter to form the ejaculate. The prostate is attached to two muscular bands called sphincters (closers), one at the base of the bladder and one at the other end of the prostate.

❝The prostate gland is a unique structure, specific to the male anatomy. It is also poorly understood in medical circles and has many unknowns attached to it. ❞

At puberty, the prostate grows to its adult walnut size and for about 30 or 40 years nothing much happens to this gland. It functions basically to provide the bulk of the ejaculatory fluids. Then, beginning around the ages of 45 to 55, the prostate in most men begins to enlarge. The condition is called Benign Prostatic Hypertrophy (BPH). By age 90, 100% of men have enlarged prostates.

Sometimes the enlargement is due to benign tumors in the glandular portion of the prostate called adenomas. Sometimes the overgrowth is just in the muscular portion, with the cells getting larger not necessarily multiplying in number. And sometimes the BPH is a combination of both.

BPH by itself does not always cause trouble. There are many men who have no changes in urination or sexual functions relating to enlargement of their prostate glands. However, most men over age 60 have some symptoms of this BPH overgrowth. I will be going over the full list of prostate problems soon, but first we still need a little more background information.

The annual death rate from prostate cancer is the same as the breast cancer death rate is for women, around 50,000 deaths per year in the U.S. Besides enlargement and cancer, the prostate gland has one other major disease potential called prostatitis. This is a unique form of infection in the gland (different from other common infections like sore throats) and occurs usually in younger men.

WHAT DOES THE PROSTATE DO?

It is a strange beast, the prostate. From birth to age 15 it is small and dormant. It grows to full adult size at puberty along with the penis and testicles. From ages 15 to 45 it is extremely active (for sexuality and fertility) and essentially, but not perfectly, trouble-free. From ages 50 through 90 it can be a major source of stress in men's lives. There are many theories offered as to the exact function or functions of the prostate gland. A few of them are listed below.

Lubrication of the urethra

There is a tiny stream of prostatic fluid continuously draining into the urethra running through it. During ejaculation a large amount of this fluid (around one ounce) is moved into the urethra where it is mixed with the sperm and shot out the end of the penis. According to this theory the mucusy prostatic fluid is constantly coating the urethral tube and protecting it from any damage caused by the flow of urine. This helps to maintain a smooth urethral lining and prevents any urethral scaring or strictures.

The theory is credible because there is always a dribble of prostatic secretions into the urethra. However, there appear to be gaps in the theory, which require explanation. First, the prostate is barely functioning before puberty, yet boys do not have any urethral burning problems. Second, many men with BPH who have undergone corrective surgical removal similarly do not have trouble with chronic urethral burning conditions while voiding (at least not as a common complication of the surgery).

Extra bladder sphincter

The prostate gland is linked to two sphincters, or muscle bands, that squeeze the urethra shut at both ends. These sphincters work just like the anal sphincter in your rectum and the gastro-esophageal sphincter where your esophagus joins with your stomach. The sphincter lying just under the urinary bladder is called the bladder sphincter, and the one at the farther end of the prostate is called the prostatic or distal sphincter.

This theory proposes lending a helping hand to bladder function. Since men have a much larger urinary bladder than women do, men can hold a much larger reservoir of urine. This would require an extra sphincter to avoid leakage. It is very common for women to lose a few drops of urine, while laughing or coughing. Not so for men.

Once again, however, pre-pubertal boys are without a fully functioning prostate and have no trouble holding back large quantities of urine, unless they have enuresis (bedwetting). Also, for many men who have had the prostatic surgery (called transurethral resection of the prostate or TURP for short), there is frequently some degree of difficulty with bladder control in the post-operative period. So, it appears that this sphincter function has been interfered with. However, within days to weeks, the bladder control reverts to normal. Good for the bladder, bad for the theorists.

Pressure cooker

The glandular portion of the prostate manufactures and concentrates specific fluids forming the bulk of the total amount of ejaculate. The seminal vesicles supply the remainder, and then each of the two epididymi (sperm tubes leading out of the testicle) transfers the sperm into the ejaculate. The process of ejaculation then propels the whole mass into the vagina. This propulsion is necessary to land the sperm directly onto and into the cervix, which then promotes fertilization of the ovum farther inside the woman's reproductive system.

Because there are two sphincters, the theory describes both sphincters simultaneously clamping down tightly on the urethra. This prevents urine from mixing with the ejaculate, and also builds up pressure in the urethra running through the middle portion of the prostate. Since the prostate has a large supply of smooth-muscle fibers like the those found in the walls of the arteries, a lot of pressure can be generated when they contract.

Just before ejaculation, the prostate squeezes and contracts while both sphincters are held in the closed position. The bladder sphincter does not lose its grip and maintains continuous closure. At the instant of ejaculation, the distal sphincter suddenly bursts open and the ejaculate shoots out. The action resembles a pressure cooker having its lid suddenly opened.

Men who have had the TURP procedure still have the sensation of ejaculation, but no forward ejaculation occurs. The ejaculate, comprising the sperm, seminal fluids, and a little bit of prostatic fluids, are ejaculated in retrograde fashion. This means they go back into the urinary bladder, not forward into the vagina.

Again, since most of the gland has been removed (some of the glandular as well as most of the muscular portions), what is providing the ejaculation spasm and sensation now without the pressure-cooker effect? I told you the prostate is a mysterious part of men's anatomy.

WHAT CAN GO WRONG?

The conditions BPH, prostate cancer and prostatitis are the three main problem areas for the prostate gland. Urologists, instead of internists or family doctors, tend to deal with both the straightforward and complicated cases.

Treatments abound, from pills to potions to procedures. Newer ones are being developed and tested all the time in the hopes of improving men's ability to urinate without concern or discomfort. It is a sad comment on the aging process for men that the simple act of urination becomes a priority issue. The main reason lies within the prostate.

A healthy prostate gland is vitally important to a man's health, well-being and erections. Unfortunately, by the time men become concerned about their prostates, it is sometimes too late to reverse any damage. As in other areas of medicine, but especially when it comes to the prostate, "an ounce of prevention is worth a pound of cure."

I will not present the full range of treatments available for BPH or for prostate cancer. That's beyond the scope of this book. I will instead concentrate on the treatments and procedures for the prostate gland that have a direct impact on ED. For additional information on prostatic function and dysfunction, there are excellent resource books available at the library. A few that I recommend reading are:

- *The Male Body,* by Abraham Morgentaler, M.D.
- *Prostate Disease,* by Scott McDougal, M.D.
- *Private Parts,* by Yosh Taguchi, M.D.
- *The Prostate Sourcebook,* by Steven Morganstern, M.D. and Allen Abrahams, Ph.D.
- *The Prostate Book,* by Stephen N. Rous, M.D.
- *The Natural Way to a Healthy Prostate,* by Michael B. Schacter, M.D.

CLOSING JOKES

Here are a couple of Woody Allen's favorites:

"Love is the answer, but while you are waiting for the answer, sex raises some pretty good questions."

"Sex is dirty, only when it is done right."

And then there was the joke by Joan Rivers:

"A man can sleep around, no questions asked. But if a woman makes 19 or 20 mistakes, she's a tramp."

Q: Do you know the difference between a clitoris and a golf ball?
A: A man will spend an hour looking for a golf ball.

CHAPTER EIGHT

Prostatitis

It's a man's nightmare.

M r. P.A. was a 37-year-old patient of mine. He did not have ED; however, he had suffered from prostatitis for the past 10 years. He was seen by two urologists, and had numerous cystoscopy procedures (diagnostic visualization of the inside of the bladder with a special type of periscope inserted through the penis!). He took pills, pills and more pills, and was still suffering.

Mr. P.A.'s erections were fine. His complaints were with the functions of ejaculation and urination. During ejaculation he often experienced pain and noticed a pinkish or bloody tinge to his ejaculate. When Mr. P.A. urinated, it would sometimes burn or sting. Medications helped for a while, but the symptoms kept recurring. The recent cystoscopy tests showed some urethral strictures (scar tissue – rough areas in the lining of the urethra).

Mr. P.A. was very unhappy because, like most men with chronic prostatitis, the available treatments are not always satisfactory. His urologist was frustrated, his wife was frustrated, and Mr. P.A. was frustrated. Welcome to the world of chronic prostatitis.

WHAT IS IT?

Prostatitis is an inflammatory condition of the prostate that can be acute (occurring one time only) or chronic (returning over and over).

Sometimes there are germs associated with an infection, but quite often there are no germs found at all in the culture tests. The symptoms include pain and burning with urination, sometimes frequency (having the urge to urinate every few minutes), pain and discomfort with ejaculation, and sometimes a dull aching in the prostate, beneath the testicles.

The treatments include a variety of antibiotics, anti-inflammatory medications, analgesics (pain pills), hot packs, cold packs, rest, and prayer. Treatments are not always curative, and the condition tends to run for many years, off and on.

CAUSES AND CURES

Unknown
There is no definitive etiology for prostatitis. Although theories abound, in many urology textbooks the authors ultimately give up and proclaim that, as yet, the exact cause is unknown.

Infection
Some prostatic fluid samples have grown colonies of bacteria which have been implicated as the cause of this condition. Treatments with specific antibiotics can be helpful. Sometimes when the cultures are negative for bacteria, a course of treatment with antibiotics relieves the symptoms just the same.

This could be because the bacteria are in a sense hiding in the prostate and do not venture into the prostatic fluids. It could also be that these particular germs do not reproduce well in the culture mediums in the laboratory, but only in the prostate.

The antibiotics do afford relief in most cases, but not like penicillin for a strep throat. The course of antibiotics for prostatitis can last for one month or longer. Relief can begin in weeks, instead of a few hours or days with medication for a strep throat.

Immune dysfunction
There is always an inflammatory component to prostatitis, and so a theory proposes that prostatitis is an immune system irregularity. This means either allowing germs to grow or inflaming the prostate by mistake, as seen in certain auto-immune diseases. Auto-immune disorders are conditions of the immune system, where the normal turn-on, turn-off mechanisms are not properly controlled.

Immune dysfunctions are very difficult to treat. Sometimes they can be due to genetic predispositions, cortisone depletion, stress and finally, unknown factors. Cortisone (trade name Prednisone™) and/or chemotherapy drugs are designed to slow down the immune system. They are very effective and are sometimes used in highly resistant cases of prostatitis. However, here again anti-inflammatory medications act as a double-edged sword by causing troublesome side effects or even prostatitis! When used as treatments for auto-immune disorders or in solving one specific problem, such as to prevent the rejection of a transplanted kidney, other conditions such as prostatitis can arise. This is due to the immune system alterations caused by the drugs.

One theory for chronic inflammation suggests that urine enters the glandular portion of the prostate gland through the prostatic ducts. Urine is toxic and inflammatory to any other part of the body except the kidney, bladder and urethra. It is an interesting theory. Unfortunately, there is no treatment available.

Sexual frequency

Too much and too little sex have both been implicated as causes of chronic prostatitis. Many men are ready, willing and able to have sex every day, 365 days a year. Many men boast that they can have sex three or more times a day, any time they want.

For most men, very frequent sex involving ejaculation puts a strain on the glandular portion of the prostate. It can take hours or days (depending on your age) to prepare more ejaculatory fluid. If your system is decompensating because of frequent sexual activity, then backing off and allowing sufficient rest and recuperation time for the prostate is usually all that is required.

On the other hand, infrequent sex and insufficient releasing of the prostatic fluid can create a "backup" pressure in the prostate glands of some men. This can cause damage to the glandular cells and promote chronic inflammation. Glands anywhere in the body are meant to secrete what they make and they function most efficiently when used as designed.

The analogy here goes back to the car or truck engine. These engines perform better and last longer when used for highway driving exclusively. Unfortunately, most vehicles are used for short city driving trips and costly engine problems are a frequent result.

One final point about sexual frequency. When a sexual act is initiated, the entire ejaculatory system is primed. If the ejaculation is withheld due to misunderstandings, interruptions from a telephone call, parents coming into the room if you are a teenager, or kids coming into the room if you are a parent, then trouble can ensue.

There is a condition called, "blue balls," where the man (usually a teenager) is unable to ejaculate, but gets pretty close. This presents as pain under the testicles (in the prostate gland) from prostatic congestion. Nothing actually turns blue, but the nickname for this condition has stuck.

The body of course is prepared to deal with prostatic congestion through nocturnal emissions (wet dreams). These begin in the early teens and can last well into adulthood. One way around the frequency and congestion issue is to have a regular sexual release, with or without a partner (intercourse or masturbation) every two to three days. This means, of course, whether you are in the mood or not. But don't worry, because once a man gets started, he tends to get in the mood fairly quickly.

Male menopause

Testosterone is the kingpin hormone required for proper functioning of the male reproductive system. Many men as you have already seen in the chapter "Male Menopause," have premature lowering of their testosterone levels. Since the prostate responds intimately to testosterone, fluctuations of testosterone levels (up or down – likely down is worse) can cause chronic inflammation. The exact mechanism showing how decreased levels of testosterone predisposes to prostatitis is as yet unknown.

It is a good idea at any age when faced with prostatitis to have your testosterone hormone level evaluated. Treatment with a trial of testosterone hormone supplementation would be up to the urologist.

Allergies and sensitivities

Allergies cause inflammatory reactions. This means that a particular substance (an allergen) triggers a specific immune response somewhere in the body. Usually the allergic response manifests on the skin as hives; however, prostatitis can sometimes be a type of allergic condition.

Allergy testing might be helpful, although greater benefit is found in the elimination of certain foods and other products from the environment, such as irritating cleaning products. A few foods, which are known to be highly allergic and/or sensitizing include dairy products, wheat, chocolate, peanuts and shellfish. These particular foods and many others can cause allergic responses that range from mild to life-threatening. The prostate has also been shown to be highly sensitive to certain foods such as coffee, spices and alcohol. Elimination of any offending foods is sometimes the only way to alleviate chronic prostatitis symptoms.

66 *The prostate has also been shown to be highly sensitive to certain foods such as coffee, spices and alcohol. 99*

Finally, the environment we live in, the air we breathe, the clothes we wear and the water we drink, expose us to invisible forms of pollution and other sensitizing chemical agents. Want a few common examples? Cigarette smoke (direct and second-hand), perfumes, hair sprays, shoe polish, and car exhaust fumes can all wreak havoc on our immune systems and could be involved with prostatitis.

I know this section is a little (or a lot) depressing, but I didn't design the immune system. The allergic response is just one part of the natural sensitivity we have to our environment. *Sometimes, however, some simple lifestyle modifications (like stopping smoking) can bring enormous benefits to our whole lives, not just our prostates.*

Trauma

Here's an area that has been shown to lower sperm counts, lower testosterone levels and might also be involved in prostatitis. It is trauma to the prostate from too much pressure, such as long bike rides. While there are not enough studies confirming the relationship of long-distance bike riding to chronic prostatitis, there is still a direct association. My advice – if you are a bike rider *and* you suffer from prostatitis – is try to back off a bit from the riding and see how your prostate fares. You might be pleasantly surprised.

Vitamins, minerals and herbal supplements

Perhaps for some men, vitamin, antioxidant, and specific mineral deficiencies are related to their prostatitis and other prostatic diseases. Zinc has been shown to be an important mineral for proper functioning of the prostate gland. Of the total selenium content in a man's body, 50% is concentrated in the prostate.

❝*Zinc is an important mineral for proper functioning of the prostate gland.*❞

A simple remedy that would act as an insurance against deficiency and would not be toxic or harmful is to take a daily antioxidant cocktail of vitamins C, E, beta-carotene (precursor to Vitamin A), and the minerals selenium and zinc. For specific recommendations, please refer to the information on vitamins and supplements found in previous chapters.

The herbal preparation Prostatonin™ which contains standardized extracts of PY102 (Pygeum africanum) and UR102 (Urtica dioica, commonly known as stinging nettle) has been shown in European urological journals to be beneficial for BPH. The mechanism of action appears to be from blocking the conversion of testosterone to the more potent dehydrotestosterone.

Since the side effect profile of Prostatonin™ is favorable and the toxicity is essentially nil, it is worthwhile to use it for a three-month trial to determine its effectiveness.

Psychological and stress-related causes

Prostatitis, like any inflammatory process, is worse during stress and stressful reactions. Eliminating stress and dealing with stress in better ways can help this chronic condition. Various programs for stress management are found throughout this book.

Sometimes psychosexual problems can be related to prostatitis and may require psychotherapy with a psychiatrist, psychologist, or sexologist. Post-traumatic stress disorder, whether sexually based or not, is another area that could be looked at through an appropriate psychotherapeutic approach.

There is one final area I have found that has literally worked wonders with some of my patients who have a particularly recurrent and incapacitating form of chronic prostatitis. I ask these men if there is some stress-related issue in their lives that they would like to get rid of and in a figurative way, "to piss on it." Or if they would like someone to leave them alone and, "piss off." When I ask my patients to think about what I just said they become very quiet and seem to zero in on exactly what is troubling them.

They do not tell me what the issue is, nor I do need to know, unless they want to tell me. But, I have found this stress-reducing technique to be very effective, especially when all else fails. This sudden jolting in the brain of some emotional problem seems to do the trick in some men.

CLOSING JOKES

Q: What's the difference between anxiety and panic?
A: Anxiety is the first time you can't do it a second time; panic is the second time you can't do it the first time.

Did you hear about the flasher who wanted to retire? He changed his mind and decided to stick it out one more year.

Did you see this bumper sticker?
MARRIED MEN DON'T LIVE LONGER,
IT JUST SEEMS LONGER.

Did you see the woman wearing this T-shirt?
I'M OUT OF MY ESTROGEN AND I HAVE A GUN!

Did you see the feminist T-shirt slogan?
What women want:
to be loved, listened to, desired, respected, needed and trusted.
What men want:
tickets for the World Series.

CHAPTER NINE

Benign Prostatic Hypertrophy

I'm up all night peeing.

Mr. P.B. was a 72-year-old man who'd had ED for over a year. He'd had a TURP (the standard surgery for BPH) done six years earlier. He was fine with his ability to urinate and his erections were acceptable until last year. Mr. P.B. still had a desire for sex and he and his wife eagerly awaited any suggestions I could offer.

Closer evaluation revealed that Mr. P.B. did not have diabetes, but he did have a mild degree of high blood pressure, for which he was taking a daily blood pressure pill (one which luckily did not interfere with erections). His testosterone level was at the low end of normal for his age, and substantially lower for men of a younger age.

It was possible that Mr. P.B.'s particular ED trouble – getting hard and going soft too soon – was a result of either high blood pressure, low testosterone or his age. However, in many men after TURP surgery, ED can be a complication. The ED in these cases has been attributed to nerve damage resulting from the surgery. And it can often take years before the ED develops.

WHAT IS IT?

Benign prostate hypertrophy (BPH) is an enlargement of the muscular part of the prostate gland (surrounding the urethra). The glandular or secretory part of the gland does not appear to be a part of the overgrowth. It has been shown to start as early as age 30, is quite frequent by age 60 and is present in all men by age 90.

BPH can lead to a variety of problems related to voiding urine. They include:

- Frequency (having to urinate very often)
- Nocturia (getting up a few times in the middle of the night to urinate)
- Hesitation of the stream (difficulty initiating the urination process)
- Reduced force of the stream
- Substantial dribbling after urinating
- The stream abruptly cutting out in the middle
- Incomplete emptying of the bladder urine, which can result in urine infections, bladder stones and sometimes urinary back-pressure resulting in kidney damage

WHAT CAUSES IT?

Unknown

Like prostatitis, many theories are presented and many medical journals still advocate the exact cause as being unknown. It is possible that BPH is simply a genetically programmed aging phenomenon. What is known for certain is that it will eventually get all of us. The size of the overgrowth is not always related to the symptoms, and the symptoms can change, getting better or worse from time to time. I told you the prostate is a mysterious gland.

Growth factors

Numerous prostatic growth factors (chemicals and proteins) have been identified as promoting overgrowth and possibly cancer in the prostate. Research continues with animals and humans in experiments designed to help modify these growth factors and possibly help to shrink the prostate. Dogs and humans possess prostate glands that overgrow, chimpanzees and other primates do not. Most of the research on growth factors is geared towards trying to achieve a reduction of the symptoms of BPH.

Two growth factors that have been shown in medical studies to modulate the growth and size of the prostate are nitric oxide and sex hormone-binding globulin (SHBG).

Nitric oxide is the chemical that is ultimately responsible for the whole erection process. Nitric oxide is claimed to inhibit some of the growth factors of the prostate. Therefore, the more nitric oxide there is available, the better the potential condition of the prostate. And remember, the more nitric oxide, the better the erections. Nitric oxide is made from the precursor amino acid, arginine. Getting adequate protein in the diet, especially arginine, will help ensure a potential supply of nitric oxide and may improve BPH.

Urological journals suggest that SHBG is a growth factor for BPH. SHBG, the protein that binds testosterone and transports it in the bloodstream, increases with aging. This appears to be due to an age-related lowering of growth hormone levels. Getting SHBG down to lower levels by losing weight, exercising and improving any diabetic tendency will lower the potential for this growth factor to affect your prostate.

Male menopause

There is a paradox in urology. As testosterone declines, the prostate enlarges. However, the prostate is dependent on testosterone for its growth. Castration (removal of the testicles and with them the supply of testosterone) promptly shrinks the prostate. How does the prostate gland get bigger if it needs testosterone and the testosterone is on the decline? That's the paradox.

Perhaps BPH is only related to other growth factors and has nothing to do with the level of testosterone. Perhaps testosterone is required as a modulator of these growth factors like nitric oxide is; perhaps the higher the testosterone, the lower the BPH growth factors. The jury is still out on the testosterone paradox.

WHAT CAN BE DONE ABOUT BPH?

Surgery

The common surgical treatment for BPH involves going through the penis with a cystoscope and cutting out a sizable chunk of the prostate that surrounds the urethra. The procedure is tried and true, has a good success rate and a low complication rate. Other newer methods of treatment that are presently completing long-term testing are laser surgery and microwave surgery.

Medications

There are two classes of medications for BPH. One particular pill, Proscar™ (finasteride), inhibits the conversion of testosterone to dehydrotestosterone, the active metabolite for prostatic overgrowth. The theory behind this drug lies in shrinking the prostate and thereby relieving the symptoms. The beneficial effect of this medication on BPH symptoms in most studies is usually not as good as a TURP, although it has been shown to be helpful in some studies. Erectile dysfunction is seen as a complication (an iatrogenic effect) in a small percentage of men taking this drug.

The second group of drugs comes from a specific class of blood pressure pills called alpha blockers, which decrease the smooth muscle tone of the muscular portion of the prostate. These drugs have a good success rate in relieving the symptoms without shrinking the size of the prostate at all. TURP surgical rates in the U.S. have declined by 30% in recent years, due to the use of these alpha blockers.

One final point about the alpha blockers concerns their side-effects. Dizziness resulting from episodes of low blood pressure can be a nuisance with these pills. Fortunately, Flomax™ (tamsulosin), a new alpha blocker specifically designed to treat BPH was recently approved for use in Canada and the U.S. Because of its minimal side-effect profile Flomax™ should set a new standard in the use of alpha blockers for BPH control.

Herbal remedies

The herbs Pygeum africanum and Urtica dioica (stinging nettle) in combined form available as Prostatonin™ have a fairly good track record for relieving the symptoms of BPH. The physiological action is similar to the drug Proscar™, which blocks the conversion of testosterone in the prostate gland. The net effect is to possibly shrink the overgrowth in the gland.

Prostatonin™ (the brand available in Canada and the U.S.) contains standardized herbal extracts. Prostatonin™ has been extensively researched in many European studies for the treatment of BPH and is a preferred choice by German urologists.

❝ *Prostatonin*™ *has been extensively researched in many European studies for the treatment of BPH and is a preferred choice by German urologists.* ❞

These herbal preparations appear to have few if any side effects and do not seem to interfere with erections, whereas Proscar™ can contribute to ED. When considering herbal products to relieve the symptoms of BPH it is important to discuss your needs with your doctor or urologist. Many doctors prescribe herbal preparations for BPH when the symptoms are mild or even as a preventive strategy.

Saw palmetto is an herb that has shown positive effects in several clinical trials for treating the symptoms of BPH. It is important to make sure that the brand you select contains 85% - 90% fatty acids and sterols to ensure potential benefit for your prostate.

Lifestyle changes

Cutting down on nighttime fluid intake, especially coffee, will help alleviate the symptoms of BPH. Having regular sex, with or without a partner, is beneficial to the prostate. Less stress helps too, by stabilizing the immune system. There are studies showing no association of smoking to BPH problems, however, that is not an endorsement to continue smoking.

SUMMARY

Benign prostate hypertrophy as a medical condition does not have a great influence on erections. It can interfere with ejaculations a little, but BPH for the most part irritates bladder functioning. As the prostate overgrows, it also compresses the urethra and as a result restricts the easy flow of urine. There usually is a compensatory increase in the muscular tone and strength of the urinary bladder to help force out urine. These changes in the bladder neck are believed to be the cause of many nighttime urinary spasm symptoms.

Here's an interesting aspect about BPH. While BPH is an inevitable feature of aging, many men are not even aware that their prostate glands are enlarged and will never experience any trouble. Size of the prostate, big or small, does not correlate to obstructive symptoms.

Research continues to find better medications or other treatments that will slow down or shrink the overgrowth with fewer side effects while at the same time preventing any association with ED. Quality herbal products can be used in addition to prescription medications to try to keep the prostate functioning at a youthful resiliency. A healthy prostate leads to one less area that can interfere with erections.

66 *A healthy prostate leads to one less area that can interfere with erections.* 99

CLOSING JOKE

Three couples, one elderly, one middle-aged and another one newly-wed, wanted to join an out of the way, non-traditional religious organization. The religious leader told the three couples that one criterion for joining was to abstain from sexual relations for two weeks. Two weeks later, they all returned and reported their experiences. The elderly couple said that it was no problem to abstain for two weeks.

"Okay. You can join," said the leader.

The middle-aged couple said that the first week was fine, but they had to sleep in separate bedrooms for the second week, to keep away from sex. The leader said they could join too. Now it was the newlyweds' turn.

The young husband said that after three days he was so horny that once, when he saw his wife reaching for a box of cereal from the top shelf, he couldn't help himself, he grabbed her and the two of them made passionate love together.

The leader then said, "Well I certainly cannot let you join our organization. And in addition, I am going to ban you from ever coming in here again."

The young wife then said, "I understand. That's exactly what the store manager told us, too."

CHAPTER TEN

Prostate Cancer

A man's equivalent to breast cancer?

Mr. P.C. was a 68-year-old man who had radical prostatectomy surgery performed four years previously for cancer of his prostate. After the surgery, Mr. P.C. had urinary incontinence (trouble holding back the flow of urine) for about three months, but that cleared up. Unfortunately, the surgery resulted in permanent ED for Mr. P.C.

Regardless of whether Mr. P.C. had diabetes, high blood pressure, conflicting medications or low testosterone, alleviating these conditions would not be able to bring his erections back. Sadly, the removal of his prostate cut the nerves connecting the penis to the spinal chord and resulted in permanent ED. Only the use of the hardware – injections, pumps or implants and possibly Viagra™ – would help this man have intercourse again.

PROSTATE CANCER TREATMENTS CAN CAUSE ED

Prostate cancer can be a fatal disease. On the other hand, it can also be a slow-growing malignancy which does not require any treatment. Your urologist will be able to give you the best advice as to how to treat prostate cancer.

From the book *Going the Distance*, by George Sheehan, M.D. (who himself died of prostate cancer), comes a useful concept. "There is a saying about prostate cancer: if it is possible to treat prostate cancer, it is necessary; if it is necessary to treat it, it is possible. Often the *biology* of the tumor (one slow-growing, the other a prairie fire), not the treatment, is decisive."

If surgery is recommended, it usually requires a total removal of the prostate gland. To do this properly, most of the nerves coming into the prostate and the penis from the spinal chord are often cut. These nerves control the erection and ejaculation processes. When they are cut, it is as if an electrical cord has been pulled out of a wall socket. The light goes out immediately.

Fortunately many urologists have been trained in the newer surgical techniques that protect and preserve the majority of the nerves coming into and out of the prostate. The newer prostatectomy procedure is identical to the previous type of surgery in removing the prostate with the cancer, but it spares the nerves and does not interfere with erections.

Sometimes, if the tumor has spread beyond the prostate gland, medications and/or radiation treatments can be used to try to arrest more growth and spread of the cancer. The usual medications used in the treatment of advanced prostate cancer cause a sudden drop in testosterone to zero. This sudden decline in testosterone can slow the growth of the tumor, but it also eliminates erections, practically in every case. Radiation can interfere with the erection process because the resultant local scarring can interrupt both the blood supply and the nerve impulses.

THE CURE FOR ED AFTER PROSTATE CANCER TREATMENTS

As I mentioned in the case example of Mr. P.C., the pumps, injections or implants are acceptable treatments for the ED-related side effect of prostate cancer treatments. Clinical trials using Viagra™ for men with ED resulting from prostate cancer treatments are very encouraging. Viagra™ might become the initial treatment of choice for these men.

The other form of treatment is formal sexual re-education with a sexologist (sexual therapist) to learn to enjoy closeness and sexual contact with a permanently limp penis. Although this approach requires certain adjustments for both men and women, some couples have found this style of sex to be quite rewarding and satisfying.

In a recent study conducted at Dalhousie Medical School in Halifax which assessed sexual functioning after radical prostatectomy, it was found that over 80% of men had a total loss of their erections. Follow up questioning about the impact on their sex lives revealed that the majority of men chose not to get involved with any hardware options. For the men in this particular study (mostly older men) regaining erections was not a priority.

PREVENTION OF PROSTATE CANCER

Prostate cancer rates are equivalent to female breast cancer in the U.S., where statistics show nearly identical rates for occurrence and mortality. Most of the research for both forms of cancer centers on the treatments but prevention is foremost on the minds of younger men and women at risk.

Slowly and steadily, clinical studies are pointing towards lifestyle modifications that include lower fat diets, exercise, moderate alcohol intake, no smoking and stress management as prevention strategies for both cancers. Eliminating exposure to toxins and pollutants from the environment is also suggested.

The daily use of antioxidant vitamins as previously outlined for prevention of heart disease is advocated to help prevent breast and prostate cancers. A newly discovered antioxidant called lycopene has been shown to protect against prostate cancer. Lycopene is a natural plant chemical (phytochemical) found in tomatoes and is now available in tablet or capsule form.

66A newly discovered antioxidant called lycopene has been shown to protect against prostate cancer. 99

CLOSING JOKE

There's the story about the teenager who was caught in the act of masturbating by the pastor in the local church.

"Can't you save that until you're married?" roared the pastor angrily.

The boy ran away in a hurry. Ten years later the boy, now a handsome man, was getting married and the ceremony was being performed by the same pastor.

"Don't you remember me, father?" Asked the young man.

"No, my son" replied the pastor.

After reminding the pastor about the incident 10 years earlier, the man said, "You told me to 'save' it until I got married. Well, I've saved eight quarts of the stuff. What do you want me to do with it now?"

CHAPTER ELEVEN

Metabolic Abnormalities

Modern medicine to the rescue.

Mr. H.A. was a 49-year-old man with ED. He looked tired, moved slowly and spoke quietly and softly. Mr. H.A. had had ED for one year.

"It goes soft very quickly, Doc. It never gets really hard anyway to start with. And to tell you the truth, I'm too tired to have sex. After work, I eat dinner, watch TV and usually fall asleep on the couch. Weekends are no different."

Mr. H.A. had low blood pressure and normal blood sugar and testosterone levels. He was satisfied with his job and his marriage was stable. Another blood test revealed a very low thyroid level. Thyroid is a hormone that provides every cell of the body with the ability to metabolize calories as fuel for energy. Women commonly have hypo or low thyroid conditions, but men can also. In the case of Mr. H.A., after establishing that his thyroid condition was not something more serious, he was started on thyroid replacement medication. Within two weeks he was back in the saddle again.

Mr. H.B. was a 46-year-old man who presented with a typical case of male menopause – fatigue, increased stomach fat, depression, low sexual desire and ED. His testosterone levels were indeed low, but his prolactin blood levels were sky high. Prolactin is a hormone produced in the brain that is designed to stimulate breast development and breast milk production in women. Men have prolactin produced from their brains as well; however, men do not have sufficient breast receptors necessary for breast enlargement and milk production.

Excessive prolactin levels in men turn off the production of testosterone and can result in ED. In Mr. H.B.'s case, his high prolactin levels were a result of a small brain tumor called a prolactinoma. Corrective surgery after a trial of prolactin-reducing medications was successful for Mr. H.B. and his sexual functioning was restored.

CHECK WITH YOUR DOCTOR

Erectile dysfunction can be caused by common metabolic abnormalities such as diabetes, high blood pressure or low testosterone. It can also be caused by rare metabolic abnormalities and other common disease processes. Only your doctor or a hormone specialist (endocrinologist) will be able to determine if ED is related to a metabolic or a disease dysfunction. And only appropriate treatment, like the thyroid replacement for Mr. H.A., can correct the ED problem.

Some medical conditions that your doctor might want to investigate and rule out as a potential contributing factor in your ED are the following:

- Systemic diseases – renal failure, cirrhosis of the liver, scleroderma
- Neurological – cerebrovascular accidents (strokes), multiple sclerosis, Alzheimer's disease
- Metabolic – hyper/ hypothyroidism, hyperprolactinemia
- Hematologic – sickle cell anemia, leukemia, hemochromatosis
- Respiratory – chronic bronchitis, emphysema
- Infections – tuberculosis, AIDS

CLOSING JOKE

Did you hear about the 70-year-old mohel? That's a Jewish doctor who performs ritual circumcisions. He was getting nervous because as he got older his hands were shaking and he didn't want to make any mistakes. So he asked his insurance agent if there was any insurance he could buy to protect himself. The agent came back with some good news and some bad news.

"What's the good news?" asked the mohel.

"The good news is that the policy only costs $500 a year," replied the agent.

"And the bad news?" asked the mohel.

"The bad news is that there is a two-inch deductible."

CHAPTER TWELVE

Male Infertility

Tonight's the night – are you up to it?

Mr. M. came in to see me because he and his wife wanted to have a baby. Both were in their late twenties, married for five years and were having unprotected intercourse for the past six months. Mr. G. came in because he also was having difficulty with fathering a child. Mr. G. was in his early forties, in his second marriage to a much younger woman. Mr. F. was another fellow complaining about infertility. He was in his mid-thirties and his wife was not conceiving as quickly as she had for her first two pregnancies.

Mr. M., Mr. G. and Mr. F. represent typical stories from the 10% to 15% of North American couples who have infertility, or difficulty in conceiving a child. What used to be regarded in ancient times as strictly a woman's problem is now known to be caused by male (mostly sperm) factors in approximately 40% of cases.

"The number-one cause of infertility is not having enough sex. "

Why write a chapter about male infertility in a book dealing with ED? Because one of the causes of infertility for a couple is ED. The number-one cause of infertility is not having enough sex. Men have to be able to perform consistently and regularly for conception. Sometimes they can't and when that happens, the couple might miss the opportunity to fertilize the ovum that particular month.

One of the effects of prolonged infertility in men is ED due to performance anxiety. Therefore, infertility is a necessary topic to explore in this book because of its cause-and-effect relation to ED. And since this is a comprehensive book on men's health, I have included male infertility as a separate chapter.

TESTING FOR MALE INFERTILITY

What causes male infertility and what can be done about it are two questions that are best handled by highly trained medical specialists, usually reproductive urologists and endocrinologists. The waiting period is long, the success rate is variable, the costs are usually high, but when a pink or blue bundle of joy is the product of sometimes years of infertility treatments, it's all well worth it.

In some ways, evaluating men regarding infertility is much easier than it is for women. In one simple test, a sperm analysis, the doctor knows if the man is responsible for the couple's infertility. With women, a variety of tests have to be performed, ranging from repetitive, hormonal-assay blood tests to surgical procedures. In addition, the treatments for male infertility can sometimes be easier to treat than for women because the doctor is only dealing with sperm and not with hormones, blocked fallopian tubes, uterine fibroids and other unknown factors.

When a man is suspected of being the cause of infertility, he first must have his semen checked from a masturbated sample, within one hour. Often three samples with three- to four-day intervals are required. The semen is a mixture of sperm from the testicles with prostatic and seminal vesicle fluids. Analysis of the semen reveals the following:

- The volume can vary from one-quarter to just over one tea-spoonful. Low volumes point to blockages or infections in the seminal vesicles or the prostate gland.
- The semen sample should quickly coagulate and then lique-fy within half an hour. Semen should pour easily. If it's too thick, it prevents the sperm from moving.
- The sperm count ranges from 20 million to 200 million per cubic centimeter. Over the past 20 to 30 years, due to pollu-tion, other environmental factors and hormonal changes, male sperm counts have been steadily declining. If the level is lower than 20 million, pregnancy is extremely difficult if not impossible.

- Sperm motility, or how the little guys swim with their whip-like tail action, is the most important single gauge of semen quality. Some sperm swim straight, some go around in circles and some don't move at all. The sperm have a long way to travel up the uterus through the tortuous fallopian tubes, after which they must bang away at the woman's egg and impregnate it.
- The morphology of the sperm or the shape is evaluated next. Over 60% should appear normal. Sometimes the sperm are too large, too small, and/or have multiple heads or tails.
- The pH of the semen should be slightly alkaline – 7.0 to 8.5 – to combat the normal acidity of vaginal secretions.
- If some sperm are clumped together it often is due to the presence of antibodies. This can result from previous infections in the testicles or prostate gland. Antibodies act like handcuffs for the sperm, hampering their swimming ability.

TREATMENTS FOR MALE INFERTILITY

When a man has a lowered sperm count or inappropriate morphology, a number of procedures are attempted to rectify the problem. They include:

1. If the sperm tube leading out from the testicle, called the epididymis, is blocked from a previous sexually transmitted disease, then surgical correction can be attempted. The success rate in this microsurgical technique is still low because the sperm must spend time in a healthy epididymis to fully mature, and usually there is other damage further along the tube from the infection.

2. The testicles, which produce the sperm, must be 2° F cooler than the rest of the body in order to manufacture healthy and abundant sperm. Often, the veins draining the blood away from the testicles back up into a varicose vein inside the scrotum called a varicocele. This elevates the temperature in the testicles and kills the sperm. A simple surgical ligation or tying off and redirecting the blood flow has a dramatic improvement on sperm counts.

3. Sperm counts can be low due to hormone irregularities, usually lowered testosterone hormone. This can sometimes be

rectified with fertility drugs, such as clomiphene or bromocriptine to reduce elevated brain prolactin levels (abnormally high prolactin levels can reduce testosterone production, which reduces sperm production). Unfortunately, supplemental testosterone does not improve sperm production – it suppresses it.

4. When the volume of semen is low, along with poor morphology, pH problems and poor motility, it may be necessary to use the high-tech systems. Reproductive clinics employ very sophisticated mechanisms and maneuvers to improve the chances of fertility. A few are:

- Artificial insemination, where the semen is either deposited directly into the uterus, or in vitro fertilization, where the eggs are surgically removed from the ovaries and mixed with the sperm in a lab Petri dish, incubated, and then placed back into the uterus.
- Zona drilling, where a surgeon uses chemicals, a laser beam or a needle to open part of the outer layer of the egg so that sperm have a better chance of penetration.
- Microinjection, where a thin needle is used to insert a single sperm into an egg; sperm-enhancement and sperm-washing laboratory techniques to raise the sperm counts.

What's left? For about 50% of men, all of the above treatments fail to result in either higher sperm counts or the ultimate, a baby. Here are a few suggestions for men to try that can improve their chances of fathering a child.

- Wear loose, cotton boxer shorts, to lower the temperature of the testicles.
- Avoid hot baths and saunas.
- Reduce alcohol intake – preferably to zero. Forty percent of male infertility is linked with drinking four ounces of alcohol, due to lowered sperm counts and erratic sperm swimming behavior. Cut down to one, and no more than two drinks per day.
- Reduce caffeine intake – coffee, tea, cola.
- Stop smoking. Smoking increases the amount of free radicals generated, and has been linked to sluggish sperm, low sperm counts and higher rates of miscarriages when conception does occur.

- Be careful with certain antibiotics that can lower sperm production. The erythromycin group should be avoided. Substitute (only if necessary) penicillins or quinolones.
- If you are overweight, lose a few pounds, since the fatty tissue can surround the testicles, increase the temperature and kill the sperm.
- Avoid sexual relations for two to five days before your spouse is expected to ovulate. It will increase your sperm count and provide a higher amount of morphologically healthy sperm. In addition, avoid the use of lubricants that may make sex easier but can impair sperm motility.
- Try to avoid exposure to heavy metal pollution, lead in particular, which can disturb sperm production. Men in certain occupations have higher rates of male infertility, such as welders, painters, battery factory workers, and stainless steel workers.
- Try to get excited about having sex. Men who are more aroused ejaculate larger amounts of semen and have more active sperm.
- Be careful with exercise. Moderate is good, but extreme exercise such as long distance running (more than 65 miles per week) results in lower sperm counts and more immature sperm cells. It can also lower testosterone levels, thereby lowering sperm production.
- Consider vitamin and mineral supplements. Low levels of vitamin C can cause sperm to clump together. Vitamin C stabilizes cell membranes and may have a beneficial effect on sperm production and morphology. Recommended vitamin C doses are a minimum of 1,000 to 1,500 mg per day. Beta-carotene (15,000 to 25,000 IU daily), vitamin E (100 to 200 IU daily) and selenium (50 mcg daily), are also important to help neutralize free radicals and potentially improve sperm counts. Zinc (chelate or citrate) at a dose of 10 to 20 mg per day is a necessary mineral for proper prostate function. Adequate zinc can help improve the prostatic fraction of the semen and in turn may help to improve fertility.

SUMMARY

The male testicles produce about 160 million sperm each day. It is a tireless job. It is also a job that can last a lifetime, and some men can still father a child well into their eighties, provided of course that there are no erection difficulties (but that's another story).

When everything is working as it should be and 300 to 400 million sperm are shot into the vagina, an uphill struggle takes place to find the waiting egg. At the very end, and many hours later, only two to three hundred sperm are left to reach the prized egg. And only one is selected and allowed to penetrate and fertilize the ovum. Why so many are needed and so few survive to the final stages and why only one out of hundreds of millions is privileged to pass on the male's genetic code, no one knows.

When conception works, it's a miracle to behold but when infertility cannot be repaired, it can be devastating for a couple. Modern medical reproductive scientists are working overtime trying to improve the odds for couples to conceive. When the infertility problem originates with the man, many systems can be investigated and treated. Very often, these treatments will eventually bring smiles and tears of joy onto the faces of a husband and wife at the moment of birth of their long-prayed-for baby.

CLOSING JOKE

There was once a urologist who specialized in adult circumcisions for various medical conditions. He would keep the foreskins in formaldehyde jars after the operations. When he was about to retire he found he had hundreds of these jars and he didn't know what to do with them. So he went to a tailor that he knew and asked him to make him something from the foreskins.

One week later, the tailor proudly presented the doctor with a wallet.

"Wait a minute," protested the doctor. "You had hundreds of foreskins to work with."

"Don't worry," said the tailor excitedly. "When you rub the wallet a little bit, it turns into a briefcase."

CHAPTER THIRTEEN

Premature Ejaculation

Quick-draw McGraw.

Mr. K. answered my newspaper advertisement. He was in his mid-forties, slim and trim. We shook hands and I gave Mr. K. my questionnaire to fill out. His erection ability was fine. He could get it up every time. But Mr. K. had a problem where he came too fast, a condition called premature ejaculation which sexologists are now referring to as rapid ejaculation. He was not only embarrassed but I sensed there was also a hint of anger (at his penis) with this condition. The sadness and despair, though, was clearly evident.

Most men with premature ejaculation who come in to see me are in their late twenties or early thirties. Since Mr. K. was over 40, he and his wife had suffered for 25 years without the full enjoyment of sex.

I told Mr. K. that I could help him with some targeted sexual counseling. When I said that it would not take that long to correct a lifetime of unhappy sex and turn it into enjoyable sex, he looked skeptical but also a little curious about the treatment.

I discussed with Mr. K. the pills we could use, but first I wanted to initiate a special sexual counseling program that could work wonders. And I was right!

THE CAUSES

The usual course of premature ejaculation (PE) runs something like this: initially it affects most teenage boys, gradually declines as they gain sexual experience and never returns during sexual maturity. A small percentage of men, however, never outgrow their initial PE and suffer their whole lives with embarrassment and inadequate sexual pleasure.

The causes of PE include:

- Psychological problems or specific psychosexual difficulties
- Never mastering the neuromuscular control mechanism, whereby the brain's inhibiting or enhancing nerve circuits interact with the reflex nerve pathways of the spinal chord
- Infections of the prostate (referred to in previous chapters as prostatitis)

Psychological problems leading to PE can be in the form of general personality disorders or more involved psychiatric conditions. However, most of the time PE is not related to serious mental disturbances. Instead, psychosexual traumatic experiences, such as sexual assault, incest and concerns about the size of the penis, can result in PE.

Regarding neuromuscular control for sexual functioning, the analogy is comparable to toilet training for bladder and bowel control in a two- to three-year-old child. Under the age of two, the neuromuscular brain pathways cannot interfere with the reflexes of the spinal chord. After age three, however, the influence of the brain's circuits always allows for timely adjustments of the involuntary toilet habits. The end result for everyone is lifelong voluntary control over urine and bowel requirements.

Enuresis (bed-wetting) is another common childhood condition. It can continue for many years in children who have not developed the necessary nighttime neuromuscular regulation over their spinal chord reflexes for the urinary bladder. By puberty, because of the enlargement of the urinary bladder the enuresis resolves itself. Not so with PE. It can continue to be troublesome for a lifetime.

Prostatitis, as mentioned earlier, can be very resistant to available treatments. This causes a chronic irritation in the prostate gland which sometimes results in loss of ejaculatory control even when the mind is in the right gear. It is still worthwhile to treat chronic prostatitis repeatedly in the hope that its resolution can also improve PE.

For many teenagers, the sudden rise in testosterone production initiating puberty and sexual development caused instant erections and fast ejaculations. This was most evident during masturbation, which was often performed in secret and in haste to avoid getting caught.

Similarly, if the teenager or young man was having intercourse, he often needed to ejaculate quickly, because:

- The girlfriend could change her mind and not go through with "it."
- His or her parents could interrupt them.
- He was just so happy to be able to actually have intercourse that he could not control his excitement.
- Not having much (or any) sexual experience, he did not want to disappoint the girl by going on for too long and appearing inexperienced.

As a result, the sexual programming that promoted quick ejaculations became fixed and ingrained in many men early on in life. Plus, since men rarely if ever talk to each other about sexual concerns or problems, the patterns are never changed.

In addition, when PE is present another psychological condition called performance anxiety can develop. Worrying if the ejaculation will be too rapid can often lead to ED in young men and of course, does nothing to improve the control of the ejaculatory response. I commonly see young men in my clinic with both PE and ED. The ED usually resolves itself once the PE is under control.

❝The sexual programming that promoted quick ejaculation became fixed and ingrained in many men early on in life. ❞

There is another possible cause of PE, especially in the 30- to 40-year age group of men. Remember that the erections are under the control of the parasympathetic nervous system (PSNS) and ejaculations are under the control of the sympathetic nervous system (SNS). A disturbance in the balance of the PSNS and the SNS can contribute to PE. In other words, too much SNS drive and/or not enough PSNS drive can lead to the sexual program favoring ejaculations over erections.

This PSNS/SNS imbalance can result from the stress response being activated unnecessarily. This all too often is a sign of the times for men. What are the sayings? "It's a dog-eat-dog world," "It's a rat race," "It's a jungle out there."

Things are much different today than they were a generation ago regarding sexual functioning for both men and women, but there is still significant PE among young men and significant concerns about orgasms among young women. The difference today lies in the amount of knowledge available on sexuality in the form of books, magazines, talk shows and the Internet. *It is only through the application of this knowledge of sexuality that young men and women can have more confidence in their personal sexual functioning.*

THE CURE

Premature ejaculation can sometimes be helped with certain antidepressant medications, such as serotonin-specific reuptake inhibitors SSRIs). In a low dosage, the side effect of these drugs is a slowing of sexual performance. This can sometimes mimic the brain's inhibitory influence on the spinal chord's reflex actions by increasing serotonin levels in the brain and dampening the libido.

Premature ejaculation can also be treated with a psychological program called "peaking." The peaking technique is a 10-step program of sexual exercises. It takes time and practice to master all the steps. It also temporarily takes a little (or a lot) of the fun away from sex, making it very clinical and mechanical. However, peaking has been shown to be very effective in correcting PE.

Please note that it is necessary to complete one step of this program before proceeding to the next step. If you get stuck, backtrack two steps and begin again. Remember, practice makes perfect.

THE 10-STEP PROGRAM FOR TREATING PREMATURE EJACULATION

1. Begin with self-stimulation (masturbation) until an erection is produced. Then stop and wait. Just hold your erect penis. Don't move. If the erection falters, stroke until firm again. Then stop and just hold it. Continue until a minimum of 10 minutes is achieved without ejaculation. Now go to step two.

2. Again, self-stimulate until erect. Stop and hold your penis for one minute. Stroke for a few seconds and stop. Wait for one minute. Stoke a few seconds. Wait for one minute...continue with the same pattern and when you are able to hold back ejaculation for ten minutes, move to step 3.

3. Self-stimulate until erect. Stroke for one minute, rest and hold one minute. Stroke for one minute, rest and hold one minute. Continue with the same pattern and when you can sustain this for 10 minutes, move to step 4.

4. Self-stimulate until erect. Stroke for one minute, rest and hold a few seconds. Stoke for one minute, rest and hold a few seconds. When you are able to sustain this pattern for 10 minutes, you can move on to step 5.

5. Self-stimulate until erect. Stroke continuously without stopping for 10 full minutes. When you can achieve this level of control you are ready for the intercourse schedule, beginning with step 6.

6. Stimulate until erect. Enter your partner vaginally. Don't move. If you feel the erection softening, move in and out until erect again. Stop. Don't move. When you can remain inside the vagina for 10 minutes without ejaculating, progress to step 7.

7. Stimulate until erect. Enter vaginally. Move for a few seconds. Wait one minute. Move for a few seconds. Wait one minute. Continue with the same pattern, and when 10 minutes are achieved at this pattern, move on to step 8.

8. Stimulate until erect. Enter vaginally. Move for one minute. Wait for one minute. Move for one minute. Wait for one minute. When you are able to continue this pattern for 10 minutes, go on to step 9.

9. Stimulate until erect. Enter vaginally. Move for one minute. Wait for a few seconds. Move for one minute. Wait for a few seconds. When you can sustain this pattern for 10 minutes, move on to step 10.

10. Stimulate until erect. Enter vaginally. Move in and out for 10 minutes straight without stopping. Slowing down is acceptable if you feel like it, but no stopping. After 10 minutes you can allow yourself to ejaculate.

Now go for it! You've graduated with honors.

SOME FINAL THOUGHTS

Premature ejaculation is still the most common sexual dysfunction among the young men I see in my men's clinic. This is confirmed in a survey of 600 young men in the U.S. published in *Cosmopolitan* magazine's, "All About Men Special Issue" (Summer 1998). The survey revealed some thought-provoking and enlightening results. The results have not been verified or standardized, but as a general sampling of young American men the results do corroborate many consistent facts found in other sexology studies. Check out the following questions and answers:

How often do you usually have sex?

- At least once a day   8%
- Three or four times a week   32%
- Once or twice a week   29%
- Three or four times a month   19%
- Three or four times a year   12%

How old were you when you lost your virginity?

- 15 or younger   21%
- 16 – 20   69%
- 21 – 25   8%
- 26 or older   2%

What is the maximum number of times you have ever had sex in one day?

- One to three   31%
- Four to six   51%
- Seven to ten   13%
- More than 10   5%

The above three questions reveal that young men are actively involved with sex on a regular basis. The next group of questions will show that PE is a major concern for many young men today.

What are you most self-conscious of sexually?

- Penis size   8%
- Coming too quickly   38%
- Not getting her off   32%
- My body   22%

What sexual activity do you like best?

- Intercourse 38%
- Getting oral sex 23%
- Giving oral sex 17%
- "69" 17%
- Anal sex 5%

What is your favorite position for intercourse?

- Missionary 12%
- Woman on top 55%
- Doggy style 14%
- Side-by-side 3%
- Standing 2%

Did you notice that the missionary position was championed by only 12% of the men interviewed, while 55% preferred the woman on top? And while intercourse was favored by 38% of men, oral sex was the choice of 57%? Oral sex does not have the same direct all-around stimulation of the penis that intercourse has. In addition, when the woman is on top, she is the one who controls the sexual rhythm and friction, again decreasing the direct stimulation of the penis and slowing down the ejaculation.

It is interesting to note that many of the young men in this sex survey have chosen to adjust their styles of sexuality (preferring oral sex and the woman on top) instead of mastering the neuromuscular control of the ejaculatory process. Perhaps the knowledge gained in this chapter on PE can be used to relieve the anxiety of performance control and prevent future problems with ED as well.

CLOSING JOKE

A little old man entered a church and headed straight for the confessional.

He said to the priest, "Father, I'm 80 years old. I have a wife, bless her heart, four grown children and 11 grandchildren. I've just had sex with twin 18-year-old girls."

The priest asked the man, "Tell me, my son, how long has it been since you came to confession?"

The man responded, "I've never been to confession. I'm Jewish."

The priest was surprised. "I don't understand, why are you telling me?"

The old man answered, "I'm so glad, I'm telling everybody."

CHAPTER FOURTEEN

Trauma

Fracture of the penis? I'm not kidding!

Mr. J. was a 32-year-old who came in with ED. All was well until six months ago. He could get an erection easily but now lost it quickly and could not regain it. He had no diabetes or high blood pressure and was not taking any medications. He denied work stress, marital stress or past stressful problems.

When I asked about trauma in the past, at first he denied any, but then he remembered something. Mr. J said, "I remember when I was about 10 years old. I was riding my bike. I hit a rut in the road and fell, straddling the crossbar of the bike. I was going pretty fast and landed heavily on the crossbar, right between my legs. I remember I was so sore, I couldn't walk for a week." Then Mr. J. asked me, "Do you think that accident long ago is causing my impotence now?"

THE CAUSE AND THE CURE

Trauma to the perineum (the tissue structures supporting the penis and testicles, and attached to the pubic bone) can produce serious damage to the arteries and /or nerves that supply the penis. The arteries are so tiny that trauma can result in permanent scarring. This narrowing from scar formation in the penile arteries limits the rush of blood volume.

When too little blood comes in too slowly, the penile veins are not compressed sufficiently and the blood drains out as fast as it comes in. When men are young, usually there is more than enough blood inflow to overcome any narrowing of the arteries.

With aging, even as younger men, the blood vessel narrowing process-es caused by cholesterol and high blood pressure are progressively working to shrink the arterial supply entering the penis. In these men with past trauma, it might be enough to tip the scales and result in premature ED.

If the arteries and/or nerves are permanently damaged, the only effective treatments available at the present time are the hardware solutions. These include injections, pumps and implants. The nitric oxide-enhancing drug Viagra™ may be beneficial for traumatic injuries as well.

In addition, surgical correction with microsurgical techniques to repair the damaged arteries is worth pursuing in younger men. Results have been fair to good, depending on the extent of the initial damage to the arteries.

BE CAREFUL WITH SEXUAL GYMNASTICS

When having intercourse and the rhythm is very vigorous, sometimes the penis can slip out of the vagina. Because the in and out motion is faster than the recognition by the brain that the penis is not inside the vagina any longer, the next thrust is against the buttocks of the woman. This usually is not harmful to men or women (alarming yes, but harmful no) and is usually just shrugged off with a little laughter and a desire to return to the status quo (lemme back in).

However, if intercourse is attempted with the woman on top of the man and the woman is going up and down on the penis, the same thing can happen – the penis can slip out. The difference this time though is that the full weight of the woman comes down onto the shaft of the penis. This can cause what is termed a fracturing of the penis. Since there are no bones in the "boner," the only things that can break (or tear) are the tunica albuginea, (the cover of the corprora cavernosa and sometimes the sinusoids in the corpora).

There will usually be intense pain should that happen. The penis will also be visibly bruised but then heal within one to three weeks. However, sometimes the fracturing can heal with scarring instead of elastic tissue. The result will be a bending of the erect penis (Pyronie's disease) at the scar. This might result in painful intercourse for both the man and his partner.

The advice is obvious – avoid highly gymnastic sex. At least be careful and methodical in your lovemaking.

CLOSING JOKES

There was the story about a doctor and his wife who were celebrating their twentieth anniversary. The wife asked her doctor-husband how he would rate their marriage.

"Well, we've been through some good times and some bad times but I feel we have weathered the storms together very well. You're also a marvelous cook and a wonderful mother to our children."

The doctor continued, "There is one area on our marriage that I feel is just not as good as I would have liked and where I feel you have let me down. It is the sexual area of our marriage. However, in every other aspect I feel you are just terrific."

Two weeks later the doctor came home early from his clinic to find his wife in bed with another man.

"What's going on here?" shouted the doctor.

"Don't get upset," replied his wife. "I'm just getting a second opinion."

Here's a joke from Max Kauffman:

The husband said to his wife, "Guess what I heard in the pub? They reckon the milkman has made love to every woman in this district except one."

The wife replied, "I'll bet it's that stuck-up Phyllis at number twenty-three."

Here's a joke from Henny Youngman:

"Some people ask the secret of our long marriage. We make sure we go out to dinner two times a week. And there's always a little candlelight, soft music and dancing. She goes on Tuesdays and I go on Fridays."

PART THREE

MEN AND SEX:
THE WOMEN

*Women <u>can</u> help their men live
longer and have better erections*

Women _can_ help their men live longer and have better erections.

M rs. Y.A. was an attractive 35-year-old woman who made the appointment for her 37-year-old husband. In fact, Mrs. Y. A. kept me on the phone for 20 minutes while she made sure that I was the right doctor for her husband. When the couple arrived at my clinic, it was Mrs. Y.A. who did most of the talking. She wasn't dominating her husband, it was just that she genuinely cared about him. Mrs. Y.A. wanted to be involved in all areas of his life, including troubled areas such as ED.

Mr. Y.A. filled out my ED questionnaire, which pointed to psychological causes for his ED (no diabetes, no high blood pressure, lots of stress). He was assessed at another men's ED clinic, where he was offered a choice of low-dose testosterone pills or penile injections. He was not offered sexual counseling or stress management advice.

When I asked about sexual frequency and sexual practices (different positions, oral sex, etc.), and Mrs. Y.A. quickly responded, "I am willing to do whatever it takes to help my husband regain his erection ability." She calmly told me, "There are no restrictions placed on my efforts to help my husband."

I thought to myself, "If there ever was a woman, who wanted to improve her man's sexual performance, here she is."

I began to suggest my strategy for resumption of sexual intimacy without resorting to intercourse. I told Mr. and Mrs. Y.A. to engage in sex, without intercourse, three times a week. I told them to concentrate for the next two weeks only on Mr. Y.A.'s arousal and stimulation, not on Mrs. Y.A.'s.

Both partners were listening attentively. Removing the pressure of intercourse (temporarily for two weeks) would decrease any of Mr. Y.A.'s performance anxiety. Focusing on his arousal and stimulation mechanisms would get his system activated again and begin the road to recovery. They agreed. So far, so good.

When I began to discuss arousal techniques for men – sexual fantasies, girlie magazines and adult videos – Mrs. Y.A. almost jumped out of her chair.

She shouted at her husband, "You mean to tell me that when we are making love, you aren't thinking of me?"

Mr. Y.A. told his wife the truth, "No, not always. Sometimes I think of other women or other situations. I'm just thinking, not doing."

Mrs. Y.A. shouted again (she didn't hear her husband or didn't want to hear him), "You mean you have been thinking of other women when we are having sex? Why? Don't I stimulate enough? I told you, I'll do anything you want. How can you think of other women when you are with me?"

Then Mrs. Y.A. spoke quietly but tearfully because she was obviously hurt. "I don't think I could make love to you again, knowing this. I never think of other men at any time. How could you think of other women when we are making love? I feel betrayed."

Both Mr. Y.A. and I spoke in unison, trying to explain that men were different than women, had different arousal and stimulation processes than women, and often fantasized about other women during lovemaking. It did not diminish a man's love for his woman. It was just a male brain phenomenon, which was different for a woman.

Unfortunately, Mrs. Y.A. wanted nothing to do with the scientific explanation of men's sexual fantasies. She was too upset and hurt to continue. Mrs. Y.A. left my office and her husband followed, offering a brief apology. I never heard from the couple again.

Mrs. Y.B. was 47 and her husband was 72. The Oriental couple came in with their four-year-old daughter. All was well with Mr. and Mrs. Y.B. until one year ago. Mr. Y.B. developed ED as a direct result of his long-standing diabetes. Mr. Y.B. was referred to my clinic by his endocrinologist (diabetes specialist) because the local urologist had almost a one year waiting period.

I have seen many men with diabetes and ED. The treatment with injection therapy, since the oral pills Viagra™, Vasomax™ and apomorphine were not available in Canada or the U.S. at that time, would be standard and appropriate treatment for Mr. Y.B. What was so special about this couple or about Mrs. Y.B.? Surprisingly, it had nothing to do with the couple's 25-year age difference. It was the fact that Mrs. Y.B. wanted to know first-hand from me everything about ED, diabetes, sexuality and men's health in general.

Mrs. Y.B. wanted to make sure that no stone was left unturned when it came to her husband's health care. She realized that Mr. Y.B. had a high risk of death due to his age, diabetes and high blood pressure. Mrs. Y.B. loved her husband very much and wanted him to be around to watch his four-year-old daughter grow up.

She wanted to know how she could help him with his diet, exercise, stress and sexual functioning. Mrs. Y.B. had come to the right place.

Mrs. Y.C. was a 53-year-old patient of mine whose husband had ED, but had never told me about his problem. She was experiencing her own menopausal complaints – hot flashes, irritability, headaches, urinary frequency and lowered sex drive. However, she was concerned that her marriage of 31 years might be in jeopardy because of her menopause.

Mrs. Y.C. had no desire for sex and did not feel as close to her husband in the past six months. As a result, sex was infrequent, painful and certainly no fun for either Mrs. Y.A. or her husband.

Mrs. Y.C. asked me, "Doctor, will hormone replacement therapy help my sexual attitude or desire? Will it help my vagina? It feels so dry. What else can I do? I don't want to get breast cancer but I don't want heart disease or osteoporosis either. Are there natural remedies that are effective?"

Mrs. Y.C. continued, "I care about my husband and I want him to be happy. I know he is embarrassed about his impotence. I don't think he'll come in to talk to you about it. He might take the pills everyone is talking about, Viagra™ or Vasomax™, but I don't think I could convince him to come and see you about it. We haven't had good sex for a long time and I know it's affecting our marriage. Doctor, can you help me to help my husband?"

SHOULD YOU READ THIS CHAPTER?

The material I will present in this chapter is intended specifically for women. It is designed for women readers who wish to make sure that their partners will have firm, long-lasting erections for effective and pleasurable intercourse. Should this be an important issue for all women? That depends. Let me share with you how I developed this chapter.

I was invited to present an abbreviated version of the concepts found in this chapter at the Eighth Annual Meeting of the International Society for Impotence Research (ISIR) in Amsterdam on August 27, 1998.

In the opening part of my presentation, I discussed the prospect of enlisting the female partner in improving or preventing ED. To help the doctors decide which women would be appropriate for my suggestions, I subdivided female partners into a classification system using inclusion or exclusion criteria.

The same rules will apply for this chapter. If you find that you match the description for the exclusion subset, then I advise skipping this chapter or even the entire book. If you find that you identify with the inclusion group, then please continue.

Inclusion criteria

- Mothering attitude: if you say, "Let me help you," you're in.
- Self-motivated: if you say, "I need a good stiff penis for good sex," you're in.
- Willing and able: if you show up with your man at the ED clinic for the first visit and say, "I'll do anything you ask," you're in.

Exclusion criteria

- Indifference: if you say, "I don't care," you're out.
- Reluctance: if you say, "It's his problem," you're out.
- Hostility: if you say, "It serves him right," you're out.

What if you find yourself with a mixture of both inclusion and exclusion criteria? You probably fall in with the majority of female partners. The criteria I outlined appear cut and dried but in the real world they would only describe a minority of female partners.

Here's my advice: read on and see how you feel about the material. If you find the information seems to make sense and you find yourself frequently nodding in agreement, then this chapter is for you. If you find yourself grimacing and shaking your head, then please stop. Trust your female intuition.

WHY A SPECIAL CHAPTER FOR WOMEN ONLY?

There are many obvious, common-sense ways to improve your sex life and love life. You're probably using many of these ways every day (or night). In addition, there are many self-help books available on the subject of human sexuality that provide extra professional advice. I have included recommended reading lists throughout this book.

What women will find in this chapter is a variety of practical techniques which will rapidly improve sexual functioning for their male partners and allow them to have sex for life. (Good title for a book, eh?) In addition, I will highlight some of the sexual differences between women and men. Hopefully this knowledge will help to bring the sexes closer together.

The strategies presented in this chapter will help you to become directly involved in sexual activities. These activities should only be done with an intimate sexual partner.

" *Don't worry about why your man cares so much about his erection ability. Just accept it as a biological fact of life for men. It will be easier for both of you.* "

Elaine, from the *Seinfeld* TV comedy series, once asked, "I don't get to handle the equipment as often as you guys do. How do you walk around with those things anyway?"

Here is my general advice for women: knowing the *how* (it works) and the *when* (it works) about his equipment will benefit both your relationship and his sexual performance. But don't worry about *why* your man cares so much about his erection ability. Just accept it as a biological fact of men. It will be easier for both of you.

As writer Doris Lessing once said, "There's something about a man with a whacking great erection that is hard to resist."

A MAN'S SEXUAL HEALTH IS LINKED TO HIS GENERAL HEALTH

In all honesty, the advice in this chapter is geared towards improving your man's health in general and sexual health in particular. It will not improve your health or your sexual enjoyment directly. Remember, the focus of this book is about sex for life – men and their erections – and the focus of this chapter is *what you can do for your man* to improve his health and sexual ability.

However, both your health and your sexuality will benefit indirectly, which is good news for you and your man. If Mister has dependable erections, your sex life will improve. If Mister feels better as a man, from improvements in both his health and sexual ability, suddenly you will find him looking for ways where he can improve your life. This will become especially evident if he becomes aware that you were substantially responsible for his improvement.

As a woman, if you want to learn to enrich your life in any way (health, sex, fashion), there are ample sources of information at your fingertips in books, magazines and seminars. Unfortunately, there is a dramatic lack of information promoting men's health. Hopefully, this book will help to change men's whole lives – not just their sexual lives – for the better. All this can be achieved without any compromises to women's health issues or women's lives.

This chapter will also benefit those women who want to help their husbands and boyfriends close the seven-year gap that has their men dying before they do. Medical studies keep confirming that too many men are dying needlessly before their time. So, to help keep hubby around and kicking, you will find additional longevity information placed throughout this chapter.

> **66** *Medical studies keep confirming that too many men are dying needlessly before their time.* **99**

Finally, the majority of information contained in this chapter is intended to at least maintain and possibly increase men's testosterone levels. This one area in men's lives alone will provide men with improvements in coronary artery disease, osteoporosis, erections and possibly Alzheimer's disease and diabetes.

WOMEN ARE BORN NURTURERS

One final point before we get to the essence of this chapter. I have studied quite a few books and articles in my research on breast cancer and hormonal replacement. I have yet to find any sources with information designed for men to help improve the health status of their female partners.

Many books have sections that discuss how important it is for men to be supportive of their female partners if they have breast cancer or other serious female health concerns. It is rare, however, to find a chapter just for men in a book entirely designed for a woman's health benefit.

The reason I included this particular chapter relates to one of the profound differences between men and women that I discovered from my work in my men's clinic and my breast cancer prevention clinic. Women care about their men in a different way than men care about their women. Not better, not worse, just different.

Women are born nurturers. They will go out of their way to try to correct any health problems affecting their men. Men will usually delegate the job of fixing a health concern to their women, to someone else, like a doctor, a mother-in-law or a support group. Also, men will not volunteer to lend a helping hand on their own *as fast* as women will.

Men need to be guided and told to do things a little more (sometimes a lot more) than women do, especially when it comes to health and family. The three case histories of wives of men with ED at the beginning of this chapter show female readers that many men are often dependent on their wives for nurturing and support. Of course, most men will never admit that, even though it's true.

SEX, SEX AND MORE SEX

Men need regular sexual activity. Men can have solitary sexual servicing (masturbation), but the vast majority prefer intercourse over masturbation any day. Men in general have much higher needs for regular sexual relations than women do. This is simply a biological phenomenon related to the daily fluctuations in testosterone for men and the monthly fluctuations of estrogen for women. Some men want sex every day and some are satisfied with once a week. However, men in general prefer a sexual routine of every other day (and don't forget the Saturday night special).

Men's Fitness magazine (March 1998) asked 1,400 men, "How often do you feel sexual attraction?" Here's how they responded:

- Once an hour   28%
- A few times a day   63%
- Once a day   5%
- Less than once a day   4%

The numbers obviously speak for themselves. Since the average reader of *Men's Fitness* is around 35 years old, men in this age group *experience sexual attraction even when you are not around.* This likely applies to middle-aged men as well. During these thoughts involving sexual attraction, he may be thinking of you or he may not be.

One thing we know for sure – Mister is thinking of sex.

Of course, sexual attraction is not a one-way street – women are also sexually attracted to other men. If you recall the section on sexual fantasies in the chapter "Psychosexual trauma," I showed evidence that *younger women are catching up to men in the area of sexual fulfillment through the use of sexual fantasies.*

Here is more evidence that younger women (average age 30 to 35) have sex on the brain a lot more than we might think. In a survey by *Cosmopolitan* (August 1998), 1,000 women were asked, "How many times a day do you think about sex?" Here are their responses:

- I lose count   23%
- 11 – 20   9%
- 6 – 10   20%
- 2 – 5   40%
- 1   7%
- None   3%

The numbers are not identical to the men's survey, but they sure are close. This just makes it easier on women to have more sex for *his* benefit. It also means that many women will be eager and willing to try out the upcoming suggestions on how to increase sexual activity at home.

Increased sexual activity for men that occurs on a regular basis, is enjoyable, and leads to an orgasm, helps promote improved prostate health, testosterone levels, sleep, self-esteem and health in general. When your man is happy and healthy (because of more regular sex), you have a better chance of being happy and healthy too, partly from more regular sex as well, but also from more love and affection.

How can you, as his female partner, make sure his quota of sex is a number that is acceptable to both of you and can also be maintained on a regular basis? Here are 12 ways:

1. Quickies

Sex can take 20 minutes or two minutes – for a man, not for a woman. The man is just waiting for you to tell him when he can "do it." If you arrange to have sex with your man two to three times a week, every week, some of those sessions will have to be quickies. As long as you are getting your share of romantic, slow and loving 20- or 30-minute sexual encounters, try to live with a few quickies to make up the quota.

Remember, with a quickie, you may not be getting as much pleasure from it, but that's acceptable to him if you're comfortable with it.

Quickie sex does not diminish your man's love for you. It's simply that men are able to have sex without romance and even without love. A quickie is strictly a physical thing, a quick release of sexual tension. But it sure feels good to a man (and to some women).

2. Try something new

Try a different position. How about creative sex, like you may have practiced when you were pregnant? Try out different sex games, whips and chains, if it pleases both of you. Don't do anything you feel uncomfortable with, just see what the two of you can come up with. Sexual variety is the spice of life, and sometimes in marriage, sexual practices tend to get stale.

Sex therapist Dr. Patricia Love suggests setting the stage for sex with the proper music, the use of candles, massage oils or a shared shower. Dr. Love describes a particular style of sex she calls adventuresome sex – using various props, such as food (to be put where...?), seductive clothing, feathers or ice (also to be put where...?). You could greet your man at the door when he comes home from work, dressed only in clear plastic wrap. Just make sure it's hubby at the door before you open it!

3. Don't state the obvious

It happens to every man, young and old, at one time or another. The penis gets soft and won't regain sufficient firmness to allow for effective intercourse. He knows it. He doesn't need your comments. From his perception and vantage point all comments are negative comments. And they will likely finish him off for good.

Give him a few minutes without any words, gestures or sighs that imply disappointment on your part. You can instead say something like "Let's not have intercourse just yet. I have something else in mind (sex games, revealing clothing, sexual videos, food, ice)." It might stimulate him enough to get back in the ball game. If not, it will distract him and you won't have to say, "It doesn't matter." It does matter to him.

4. Think about hormone replacement therapy

Most doctors and gynecology specialists in North America and Europe advocate the use of hormone (estrogen) replacement therapy (HRT) for a large percentage of menopausal women. Unfortunately, the compliance rate for women who continue to take HRT after three months is only 14%.

Estrogen replacement will directly improve women's sexual desire and vaginal lubrication. Sex is therefore not only easier, it is more enjoyable for both partners. Sometimes, if estrogen does not do the trick to stimulate sexual drive, gynecologists often add a little testosterone to the HRT cocktail, with dramatic results in sexual performance. My advice is to think about HRT, read books about HRT, and talk to your gynecologist. You are the consumer, so make an informed decision for yourself.

5. Mini-honeymoons

Honeymoons are understood to be a time of frequent if not continuous sex. When was the last time you and your man had continuous sex together? Did you say your honeymoon? Here's the plan: 1) arrange a weekend retreat, 2) without the kids, 3) during your midcycle, and 4) make sure that sex is a top priority.

Talk to your man in advance about you wanting the weekend to be a time with lots of sex so that his mind is in gear (and yours too). This way both of you are on the same wavelength and there will not be any misunderstandings. Remember to pack some massage oil, sexy lingerie, garter belts and black stockings. Don't forget the kind with the seam. They can really turn up the heat fast for him. Watching X-rated movies provided for private viewing on your hotel TV won't hurt either.

6. Consider using an erotic aid

You've heard about them, but you may not have considered using them – sex toys for women. I am referring to vibrators and dildos. A 1978 survey of married women by *Redbook* magazine showed only 20% used an aid. Fifteen years later, another survey by *Ladies' Home Journal* found that almost 50% of women were using them.

Vibrators, the most common erotic aid sold, are usually designed for female masturbation, but can also be used during lovemaking with a partner. They can get you going if you require some specific clitoral stimulation, or can come in handy if Mr. Softee appears and you want to give him a break for a while. One thing is for sure – they will help to satisfy you just in case he can't, which takes the pressure off hubby to perform.

7. Safe sex

Sex in the nineties is not like it was in the seventies. We now have more sexually transmitted diseases (STDs) such as VD (venereal diseases – syphilis and gonorrhea), herpes, chlamydia, genital warts and of course the big one, AIDS. The use of condoms dramatically reduces the incidence of STDs. Condoms are also 100% effective for birth control if they are applied correctly. In monogamous marriages, STDs are rarely an issue but birth control sure is. In open marriages or while dating, condom use and other safe sex practices are mandatory.

But as all women know, men hate condoms. The main reason is that men sacrifice a lot of tactile sensation and friction when a condom is used during intercourse. Here is my advice. In monogamous marriages, try to arrange permanent birth control with either a tubal ligation or a vasectomy when your ages and number of children are appropriate. In other sexual relationships where there could be the potential spread of STDs you must continue with safe sex, but be aware that his sensation is significantly reduced with a condom. So try to stimulate him a little longer before it's time for him to slip on his raincoat.

Susie Bright, in her book *Susie Bright's Sexual State of the Union,* writes about integrating safe sex practices with sexual stimulation and sexual gratification. "If safe sex is offered like cod liver oil, it's not going to be swallowed. Safe sex doesn't work without sexual fulfillment – that's why I started to do workshops (called Safe Sex for Sex Maniacs), because I had to do something dramatic to break through the forbidding qualities of so many safety do's and don'ts."

8. Sexy lingerie

From the book *Hot Monogamy,* by Dr. Patricia Love and Jo Robinson, come these results of a survey done on 1,000 men who were asked, "What is the most sexually arousing – dirty talk, X-rated videos, pornography, female masturbation, sexy lingerie, or 'other'?" These are the results: 92% were turned on the most by sexy lingerie. In addition, 73% of these men relied on this particular type of stimulation to maintain sexual interest in a long-term relationship.

Don't let hubby buy you these items (they probably won't fit). It's better for you to shop for what you feel flatters your shape and size. And guess what? You might even get turned on a little yourself. Like I said in the section on honeymoon sex, black stockings with a garter belts does the trick every time for him (and you will likely feel sexier yourself).

9. Enjoy sex

Men are stimulated by women who are not only interested in sex but who are also motivated to achieve orgasm. In the book *Mars and Venus in the Bedroom,* by John Grey, the author states that women enjoy sex the most *when women have orgasms.* He says that men, too, also enjoy sex the most *when women have orgasms.*

One way to ensure female sexual excitement is to do what over 20 million American women do every year – read romance novels. Research presented in the book *Hot Monogamy* showed that romance novel readers experience greater sexual satisfaction, but more important for hubby, these women have sex *twice as often* as non-readers do. I may be preaching to the converted here, because romance novels account for almost 50% of the mass-market paperbacks sold in the U.S.

I would suggest two more books to read or perhaps have handy. *Super Sexual Orgasm* and *Sex Tips for Straight Women from a Gay Guy* are both up-to-date sexual manuals (published in 1997) that will allow you to finally experience the fireworks of orgasm, or to soar higher than ever before.

Super Sexual Orgasm is just for women, written by a female sex therapist who was at one time a sex surrogate. This books helps you discover your "cul-de-sac," a collection of sensitive nerve endings deep inside the vagina. Following the clearly outlined exercises contained in this book will produce exceptional orgasms through intercourse. In addition, you can teach hubby (or yourself) where your "G" spot is hiding. Get ready for the fireworks display!

Sex Tips... is a light-hearted yet comprehensive manual for women to learn the proper maneuvers for the basic hand job, oral stimulation, ball play, intercourse positions and things you never would have thought of! The author is correct when he states that no one knows more about the sexual pleasure of a man than a gay guy. This book will open up new vistas for mutual sexual excitement and is a lot of fun to read at the same time. Remember, better sex equals a better marriage equals better erections equals better sex... You get the picture?

10. Oral sex

I don't want to get into hot water here, but I have to say it, because **this is what men tell me they want** – oral sex. And I am talking about all men, of all ages, nationalities and backgrounds! If it already is a part of your sexual practice, enough said. If it is not, and has never been, could it be? If it seems out of the question, could you begin to contemplate it? Remember, *it's for him and it turns him on.* There is no single sexual practice that works so consistently for men. I am just stating a fact and I don't want to use guilt or make you uncomfortable. However, if you want your man to really enjoy sex and/or maintain good erections, this is the single most effective strategy you can do for him. But, dare I say it? He is more than ready to get involved with oral stimulation for you too. And that can increase your sexual pleasure to a level that you might never have experienced before.

For those of you out there, who would like a few suggestions on techniques for better fellatio (oral sex), here is an excerpt from a recent book, *Just Between Us Girls,* by Sydney Biddle Barrows, an ex-prostitute:

"Men are visual creatures. One of the reasons they love X-rated movies is that they like to watch the action – in particular, they like to watch *you.* So it's nice to be rather elaborate about fellatio. Don't just put it in your mouth and start moving up and down. Men like a little foreplay down there; they like a show.

"First work your way down to it, kissing down his chest, stomach and inner thighs. Tease him a little, start to kiss it, then pull away. You might try licking his testicles and massaging them a bit. Next start to swirl your tongue around the head and the shaft of the penis. You might also want to take it, stroke it across your face, give it some light kisses, almost as if you're worshiping it.

"Some of you may be thinking, *Please Sydney, are you serious?* Believe me, he'll love this stuff. If you're still not sure you're doing this right, rent an X-rated video and see how the actresses do it. They lick and they swirl."

11. Attitude and personality

This is almost the last one, I promise. I appreciate the fact that I have painted a picture of men requiring nearly perfect women for their sexual stimulation and firm erections. And to this ideal sex object, I will add one more thing for you to do. No, it is not dying your hair blond. It is, however, acting the opposite of the stereotypical "dumb blond."

From the *Men's Fitness* magazine survey (March 1998) come these responses to the final question in the survey: "What other qualities cause you to feel sexually attracted [to a woman]?"

- Personality   63%
- Smile   51%
- Intelligence   33%
- Unattainability   17%
- Availability   14%

Remember, the question was "other" qualities for sexual attraction. We know that a woman's physical qualities are the number one attraction for men but the personality and the smile come in a close second. Women should readily understand that men are also attracted to personality because when the roles are reversed the man's personality is still a strong sexual attraction to women.

Here's the first question from the August 1998 *Cosmopolitan* survey of 1,000 female readers in the "Sex is the Theme" issue: "What is it about men that attracts you the most?" The respondents answered:

- A guy's general attitude   37%
- A good personality   32%
- The way a man moves   22%
- A man's chest   35%
- A man's face   34%
- A man's buns   27%
- A man's shoulders   17%
- A man's penis   16%

For the men reading this section, have a close look at the statistics. Women at the average age of 35 are more than twice as attracted to your chest than to your penis. And the penis has about the same attractive potential as your shoulders. If you want women to notice you for a sexual relationship, get working on your attitude, personality and those chest and shoulder muscles! It's true. Women care more about the size of your other muscles than your penis muscle.

12. Shape up

As a general rule, many men will admit that they like slim, lithe, big-breasted women. Being blond wouldn't hurt either. The pressure comes from the advertising industry, to be sure, but it doesn't change the reality for men – when women are overweight it turns many men off.

I am well aware that quite a few men are not studs anymore either and they don't seem to care too much whether or not a big beer belly turns women off. But men's sexual arousal mechanisms are more sensitive to visual and fantasy stimulation, and excess female fat on the buttocks and hips can be a downer for men.

I don't mean to offend any female readers, but I have to say the obvious: a weight reduction program for **both** partners, but especially for women, will be more of a sexual stimulant for hubby than for you.

In the summer 1998 *Cosmopolitan* magazine's "All About Men" issue, 600 young men were asked : "Which of these famous females has the body type you most love?"

- Salma Hayek – curvy and voluptuous   46%
- Demi Moore – athletic, rock-solid and tight   24%
- Winona Ryder – petite   15%
- Gwyneth Paltrow – tall, lanky and featherweight   9%
- Kirstie Alley – big-boned and large-scale   6%

Did you notice that the big-boned and large-scale actress was Kirstie Alley? Would you say that she is fat or large-scale?

Now, guess what the *Men's Fitness* survey (March 1998) had to say in answer to the question: "Which female body parts arouse you sexually?"

- Butt   71%
- Legs   65%
- Breasts 52%
- Eyes   42%
- Waist   37%
- Hair   26%
- Feet   13%

(Most respondents selected more than one and some selected everything.)

According to this survey, men are most aroused by a woman's butt, legs and breasts, yet women spend a lot of time and money on their hair, lipstick and nails. If you are one of those women, it won't be for his benefit. You and Mister will have more successful sex if you spend some time and effort trimming and shaping your butt instead.

THIS REALLY TURNS HIM OFF

To end this section on *sex, sex and more sex*, I would like to propose one final area for your consideration. It has to do with the way you reject, criticize, question and finally give advice to your man. Men, in general, hate to be rejected and criticized. They also prefer to give advice rather than receive it.

And when it comes to sex, rejection on your part can be very devastating on his part. Instead of saying, "I can't have sex now, are you crazy? The Jones' are coming over in 30 minutes!" try saying this instead: "Well, sex right now would be exciting for me too, but I don't think we could get the house ready for the Jones' who are coming over in 30 minutes. How about if we get into it after they leave? I have something in mind I want to try with you." At that point, give him a little grab, you know where, so he knows you mean business.

Repeated rejections and criticisms are demoralizing to men. They also turn off his sex drive because a man does not want to face being rejected for sex. As a result, if he subconsciously turns off his sex drive then he won't be rejected, because he won't be asking for it. This is bad for him and bad for you. Less sex leads to less closeness leads to less sex… As I said previously, it's either an upward spiral or a downward spiral.

> **“Repeated rejections and criticisms are demoralizing to men. They also turn off his sex drive. ”**

Here's another area to consider regarding rejections and criticisms. Men are sensitive creatures even though they don't often admit it or show it. If your criticisms are directed towards your man's friends, sports interests or work environment, he will often see these as personal threats. This creates a conflict for your man because he is somewhat torn with his allegiance to you and his buddies or his desires. Be careful and considerate with your words, actions and tone of voice. Mister can be very upset and never show it at all except for a sudden case of ED.

Finally, never criticize his sexual needs, frequency and personal arousal system. Either it will lead to arguments or the opposite – held-in hurt feelings – for both of you. If he has a personal collection of girlie magazines or erotic videos, as long as both of you are having a happy sexual and loving relationship, try to look the other way. Tolerance and acceptance will go a long way in any type of relationship, but especially in a love relationship.

Women, I don't envy you; you have your work cut out for you. I know that if the tables were turned, hubby would probably not invest a fraction of the time or effort that I am suggesting you do to help him with his sexual functioning. Whether what I am proposing for women seems fair or unfair, remember, this is a book devoted to examining all areas that can affect a man's erections. And this chapter is one of those areas.

Here's my best short-list of priorities:
- Engage in more oral sex.
- Wear nylons, garter belts and high heels.
- Be careful with criticism and rejection.

GO TO THE GYM WITH HIM

Join a gym or fitness club and go with your man. Try to do similar exercises with him, both aerobic and anaerobic. Plan to work out on a regular basis, and arrange a schedule where both of you can go at least three to four times a week. It might be an idea to invest in some home exercise equipment, such as a stationary bike, treadmill and free weights. Home exercise can be done when the weather is bad, when your schedules collide or when you are just too tired to go to the club for a full workout.

Make sure your man gets involved with a weight-training program. You can start one too, and don't worry, you will definitely not get large muscles. You will, however, get shapelier, especially where it counts. Ask his advice about specific weight-lifting exercises and ask him to show you how the special weight machines work.

*66 **Once he sees himself in the mirror with larger, firmer muscles in his chest and biceps, his masculine vanity and striving for excellence will take over.** 99*

Get him interested, get him started, and nature will take over. Your job is to get him thinking about weight training. Once he sees himself in the mirror with larger, firmer muscles in his chest and biceps, his masculine vanity and striving for excellence will take over. Men and muscles go together. It's built-in desire for all men, but for many couch potatoes the desire to be more muscular needs to be rekindled.

Buy your man muscle magazines such as *Muscular Development* and *Men's Health*. These magazines are not just for power lifters, although the pictures are almost always showing the finalists in weight-training competitions. There are usually articles for beginners in every magazine, as well as valuable information on proper techniques for all basic exercises using weights.

Here's something to try. Be a little competitive with your man when it comes to the weights. He should be able to lift, push and pull three to four times what you can. If your pounds off the ground begin to rise, he will have to increase his workouts accordingly.

Some men, when they get a little older don't push themselves enough at the club. Some trainers and fitness advisors don't push the clients either for fear of offending them, causing injuries or worse, contributing to a heart attack. Your man won't improve his testosterone or his erectile functioning unless he pushes himself to increase his workouts and weights *every* time he works out. Here are some suggestions to help him get motivated:

- Don't criticize. Instead, encourage him to strive for improvements in his body.
- Show him some new exercises you found in the muscle magazines.
- Give him a birthday present of an hour with a personal trainer.
- Make sure he does his leg press exercises every day. It improves erections.
- Compliment his new muscles. Feel them and admire them. He sweated for them, he pumped them up, and it will make him feel even better if you take some pride in them too.
- If you see your man slouching, remind him to stick out his chest, keep his head high and shoulders back. Remind him to strut his stuff.

IF YOU SMOKE, STOP

The worst thing for your man is smoking – this includes inhaling direct and second-hand smoke. Smoking causes high blood pressure, atherosclerosis (hardening of the arteries), increased risk of heart attacks and strokes, and above all, ED. If your man does not smoke and you don't smoke, just try to limit his second-hand exposure. Otherwise…

- *If you don't smoke and he does*, talk to him and your doctor about nicotine patches, nicotine gums or support groups to help him kick his habit. Encourage him and actively promote a smoke-reduction and elimination program for him.
- *If you smoke and he doesn't*, the onus is on you to quit and protect him from your second-hand pollution. You have to

do whatever is necessary to quit. Enlist his help in your own program for reducing and quitting smoking. He'll be happy to oblige.

- *If both of you smoke,* talk to him about both of you quitting and suffering through the withdrawal together. The techniques described in Part Two, Chapter Four, will be helpful for both of you when you finally decide to do it (stop smoking, that is).

- *If he is not interested in stopping at this time,* I suggest that you quit on your own. Leave him out of it. You just stop your own smoking and when you are successful, guess what hubby will do? He'll stop too. It won't be fun for him to smoke anymore when you have already quit. Just make him think it was his idea that he quit, he'll like that.

THE WAY TO A MAN'S HEART IS THROUGH HIS STOMACH

I won't go over the nutritional advice that is outlined in detail in Part Two, Chapter One. I will assume that you are balancing his diet with proteins, carbohydrates and fats in every meal. The extra protein will ensure adequate levels of the amino acid arginine, the precursor of nitric oxide. More nitric oxide ensures better erections. That's good for both of you.

Here are a few more suggestions to help maintain healthy nutrition for your man:

- Prepare lunches for him that are certain to be nutritionally balanced. That way he has no excuse for going off the meal plan.
- Watch what he eats at home and redirect his cravings for junk food by substituting nutritious, delicious snacks.
- There are many meal replacement bars that taste identical to chocolate bars but have more protein content and are more nutritionally balanced. Have a supply of these on hand and make sure hubby has some in the glove compartment of his car for those long road trips to keep him in a healthy state of nutrition. You can find these bars at health food stores. Avoid bars with hydrogenated or partially hydrogenated fats or oils.

- Add tofu to your diet. It is high in protein and low in fat. You can disguise tofu to taste like anything you want and he won't know the difference. A wonderful recipe I love is a mock chopped-egg salad using tofu instead of eggs. The recipe is included at the end of this chapter. All my patients love it!
- Eat the same foods your man does. The nutritional program I previously outlined is specifically designed to limit the effects of Syndrome X. It will help get you in better shape along with your man.
- Once and for all, get yourself back to a slim, trim package. Medical studies show that more women are overweight than men, especially post-menopausal women. It's not fair to your man to have him limit sweets and breads if you are not involved in conscientious eating too.

I know that women feel more pressure to lose weight than men do. That's why the diet industry is geared more to women than to men. Unfortunately, many women succumb to the pressure by developing eating disorders – bulimia, binging and anorexia nervosa. Successful treatments for eating disorders are limited and many women are suffering silently.

66 Inside every man is a Tarzan and inside every woman is an Uma Thurman. 99

What you may hear on television talk shows or read in women's magazines is this: accept yourself the way you are (overweight) and stop fighting with a diet. Want my advice? It doesn't work! You'll never accept the fact that you are overweight. Inside every man is a Tarzan and inside every woman is an Uma Thurman.

While my height, hair loss and eye color are all genetically fixed, I do have control over what I put in my mouth and how much exercise I do. And so do you! Just stop eating the bread (and cookies and cakes) and you will see the fat melt off your hips.

One more suggestion to help the Uma in you re-emerge: find a photograph of yourself when you were younger and wearing a bathing suit (preferably a bikini). Get the photo enlarged to poster-size. Now place this poster by the fridge. That's it. Your brain will do the rest. Within three months you will be well on your way to looking like you did in the picture.

MAKE AN APPOINTMENT FOR HIS PHYSICAL

Your man does not need to remind you to go to the doctor for an annual Pap smear or a mammogram. He does, however, need your reminder about his annual check-up (which likely has not been done in a few years). Men subscribe to the motto: "If it ain't broke, don't fix it." Unless they feel something wrong or they see blood, they tend to stay away from the doctor's office. I know at my office, medical visits from female patients outnumber male visits four to one. And there are many studies confirming this fact.

He might balk and complain about the appointment, but too bad for him. He needs it. It is mandatory to have his blood pressure checked, and a blood test taken for diabetes and cholesterol. And these procedures won't be performed unless he shows up at the doctor's office. Just make the appointment. He'll go – reluctantly – but he'll go.

It's usually not a good idea to check with the doctor in advance to remind him/her to do a rectal exam for the prostate assessment, and possibly perform a blood test for prostate cancer screening for the PSA antigen. The doctor knows what to do. Instead, it is easier and more appropriate to talk with your man about making sure that the doctor will perform these necessary tests. Let him take some responsibility for his health, even if you have to guide him.

What if your man has ED? Should you arrange his appointment with the doctor or not? Many men I see in my men's health clinic were encouraged to make the appointment by their wives. The wives saw the ad in the local paper, spoke to their husbands and persuaded them to see me. The women did not have to twist hubby's arm. He just needed a little prodding.

> **66 Many men I see in my men's health clinic were encouraged to make the appointment by their wives. 99**

My advice regarding an appointment to an ED clinic for men is to let him come alone the first time. Do not go with him. He is embarrassed enough to talk about ED in front of the doctor, and does not need you there prompting him to talk about his problem.

If you should attend the first meeting, you will be assuming the role of mother, which will not work well with hubby's ego. You might be required to attend later meetings, provided both the doctor and your man agree to your presence. From my experience, most men can handle the initial doctor's visit for ED just fine by themselves and the wife would just get in the way.

VITAMINS, MINERALS AND HERBAL SUPPLEMENTS

In earlier sections of this book I outlined the various vitamin, mineral and herbal supplements that have been shown to be beneficial for men's health and erections. Most likely your doctor will not advise taking any supplements. That is only because the majority of doctors are not trained in this field of medicine. Therefore, it is up to you to decide if you and/or your man should be consuming supplemental nutritional products.

Read books and magazines, go to public seminars, and ask your pharmacist or other health professional about the use and misuse of vitamins and herbal products. There is a wealth of information available on antioxidants and minerals.

Consider the use of therapeutic herbal products, especially the brands formulated with standardized extracts of herbs, i.e. Ginkgo biloba (Ginkoba™, Ginkgold™), ginseng (Ginsana™), and Pygeum africanum, stinging nettle (Prostatonin™) and saw palmetto.

A few judiciously chosen nutritional products are more than just insurance against a diet deficient in vitamins and minerals. I personally view these supplements as health-promoting products designed for long-term benefits. The more I research the field of nutritional medicine, the more I am convinced that the actual benefits of nutritional supplementation far outweigh any side effects.

STRESS MANAGEMENT

There are a variety of stress-reducing mechanisms specifically designed for women to use with their men. But before we get into these, it is important to recognize one fact – *stress* is not the boogeyman that wreaks havoc on the cardiovascular and immune systems. Stress does not directly lead to a whole host of diseases – ED being only one of them. It is the stress *response,* either over or under, which must be regulated to promote health, well-being and good erections.

Many stress-alleviating mechanisms are outlined throughout this book. The following section will outline 10 important language and behavioral skills that women can utilize to:

- Build up a man's self-esteem
- Diminish his stress response
- Improve his testosterone levels, and his erections

1. Don't complain

At least don't complain out loud so much. For women this can be called thinking out loud. For men this is called complaining. To go over and over an issue without an endpoint or a goal necessarily in mind is a common form of communication that women will use with other women. Men never use it with other men.

Men become disturbed when women complain too much because men feel an obligation to save the day when they hear women in distress. Try to limit his exposure only to those times where you truly want his advice, and not to those times when you just need to "vent."

Did you ever wonder why your man doesn't listen enough to you? Maybe it's because he interprets your words as complaining even though you don't realize that's what you are doing.

2. Don't say, "I told you so."

Your man is going to make mistakes. Sometimes it seems like he makes too many mistakes and isn't learning from them. He is, but on a different level than you do. He learns without discussions or apologies and does not want to hear the obvious – that you knew better than he did.

> **❝Criticism is much more difficult for a man to handle than for a woman. A man will retreat under the onslaught of criticism. ❞**

Help him to fix up what went wrong, and go easy on both blame and shame. Criticism is much more difficult for a man to handle than for a woman. A man will retreat under the onslaught of criticism. He will, instead, justify to himself and to you that his actions were not as bad as they seem. That will only lead to an argument, possibly escalate into a bigger fight, and then guess what – no sex!

Try to help hubby and yourself by using the words, *"What do we do now?"* or *"Where do we go from here?"* or *" How do we fix this?"* instead of *"I told you so."*

3. Don't use the "W" word

Never use the word "wimp" (it rhymes with limp) to your man. Never imply or infer it either. The word "wimp" will immediately crush and destroy a man's ego and his erections. Remember, your man is programmed to save the day. Inside every man lives a warrior and a Knight in Shining Armor.

A "wimp" is a loser and a failure. And a "wimp" does not make a good lover either! Help him to feel more like a winner and a savior. What if he isn't a winner, I heard you say? Treat him like a winner first and he will start acting like a winner second. Winners always have good erections and make the best lovers, too.

4. Your man is not a mind reader

Men think differently than women. Sometimes hubby is preoccupied with business problems or personal concerns (like ED perhaps?) and may seem to be taking you for granted. He doesn't want to talk about his troubles because he thinks he has to handle things alone.

You know he has something on his mind and he appears distracted and neglectful. Good news – there isn't anything wrong with your man. He is simply programmed to "keep his eyes on the prize" – from caveman days on the hunt or war days going into battle.

If you want your man to do something for you, even to bring you flowers, you have to remind him. He'll more than likely do it, but he won't think of doing it himself first (he is not a mind reader). This way, you will get what you want or need, and he doesn't get criticized unnecessarily.

5. Pamper him, but don't mother him

Your man needs to be babied once in a while. He might even need some mothering, and heaven knows that women make the best mothers. Just *don't let on that you are mothering him.* Try to talk to him and treat him the way you do when he is really sick in bed with the flu. Not the way he talks or treats you when you are sick.

A man is just not good at mothering. A man likes to be the king of the castle, but sometimes the stresses of life get the better of him. At work, with the kids, in sports or just with the guys, sometimes your man doesn't feel in charge. Help him to feel indispensable. Praise him, encourage him and feed his ego. A man's ego is more vulnerable than a woman's ego. Build him up a bit and you will see bigger erections. You will both benefit.

6. Cater to his sexual appetite

You know by now that when it comes to sex, men are different than women. Sex decreases stress for men. They always feel good after sex (assuming there is no ED or PE). The reason is because when men start a sex act, they know in advance that they are going to finish with an ejaculation. Women do not always have the luxury of a guaranteed orgasm.

Try not to disturb his pleasure by changing your mind. Stopping in the middle of sex and not letting him complete his sexual process, not letting him proceed to ejaculation will work against you and make him feel stressed and frustrated. He will understand what to do if you say, "You can come any time now."

❝Sex decreases stress for men. ❞

In addition, if your man needs a little extra mental arousal with a magazine or a video, don't take it as a personal insult and assume that you are not attractive to him and don't turn him on anymore. *You are his number one turn-on.* He just needs different arousal techniques than you do. It does not diminish his desire for you. If he wants (or needs) a little help from a magazine, don't worry about it.

7. Take him out to the ball game

Consider buying your man some tickets to the local baseball park, football field, hockey arena or basketball court. Men and spectator sports go together. Being at the game instead of at home allows your man to escape the stresses of daily life.

He doesn't have to go to all the games, but you will find that his attendance record will still be quite high. He will also return home from the game (especially when the home team wins) in a happy and relaxed frame of mind.

Finally, here is an added benefit for you – you will end up going to the game too, being with your man on a night out and actually enjoying yourself. The stadiums are now boasting 50% or more female attendance to virtually every sporting event (other than boxing, that is).

8. Buy a time-share

No, I am not in real estate! However, I know the stress-reducing benefits of vacationing. Many men are workaholics and will not stop until they drop (dead). To promote his health, wellbeing and good erections, vacations are at the top of the list.

The advantages of a time-share property are that the investment is small, the duration is long-term (20 to 30 years) and the opportunity to travel all over the world is readily available.

Finally, the resorts almost always have first-rate, fully furnished one- or two-bedroom condominiums. No more cramped hotel rooms with the kids. You and hubby will have your own private bedroom for you know what. No wonder more time-shares are bought because of the wife's influence. And more time-shares are sold by female real estate agents, too.

9. Take him shopping, but only for one thing

Do you know what that is? It sure isn't clothes shopping. You guessed it – new car shopping. That's where men are literally in heaven. They can be bone tired from work, stressed to the limit and cranky as can be, but when you mention that it's new-car shopping time, watch the metamorphosis take place in your man. Suddenly he is energized and attentive.

Here are a couple of tips. Go with him and let him kick a few tires, look under the hood (even though he doesn't know what he's looking at), haggle with the salespeople and above all, if you can, get a new car that comes with as many "toys" as possible.

What does the salesperson say to every man that walks into the showroom? "How many bells and whistles do you want?"

10. Teach your man how to meditate

Meditation is one of the most effective mechanisms for stress management. Women do not have a monopoly on meditation, nor do they have to change to an eastern religion to understand and gain the benefits of meditation. Many women mediate and practice yoga to reduce stress.

Yoga combines stretching, deep breathing and mind control all rolled into one. Find a yoga class that both of you can attend on a regular basis. Almost overnight, hubby will be calmer, happier, more productive at work and better in bed. Both of you will also sleep better as a result of meditation or yoga.

SUMMARY

We've covered a lot of ground in this chapter. I know it was all one-sided (his side) and it doesn't seem fair. I understand and appreciate the fact that there have been many times in your relationship when things seemed one-sided in his favor. And now I'm asking you to go out of your way and do even more for him even when he doesn't want it (or deserve it?). Is it worth it?

Yes! First, it will maintain his erections, which will make him feel good as a man. *Having a man who feels like a complete man is a good thing for* *you*. And if he has the ability for intercourse (erection on demand) any time you want sex (you, not him – he always wants it), his self-esteem will rise. Trust me, you will enjoy being with your man when he feels on top of the world (especially if you had something to do about it).

Second, you will likely find that from your efforts he will in return be more sensitive to your feelings. He might (and I say "might" sincerely, because I cannot guarantee it) start putting your needs first once in a while by following your lead. If he sees you looking after him more, he might get the hint and look after himself and you more. No guarantees, but you'll never know unless you try.

Third, there is a far greater chance that your man will get a serious disease, like heart trouble (angina) or even a heart attack many, many years before you do. Think about how you will treat him after his heart attack. How will you talk to him? How will you respond towards him? How will you criticize him? I suspect that after his heart attack, you will treat him in many of the ways that I have outlined in this chapter!

Therefore, since you have a high probability that you are going to have to resort to many of the suggestions in this chapter anyway, why not initiate some of them now, in advance, and possibly head off or postpone a potentially serious illness? At the very least, your man's health will improve as a direct result of your interventions. And that's something you can take some credit for.

CLOSING JOKE

A wife and her husband were having coffee, when the wife said, "You know honey, I haven't been feeling very well lately, so I went to the doctor."
"Uh huh," said the husband.
"He gave me a full checkup and he found out what the problem was."
"Uh huh," said the husband.
"The doctor said that to cure my problem I needed more sex."
"Oh really?" said the husband, a little more interested now.
"Well, how many times a week did the doctor say you needed sex?" asked the husband.
The wife replied, "He said I needed sex five times a week."
The husband looked very thoughtful, and finally spoke. "Okay, put me down for two."

DR. SAUL'S TOFU SALAD RECIPE
(MOCK CHOPPED EGG)

1   Pound firm tofu - 1" cubes
2   Tablespoons low fat mayonnaise
2   Tablespoons soya sauce, or tamari sauce
2   Teaspoons prepared yellow mustard

1   Teaspoon turmeric
1   Teaspoon coriander
1   Teaspoon paprika
1   Teaspoon cumin
2   Tablespoons parsley flakes (dried)
1 – 2 Teaspoons extra virgin olive oil

Salt and Pepper to taste

Blend in food processor ONLY until mixed.
Use as you would egg salad.

Enjoy!!!

PART FOUR
MEN AND SEX:
THE FUTURE

Things are looking up

Things are looking up.

Sex For Life should be used as a guide to understanding male sexuality, especially as it concerns erections. This includes:

- Being aware of and appreciating the importance of erections for men.
- Learning and implementing practical strategies for a regular and robust sexual life.
- Developing and maintaining loving relationships.

A man's desire for a lifetime of sexual activity is an inherent factor of the male experience. It encompasses seven elements, which comprise all factors and principles. What are these seven elements? *Sex For Life* is:

1. Timeless

Sex For Life represents how men have viewed sexuality from time immemorial: since the time of the caveman, the Roman Empire and the Middle Ages. Our desire for a long, sexually fulfilling life is still with us now at the dawn of the Third Millennium and will continue into the foreseeable future.

2. Universal

The desire for a lifetime of passionate sex on a regular basis resides in *every* man – rich men and poor men alike, regardless of color, race or creed. Sex was designed (rightly or wrongly) to be charged with excitement – for all men and all women.

3. Comprehensive

Sex is more than simple intercourse. It is about closeness, connection, and commitment. Sex is also designed to be full of intensity, emotion and sweat. *Sex For Life* encompasses all aspects of sexual fulfillment – from the softness of a gentle kiss to the drama of climax.

4. Significant

Sexual functioning for men and women is an inescapable part of our lives. However, sex for humans goes beyond the simple, animalistic need to procreate the species. Sex for humans is like food – we want it on a regular basis and attach a lot of emotion to it. And just like food, the better it looks, smells and tastes, the more we like it.

5. Ethical

A man who wants sex for life allows the fire of sexual desire to flame between consenting adults – as a flame of excitement with respect. Lifelong sexuality is designed to be mutually fulfilling for both partners, without coercion or dishonesty.

6. Achievable

Sex as a fact of life must not only be attainable but also maintainable. Human sexuality is designed to last a lifetime – something that sets us apart from other species. When our equipment is in working order, heightened stimulation and arousal can continue well beyond the reproductive years.

7. Uplifting

Having good sex when you want it for as long as you want it is one of the most uplifting experiences in life. As Woody Allen said, "When sex is good, it's really good. And when sex is bad, it's not too bad."

The sexual drive for men is a legacy handed down to all men in their genetic code. And it is precisely because I know many men are unhappy with their sex lives that I have written this book on the *new* and comprehensive approach to male sexuality.

But there is always more, isn't there? Let's examine where we go from here.

MORE ABOUT MEN AND SEX

I hope you have begun to appreciate on a conscious level what has always resided in your psyche on a subconscious level. I am referring to something profoundly important to men – *the ability to develop and maintain an erection on demand.* With the confidence of erection ability comes confidence outside of the bedroom and also:

- In the boardroom
- Out on the boulevard
- On the basketball court
- At the building site
- Out in the bush

It used to be strictly a man's world – in some parts of the world it still is. However, in Westernized countries, the roles of men and women are blurring. Everyone can now "wear the pants." There is no such thing anymore as "woman's work," and no job opportunities are denied to women.

If we actively pursue this newfound equality at work, or at least "work" with it, we will likely achieve more happiness and satisfaction between the sexes in other areas of life as well.

66 With the confidence of erection ability comes confidence outside of the bedroom. 99

Sex as a topic has undergone several changes as well. Radio talk-shows abound with "sexperts." Self-help books (such as the one in your hands) informing and teaching about general or specific sexual issues are now commonplace.

Then there are the books editorializing and leading into discussions about the politics of sex, without necessarily dwelling on specific sexual acts or functions. Instead, they speak to general social concerns over sexuality in society, such as teenage sex, senior's sex, safe sex, swinging sex, homosexuality, abortion and finally, the sexually abused and the abusers. Some excellent books on these topics are:

- *Talk Dirty to Me,* by Sallie Tisdale
- *Susie Bright's Sexwise* and *The Sexual State of the Union,* by Susie Bright
- *All About Sex,* by Planned Parenthood Federation of America, edited by Ronald Filberti Magolia Ed.D., and Jon Knowles
- *Our Sexuality,* by R. Crooks and K. Baur
- *Exploring Human Sexuality,* by Kelly and Byrne
- *The New Male Sexuality,* by Bernard Zilbergeld Ph.D.
- *Sexual Static: How Men are Confusing the Women They Love,* by Morton Shaevitz M.D.
- *Sex, Sex and More Sex,* by Sue Johanson
- *What Men Really Think,* by Mark Baker

Here's an excerpt from *The Hazards of Being Male: Surviving the Myth of Masculine Privilege,* by Herb Goldberg, Ph.D. This book was written in 1976 but is still very applicable today:

"Our culture is saturated with successful male zombies – businessmen zombies, golf zombies, sports car zombies, playboy zombies, etc. They are playing by the rules of the male game plan. They have lost touch with, or are running away from their feelings and awareness of themselves as people. They have confused their social masks for their essence and they are destroying themselves while fulfilling the traditional definitions of masculine-appropriate behavior. When something goes wrong, they discover that they are shadows to themselves as well as to others."

Goldberg was describing over 20 years ago how men were searching for the true meaning of masculinity, not just their desire for sex for life, but still not finding it.

Another view about men and sex, this time from a woman's perspective, comes from a brand new book, *The Improvised Woman: Single Women Reinventing Single Life,* by Marcelle Clements. It was reviewed in *The Globe and Mail* newspaper on August 1, 1998, by Marian Bostsord Fraser, a Toronto broadcaster:

"There are no men. Of course there are men. But they are all gay, or afraid of strong women, or too old, or too young (and stupid), or the right age (and stupid because they want someone younger), or "happily married" (with full-blown fields of wild oats flourishing under the noses of unsuspecting – huh!- wives). Ah, yes, we (women) have all said it; there are no men."

CYBERSEX FOR LIFE?

No one knows where on-line sex chat and cybersex will take us – will it open up a new sexual utopia, or simply add to the list of causes for sexual alienation, frustration and erectile dysfunction?

Sex via the Internet is a brand new forum that is not only catching on but mushrooming. The following is an excerpt from a 1995 book by Nancy Tamosaitis titled *Sex and the Internet net.sex...Those folks online aren't doing anything strange...or are they?*

"With an estimated 25-30 million people (in 1995) on the Internet, the experiences are bound to be wide and varied. The only definitive conclusion to be drawn from the users' anecdotal experiences is that the Internet is an avenue for people to converge, exchange ideas and information and explore tapped and untapped aspects of their personal lives. The experience of sharing ideas, erotic expression, and fantasies through the modem medium is safe and incredibly stimulating for many people.

"Although people of all ages frequent *alt.sex*, the majority of people who post are in college, logging in from their University-sponsored accounts. At times, *alt.sex* feels like a never-ending dormitory party, complete with overflowing beer mugs and horny men. Although date rape cannot take place in cyberspace, one does witness a high volume of male domination and female alienation on *alt.sex*."

Here's a personal ad found in alt.personals.bi: "Married man seeks same for e-mail. Seeking a married man who wants some release by exchanging hot e-mail. Could be about anything, your wife, yourself, another guy...I find that marriage is great but can get stagnant if you don't generate some excitement. I'm very open with my wife but I need something else to get stuff off my chest without being judged."

And how do women fare in the male-dominated world of Internet Relay Chat (IRC)? Mistress Minx Kelly, an on-line devotee, discusses the strength of IRC activity for women:

"Women can explore other sides of our sexuality that are forbidden in real life. On-line, we can flirt and masturbate with other women, hot-chatting (the exchange of erotic dialog on-line) and expressing that hidden side of ourselves that even our closest friends don't know about."

STRESS MANAGEMENT

Has this book made a change in your ability to handle stress and limit your overreactions to stress? I hope I have provided enough practical information for you to improve your coping skills to withstand certain stresses which at one time would have overwhelmed you.

Stress management is the modern-day savior for the scourge of stress. Bookstores and libraries are loaded with books and tapes on specific techniques, some new and some over 30 years old. Study and learn how you can modify or alleviate your stress response. Not only will your erections be better but so will your heart, stomach and ability to sleep.

If there is still a deficiency in your stress-coping skills, try this technique. Just ask yourself, "What should I do now?" Then wait for your brain to give you an answer. You can then proceed to do what your brain advises provided that you follow this one rule: *You are allowed to do and say anything you want to as long as you don't hurt anyone or yourself with your words or actions.*

MALE MENOPAUSE - DO YOU HAVE IT?

Has the concept of male menopause or andropause caused you to examine your life and perhaps seek evaluation from a physician knowledgeable in this field? The doctors dealing with lowered testosterone syndrome are called andrologists. They are mostly endocrinology specialists, sometimes urologists and occasionally family doctors (like myself).

Times are changing in medicine, but sometimes the gears turn rather slowly. What was laughed at and scoffed at barely five years ago (andropause) is now a legitimate medical condition, with medical societies, journals and meetings studying the incidence, epidemiology, patho-physiology, psycho-social aspects and finally, treatment options.

At the First World Congress on the Aging Male, held in Geneva, Switzerland in February 1998, where I was invited to present excerpts from my journal article, *"If he's too shy to seek help for failing sexual performance,"* the following topics of discussion were front and center:

- The need for more research into the health and disease aspects of the aging male around the world.
- Erectile dysfunction – treatments, social concerns, endocrinological and vascular changes.
- What is the safe yet effective level of testosterone for the aging male? Should testosterone hormonal supplements be used as routinely as estrogen supplements are for post-menopausal women?
- The need to expand on the medical knowledge concerning prostatic diseases, not only to decrease the death rate, but to lower the morbidity (sickness) associated with prostate hypertrophy, prostatitis and prostate cancer.

GO BACK IN TIME

Yes, times have changed and men have changed. But the old saying rings true: the more things change, the more they stay the same. I spent considerable time detailing the nutritional and exercise strategies for health improvement generally and ED improvement specifically. Are they new? Are they radical?

For today's standards and customs, perhaps they are. But what about as far back as 100,000 years ago or even as recent as 100 years ago? Not at all. Nutritional and exercise programs are bringing men back to their roots as warrior-hunter-gatherers:

- Back to the time before bread, cheese, alcohol and cigarettes
- Back to the time of lean game meat, root vegetables, nuts and fruits only in season
- Back to the time of food shortages, conservation and rationing, eating small quantities and *never* having obesity

Think back to the time without cars and without machines. In the olden days, men walked, ran and hiked for miles and miles each and every day, carrying their children and belongings wherever they migrated. Go back to a simpler life, filled with the importance of wife and family, honor and truth, purpose, and finally, a job well done.

Perhaps one continuous aspect of history we do not have to rekindle is the brutality and senselessness of war. Now, at the dawn of the Third Millennium, we can finally learn to settle our differences using brain instead of brawn, compassion over violence, and by creating instead of killing. Since it has always been men starting wars, it will have to be men who cease committing *unnecessary* aggression.

How is the world progressing today in terms of various global conflicts leading to war? Just pick up any newspaper and you will quickly find out for yourself that we are not making much headway. "Make love, not war" was a rallying cry of the turbulent sixties for both men and women. Perhaps more "Peace Now" rallies are needed today.

THE RETURN OF THE MUSCLEMAN

Muscles, muscles everywhere, but no solid muscles to be found. Men have stopped their manual labor and their farm work. Many have even stopped playing sports. Machine power is an inevitable fact of life. This means that men must go back to the gym to recondition their muscles. A man without firm muscles is like a fish out of water. The only way to regain the necessary muscular mass and strength is to work out. Muscular development must be done without the use of steroids, magic pills, or potions – just plain old grunt and sweat. *Mainly sweat and manly sweat!*

❝ The testosterone surge from weight training with heavy weights is one of the best ways to maintain an adequate testosterone supply. ❞

The hormonal benefits of increased testosterone, growth hormone and insulin resulting from heavy, physical weight-training exercises are consistent and dramatic for men but only moderately beneficial for women. The testosterone surge from weight training with heavy weights is one of the best ways to maintain an adequate testosterone supply. More testosterone means more sex, pure and simple. Your body's internal pharmacy is equipped to supply you with the exact amount of that hormone, delivered hourly to your door, free of charge.

THE RETURN OF THE MORAL MAN

Times are always changing, but for many men and women the pace may be too slow when it comes to morality and honor in love relationships. Commitment to long-term fidelity within love relationships has always been a concern for women, but are men concerned?

In the 1998 *Cosmopolitan* "All About Men" issue, 600 young U.S. men were surveyed for their responses to questions about sexuality and relationships. Here are some findings:

Have you ever blurted out "I love you" in the throes of passion, even though it wasn't true?

- Yes   41%
- No   59%

The most women I've ever simultaneously dated and slept with is:

- One – I'm a one-woman kind of guy   50%
- Two – I like to play doubles   32%
- Three – I like to have options   14%
- Four or more – I own Trojan stock   4%

Have you ever cheated during a committed relationship?
- Yes   45%
- No   55%

Have you ever had...
- Phone sex   21%
- Cybersex   12%
- Both   22%
- Neither   45%

Here is what the editors of *Cosmopolitan* had to say about the results: "Who's been naughty and who's been nice? Fifty-five percent of our males say they've never cheated during a committed relationship. Yep it's over half but not by much. That leaves 45% who deserve to have a drink spilled on them in a crowded bar. And about phone and cybersex, guys have been a little more willing to just let their fingers reach out and virtually touch someone."

THE JOY OF SEX

Sex, sex, sex. We can say it now. Even if we can't do it anymore, we can first talk about it and then maybe we can do it again. When it comes to sex, men are different from women – not better, not worse, just different. Sexual differences must be acknowledged.

Deviant, antisocial, violent and abusive sexual practices should have a zero tolerance in a civilized society. For far too long, too many men have committed crimes of rape, incest, pedophilia and other sexual deviations, and have gone unpunished for these atrocities. It's time to stop this barbaric sexual abuse of women, girls (and yes, boys as well) and instead, focus on the following five things:

1. Different strokes for different folks

The acknowledgement by men and women in marriage that husbands have different sexual urges and needs than their wives do. Couples must work out a schedule to have more sexual encounters for the sole benefit of the husband. I am referring here to the "quickies." Men need more sex. And if they don't get it at home, they'll get it elsewhere. This also means that women should demand specific times for more romantic and prolonged sexual encounters in addition to those times when he's just "getting his rocks off." Just like a healthy appetite is indicative of health in general, so is a healthy sexual appetite for both men and women.

2. What's love got to do with it? Everything!

Men can become accustomed to strictly the physical part of sex, and forget or never learn the emotional, loving aspects. Men can be expert lovers, but not know a thing about love. Women can have sex without love, but would rather not. It's not as much of a choice for men. If it became a choice (sex with or without love), and they chose the love path, the benefits are definitely there for men. They will begin to achieve heights of sexual enjoyment never experienced before. Love is a difficult emotion for most men to grasp and sometimes they need a little help in learning more about it. And who better to teach them than the experts on love? Women.

3. Don't be afraid to touch yourself

It is healthy for men *and* women to maintain some level of sexual self-stimulation in the form of masturbation throughout life. The steady increase in sales for personal female vibrators reveals that women are actively involved in pleasuring themselves as well. Most of the men I see in my men's clinic have all had self-stimulation *without* their partner's knowledge – during menstrual periods, during times of stress, or just for the fun of it. Where all the guilt and recrimination comes from, I don't know. All I know is it's one activity that is guaranteed to please, and you don't have to get dressed up for it either.

4. Learn to give her fireworks

Men need to learn what pleases a woman sexually. A woman's pleasure is not measured in numbers – inches of penis length or minutes of intercourse. No one ever taught men how to "do it," because men simply do not talk subjectively about sex. They might brag and lie about sex but men need to learn specific sexual skills and techniques that will do it *for* a woman rather than *to* a woman. Here are a few suggestions: slow down and caress her more, massage her with aromatic oils, nibble wherever she wants to be nibbled and finally, find out where her clitoris and G-spot are hiding. Men have to discover that there is a whole wide world of sexual pleasure beyond the act of intercourse. And if ED doesn't improve (yes, it sometimes happens), the joy of sex with a soft penis is a unique way to have sex that many couples happily explore.

5. To each his own

Some men are simply not happy being with a woman in a love and/or sexual relationship, and never will be. They are not attracted to women sexually; they are attracted to other men. It's not the homosexuality itself, but the homophobia that is bad for men. Women can hug and kiss each other and it does not make them lesbians. Men can only hug when the team scores a goal, not when a man is hurting or sad. If men can have different-colored skin and speak different languages, they can have different sexual preferences. No one is actively soliciting converts to any camp. Do what your heart tells you to do. And don't preach or condemn. Let your brother follow his heart, in peace.

A RETURN TO FATHERING

Good, loving fathering will improve men's self-image, self-esteem and their overall sexual ability. Fathering is not only important for fathers, it is especially important for the sons. The female mothering influence from infancy and early childhood, and the preponderance of female grade school teachers is not good for the development of complete men. Complete in mind and body. A boy requires a masculine role model and preferably one who loves him.

In addition, too many fathers today are either workaholics, in jail or have simply run off. This only leads to psychosexual trauma for many sons. As men, we are ultimately responsible for our erections, but indirectly for our sons' and grandsons' erections. As it says in the Bible, *"the children [shall be punished] for the sin of the fathers to the third and fourth generation."*

Be there for your son. Counsel and mentor him. Teach him about the natural urges residing inside all men. Listen to his concerns and fears. Advise him about the strengths and weaknesses of men. Try to explain how complicated (and hidden) a man's emotional system can be. Help your son to express his feelings without judging them. And don't ever discipline your son by using physical force. Violence only teaches further violence.

Learn about the love between a father and a son while you are a father and your son is still young and impressionable. Sadly, too many grandfathers missed out on loving their sons and lived to regret it. It was too late for their sons when they (the grandfathers) finally realized what they had missed. Instead, they do the next best thing by being there for their grandsons.

Jeb Diamond Ph.D., in his recent book *Male Menopause,* elaborates on the concept of mentoring. His challenging view about male menopause (besides the physical changes, which are well-documented in medical circles) has to do with the emotional changes that occur to men in the mid-life years.

Many men have sexual affairs, many buy motorcycles, and still others quit their jobs – all looking for some meaning in their lives. Diamond suggests that men should return to their roots as the elders or the wise men of the society. Once they become more involved in making the world a better place to live, they experience greater meaning in their lives, meaning that feeds the soul. Finally, sexual fulfillment becomes one more area that is essential to a successful passage through male menopause.

A few more books which will provide greater insight into the innate nature of men are:

- *At My Father's Wedding: Reclaiming Our True Masculinity,* by John Lee
- *Iron John,* by Robert Bly
- *Fire In The Belly,* by Sam Keen
- *What Men Really Think,* by Mark Baker
- *Man Overboard,* by Ian Brown

LESSONS MEN CAN LEARN FROM WOMEN

- *About sex* – we can learn to slow down and build up to a peak, instead of blasting off into orbit as fast as we can. Women today are enjoying sexuality beyond just the need for procreation and men can also learn to appreciate this total sexual experience. There's much more to the dynamics of sex than the physical aspects of erections, intercourse and ejaculations.
- *About feelings* – yes we have them, just as women do. We just hold them in longer, or have adult tantrums and lose control.

No one said life is always free 'n easy and positive. Sometimes it helps to blow off steam. Just be careful not to hurt anyone with your words or actions when expressing feelings.

- *About communication* – this is where women have men beat – hands down. Men close off far too fast and "bottle up" their fears, concerns and needs. Men hide in their "caves" while women garner support and advice. Remember, no idea is too scandalous, stupid or strange. Talk is cheap, but it can also be effective.

- *About connections* – women develop effective networks through their involvement in various support groups. Women go out of their way to do favors for others. Men put all their eggs in one basket (called a wife). Just keep opportunities available, instead of burning bridges, if you are not a networking type of man.

- *About selfish vs. selfless* – women are accused of being selfless to an extreme and men are accused of the exact opposite – being selfish. Try to strike a balance by considering another's feelings, opinions or behaviors. Try going out of your way for someone else without being asked.

- *About the "hurry syndrome"* – women sometimes have a habit of being late, while men tend to be early (and rushing to boot). "Type A" personality ("hurry sickness") is usually a man's problem, and can lead to heart disease. Here's a lesson from women – slow down and live.

REMEMBER THIS

No one can dispute the obvious and inherent differences between men and women. Men feel freer to get in touch with their *maleness* and all the feelings and desires that come with being a man.

❝ *Let a man be a man.* ❞

CLOSING QUOTATIONS

Euripedes, the Greek philosopher, said, "If your life at night is good, you think you have everything."

Shakespeare in Henry the IV said, "Is it not strange that desire should so many years outlive performance."

Ovid, the Second-Century Roman philosopher said, "If your wife is old and your member exhausted, eat onions in plenty."

Ayn Rand said, "Tell me what a man finds sexually attractive and I will tell you his entire philosophy of life."

Mae West said,
"A hard man is good to find."
"Too much of a good thing can be wonderful."
"It's not the men in my life that counts, it's the life in my men."
"Give a man a free hand and he'll try to run it all over you."
"Some men are all right in their place, if they only knew the right places."
"I feel like a million tonight, but one at a time."
"When I'm good, I'm very, very good. But when I'm bad, I'm better."

Gypsy Rose Lee said, "Men are not attracted to me by my mind. They're attracted by what I don't mind."

Joe E. Lewis once said, "You only live once – but if you work it right, once is enough."

EPILOGUE
MY FUTURE

Where do I go from here?

Where do I go from here?

My first year of exposure to the magnitude of men's sexual dysfunctions made me realize that I could not integrate family medicine and men's sexual medicine within the same afternoon office hours. As a result, I have phased out my North Scarborough Men's Health Center and joined the Midlife Health Center in Toronto. As the director of the men's health program at the Midlife Health Center I will be able to develop an approach to men's health (not just sexual health) that I envision to be unique and influential in this field. I am planning to work with the Midlife Health Center to become an advocate not just for men's sexual therapeutics, but for men's longevity.

My ongoing research utilizing medical journals, medical symposiums and current books and magazines on men's health allows me to keep abreast of the most recent advances in the diagnosis and treatment of men's sexual disorders.

I want to take the Midlife Health Center beyond the status quo – beyond any men's health facility in the world. The Midlife Health Center will become one of the most comprehensive, integrated and above all, one of the most effective organizations dealing with men's health issues.

Am I tooting my own horn? Is it just wishful thinking? Of course it is! It's not a *fait accomplit* yet. But if you don't shoot for the moon, you'll never get into orbit.

Thankfully I do not have to do everything by myself. Networking, delegating and asking for help – these are all avenues that will help me to provide better care for patients and allow me to create new and better men's sexual health programs.

More books are on the way, too. I'm working on two books – one about the power of the brain and the other about the power of creative writing.

I will also continue to:
- Practice family medicine
- Develop a state-of-the-art men's health program at the Midlife Health Center

- Make radio, television and public appearances to help inform the public about the importance of men's health issues
- Help teach and train other doctors through lecturing at continuing medical education seminars, writing for medical journals, and working with the Canadian Society for the Study of Andropause and The Canadian Male Sexual Health Council

Can you sense my excitement? I hope so. I also hope that some of my enthusiasm and excitement has rubbed off on you, and that you will begin implementing some of the advice and programs suggested in *Sex For Life*. If you follow my advice, *I guarantee your sex life (arousal, frequency and performance) will improve.*

66 *If you follow my advice, I guarantee your sex life will improve.* 99

I am also confident that many younger men currently without ED will avoid future ED problems as a direct result of the material found in this book. At the very least, just reading *Sex For Life* will inform and entertain you.

Whatever its cause, one thing is certain – men need to nip ED in the bud. I have seen far too many men who come into my clinic after a year or more of having ED and no sex. Too many men subscribe to the motto:

No erection = No intercourse = No sex.

That's wrong! A better view is this:

No erection = No intercourse = Other healthy forms of sexual arousal and satisfaction.

An even better approach is this:

No erection = I better get over to the doctor right away so I can get my erection back (an erection on demand).

I hope by reading this book, you are well on your way towards improvement strategies for ED, if you have it, and prevention strategies if you don't have it.

It has been my pleasure to write this book for you. I would like to thank you for allowing me to share my thoughts (and jokes) with you.

Please remember my motto, and strive to achieve it:

SEX – *Whenever you want it, for as long as you want it.*

REFERENCES

ERECTILE DYSFUNCTION

Bagley, G., Grantmyre, J. and Keresteci, A. Impotence: Treating erectile dysfunction. *Patient Care Canada* 1995 (Sept.);6(7):34-48.

Baum, N. and Rhodes, D. A practical approach to the evaluation and treatment of erectile dysfunction. *Urol. Clin. North Am.* 1995;22(4):865-877.

Benet, A. and Melanan, A. The epidemiology of erectile dysfunction. *Urol. Clin. North Am.* 1995 (Nov.);22(4):699-709.

Boolell, M., Gepi-Atee, S., Gingell, J.C. et al. Sildenafil, a novel effective oral therapy for male erectile dysfunction. *Br. J. Urol.* 1996;73:257-61.

Brock, G. A potent pill: News for erectile dysfunction. *Parkhurst Exchange* 1997 (April):64-66.

Bush, P.A., Aronson, W.J., Raifer, J. et al. The L-arginine-nitric oxide-cyclic GMP pathway mediates inhibitory non-adrenergic, non-cholinergic neurotransmission in the corpus cavernosum of human and rabbit. *Circ.* 1993;87 (Suppl V):30-2.

Buvat, J. Sildenafil (Viagra™), an oral treatment for erectile dysfunction: A 1-year, open-label, extension study. *J. Urol.* 1997;157 (Suppl 4); 204.

Catalona, W.J. Patient selection for, result of, and impact of tumor resection of potency – sparingly radical prostatectomy. *Urol. Clin. North Am.* 1990 (Nov.);17(4):819-826.

Choe, H.K., Seong, D.H. and Rha, K.H. Clinical efficacy of Korean red ginseng for erectile dysfunction. *International Journal of Impotence Research.* 7(3):181-6, Sept. 1995.

DeWire, D.M. Evaluation and treatment of erectile dysfunction. (Review) *American Family Physician.*53(6):2101-8, May1,1996.

DeWire, D.M., Todd, E. and Meyers, P. Patient satisfaction with current impotence therapy. *Wisconsin Medical Journal.* 94(10):542-4, Oct. 1995.

Feldman, H.A., Goldstein, I., Hatzichristou, D.G. et al. Impotence and its medical and psychological correlates: Results of the Massachusetts male aging study. *J Urology* 1994;151:54.

Feldman, H.A., Goldstein, I., Hatzichristou, D.G. et al. Impotence and its medical and psychological correlates; results of the Massachusetts male aging study. *J Urol* 1994; 151:54-61.

Goldstein, I. Your erectile dysfunction patient load is due to boom. *Urol. Times* 1994(Dec.):6.

Grantmyre, J. and Drachenberg, D. Erectile dysfunction: A guide to treatment. *Can J CME* 1997 (Feb.): 169-185.

Guay, A.T. Erectile dysfunction: Are you prepared to discuss it? (Review) *Postgraduate Medicine*. 97(4):127-30, 133-5.139-40 passim, Apr. 1995.

Heaton, J.P.W. et al. Resolution of erectile failure after oral treatment with apomorphine. *Urology* 1995; 45:200-203.

ˈˈˈˈ ˌˌr ˌensus development panel on impotence con-ference. *JAMA* 1993; 270:83-90.

Kim, E.D., Lipshultz, L.I. Advances in the treatment of organic erectile dysfunction. (Review). *Hospital Practice (Office Edition)*. 32(4):101-4, 107-8, 113-4 passim, April 15, 1997.

Kim, N., Azadzoi, K.M., Goldstein, I. et al. A nitric oxide-like factor mediates non-adrenergic, non-cholinergic, neurogenic relaxation of penile corpus cavernosum smooth muscle. *J. Clin. Invest.* 1991; 88:112-8.

Krame, R.J., Goldstein, I. and Saenz de Tejada, I. Impotence. *N. Engl. J. Med.* 1989;321:1648-59.

Linet, O.I., Ogrinc, F.G. Efficacy and safety of intracavernosal alprostadil in men with erectile dysfunction. *N. Engl. J. Med.* 1996; 334:873-877.

Lue, T.F. Impotence after radical pelvic surgery: Physiology and management (Reviews). *Urology Intl* 1991;476:259.

Lue, T.F. Organic impotence. *Current Therapy in Endocrinology & Metabolism*. 5:329-33, 1994.

Melman, A. Iatrogenic causes of erectile dysfunction. *Urol. Clin. North Am.* 1988;15:28.

Montague, D.K., Bafada, J., Belker, A. et al. Clinical guidelines panel on erectile dysfunction: Summary report on the treatment of organic erectile dysfunction. *J Urology* 1996 (Dec.);156:2007-2111.

Montorsi, F., Guazzoni, G., Rigatti, P. and Pozza, G. Pharmacological management of erectile dysfunction. (Review) *Drugs* 50(3):456-79, Sept. 1995

Morales, A., Heaton, J., Johnson, B. et al. Oral and topical treatment of erectile dysfunction. *Urol. Clin. North Am.* 1995 (Nov.);22(4)879-886.

Morley, J.E. Impotence. *Amer. J. Med.* 1985;80:897.

NIH Consensus Conference: NIH consensus development panel on impotence (review). *JAMA* 1993;270:83.

Padman-Nathan, H. et al. Treatment of men with erectile dysfunction with transurethral alprostadil *NEJM* 1997; 336:1-7.

Rowland, D.L., Kallan, K. and Slob, A.K. Yohimbine, erectile capacity, and sexual response in men. *Archives of Sexual Behavior.* 26(1):49-62, Feb. 1997.

Saul, D. If he's too shy to seek help for failing sexual performance. *Patient Care Can* 1997 (Nov.);8(11):64-73.

Saul, D. New oral medication for erectile dysfunction. *Mature Med. Can.* 1998;(May);44.

Schein, M., Zyzanski, S.J., Levin, S. et al. The frequency of sexual problems among family practice patients. *Fam. Pract. Res. J.* 1988;7:122.

Schover, L.R. and Jenson, S.B. *Sexuality problems and chronic disease: A comprehensive approach.* New York: Guilford Press, 1988.

Slag, M.R., Morley, E.J., Elson ,M.K. et al. Impotence in medical clinic outpatients. *JAMA* 1983;249:1736.

Spector, I.P. and Carey, M.P. Incidence and prevalence of sexual dysfunctions: A critical review of the empirical literature. *Arch. Sex. Behav.* 1990;384-408.

Tiefer, L. and Melman, A. Follow-up of men with erectile dysfunction evaluated in a urology department. *J Urology* 1985;133:327A.

Tiefer, L. and Schuetz-Mueller, D. Psychological issues in diagnosis and treatment of erectile disorders. *Urol. Clin. North Am.* 1995 (Nov.);22(4)767-773.

Vickers, M.A. Jr., De Nobrega, A.M. and Dluhy, R.G. Diagnosis and treatment of psychogenic erectile dysfunction in a urological setting. *Journal of Urology.* 149(5 Pt 2):1258-61, May 1993.

Virag, R. et al. Sildenafil (Viagra™) a new oral treatment for erectile dysfunction (ED): An 8 week double-bind, placebo-controlled parallel group study. *Int. J. Impot. Res.* 1996; 8: 116 (A70).

Virag, R., Bouilly, P. and Frydman, A. Is impotence an arterial disorder? *Lancet* 1985;1:181-184.

Vogt, H.J., Brandl, P., Kockott, G. et al. Double blind, placebo-controlled safety and efficacy trial with yohimbine hydrochloride in the treatment of nonorganic erectile dysfunction. *International Journal of Impotence Research.* 9(3):155-61, Sept. 1997.

Wein, A.J. and Van Arsdancen, K. Drug-induced male sexual dysfunction. *Urol Clin North Am* 1988;15:23.

Wiles, P.G. Erectile dysfunction in diabetic men: Etiology, investiga-
tion and management. *Diabet. Med.* 1992;9:888.

Zonszein, J. Diagnosis and management of endocrine disorder of erectile dysfunction. *Uro.l Clin. North Am.* 1995(Nov.);22(4):789-802.

EROTIC MALE SEXUAL STIMULATION

Aydogan, S., Bircan, M.K., Sahin, H. and Korkmaz, K. The importance of visual erotic stimulation in the differential diagnosis of
erectile impotence. *International Urology and Nephrology* 29
(2):233-35, 1997.

Bethany, A., Lohr, Adams, H. and Davis, J. Sexual arousal to erotic
and aggressive stimuli in sexually coercive and noncoercive men.
Journal of Abnormal Psychology. Vol. 106, No. 2, 230-42, 1997.

Cado, S. and Leitenberg, H. Guilt reactions to sexual fantasies during
intercourse. *Archives of Sexual Behavior.* Vol. 19, No. 1, 1990.

Fagan, P., Wise, T., Schmidt, C. Jr. and Dupkin, C. Inhibited sexual
excitement in the aging male. Presented at the 138th annual
meeting of the American Psychiatric Association, Dallas,
May 18-24, 1985.

Gordon, C., Hall, N., Shondrick, D. and Hirschman, R. The role of
sexual arousal in sexually aggressive behavior: A meta-analysis.
Journal of Consulting and Clinical Psychology. Vol. 61, No. 6,
1091- 95, 1993.

Hall, N. and Gordon, C. Sexual arousal and arousability in a sexual
offender population. *Journal of Abnormal Psychology.* Vol. 98,
No. 2, 145-49, 1989.

Janssen, E., Everaerd, W., van Lunsen, R. and Oerlemans, S. Visual
stimulation facilitates penile responses to vibration in men with
and without erectile disorder. *Journal of Consulting and
Clinical Psychology.* Vol. 62, No. 6, 1222-28, 1994.

Katlowitz, N., Albano, G., Morales, P. and Golimbu, M. Potentiation
of drug-induced erection with audiovisual sexual stimulation.
Urology. Vol. 41, No. 5, 431-34. May 1993.

Martins, F. and Reis, P. Visual erotic stimulation test for initial screening of psychogenic erectile dysfunction: A reliable noninvasive
alternative? *The Journal of Urology.* Vol. 157, 134-39, Jan 1997.

Monstorsi, F., Guazzoni, G., Barbieri, L. et al. Genital plus audiovisual sexual stimulation following intracavernous vasoactive injection versus re-dosing for erectile dysfunction – results of a prospective study. *The Journal of Urology*. Vol. 159, 113-115, Jan 1998.

Nutter, D. and Kearns-Condron, M. Sexual fantasy and activity patterns of males with inhibited sexual desire and males with erectile dysfunction versus normal controls. *Journal of Sex & Marital Therapy*. Vol. 11, No. 2, 91-98,Summer 1985.

Rubinsky, H., Eckerman, D., Rubinsky, E. and Hoover C. Early-phase physiological response patterns to psychosexual stimuli: Comparison of male and female patterns. *Archives of Sexual Behavior*. Vol. 16, No. 1, 1987.

Smith, A. Psychological factors in the multi-disciplinary evaluation and treatment of erectile dysfunction. *Urologic Clinics of North America*. Vol. 15, No. 1, Feb 1988.

Smith, D. and Over, R. Correlates of fantasy-induced and film-induced male sexual arousal. *Archives of Sexual Behavior*. Vol. 16, No. 5, 1987.

Smith, D. and Over, R. Does fantasy-induced sexual arousal habituate? *Behav. Res. Ther*. Vol. 25, No. 6, 477-85, 1987.

Smith, D. and Over, R. Enhancement of fantasy-induced sexual arousal in men through training in sexual imagery. *Archives of Sexual Behavior*. Vol. 19, No. 5, 477-89, 1990.

Smith, D. and Over, R. Male sexual arousal as a function of the content and the vividness of erotic fantasy. *Psychophysiology*. Vol.24, No.3, 334-39, Jan. 8, 1987.

Smith, D. and Over, R. Male sexual fantasy: Multidimensionality in content. *Behav. Res. Ther*. Vol. 29, No. 3, 267-75. 1991.

Vandereycken, W. On desire, excitement, and impotence in modern sex therapy. *Psychother. Psychosom*. 47: 175-180 (1987)

TESTOSTERONE

Baille, S., Davidson, C. and Johnson, F. Pathogenesis of vertebral crush fractures in men, *Aging* 1992, 21:139-141.

Bardin, C., Swerdloff, R. and Santen, R. Androgens: Risks and benefits, *J. Clin. Endoc. and Metabolism,* 1991; 73:4-7.

Barrett-Connor, E. and Khaw, K.T. Endogenous sex hormones and cardiovascular disease in men, *Circulation* 1988; 78:539-545.

Barrett-Connor, E., Khaw, K.T. and Yen, S. Endogenous sex hormone levels in older adult men with diabetes mellitus, *Am. Journ. of Epidemiology* 1990, Vol. 132, No. 5, 895-901.

Bosland, M. Animal models for the study of prostate carcinogenesis, *Journal of Cellular Biochem, Suppl.* 1992, 16 H; 89-98.

Cauley, J., Gutai, J. and Kuller, L. Usefulness of sex steroid hormone levels in predicting coronary artery disease in men, *American Journal of Cardiol.* 1987; 60: 771-777.

Christiansen, K. and Knussmann, R. Sex hormones and cognitive functioning in men, *Neuropsycho Biology* 1987; 18:27-36.

Effect of testosterone replacement therapy on mood changes in hypogonadal men; 77th Ann. Meeting, June 14-17, 1995, Washington, DC, The Endocrine Society.

Field, A., Colditz, G., Willett, W. and McKinlay, J. The relation of smoking, age, relative weight, and dietary intake to adrenal steroids, sex hormones, and sex hormone-binding globulin in middle-aged men, *Journ. Clin. Endoc. and Metab.* 1994, Vol. 79, No. 5, 1310-1316.

Finkelstein, J., Klibanski, A. and Neer, R. Osteoporosis in men with idiopathic hypogonadotrophic hypogonadism, *Ann. Inter. Med.* 1987: 106: 354-361.

Francis, R., Peacock, M. and Aaron, J. Osteoporosis in hypogonadal men. Bone 1986:; 7:267-268.

Giagulli, V., Kaufman, J. and Vermeulen, A. Pathogenesis of the decreased androgen levels in aging men, *Journ. Clin. Endoc. and Metab.* 1994, Vol. 79, No. 4, 997-1000.

Guezennel, C., Lafarge, J. and Bricout, V. Effect of competition stress used to assess testosterone administration in athletes, *Int. J. Sports Med.* 1995, Vol. 16, No. 6; 368-372.

Hakkinen, K. and Pakarinen, A. Serum hormones and strength development during strength training in middle-aged and elderly males and females, *Acta Physiol. Scand*, 1994, 150; 211-219.

Herbert, J. The age of dehydroepiandrosterone, *The Lancet*, Vol. 345, May 13, 1995, 1193-1194.

Hoffer, L., Beitins, I., Kyung, N.H. and Bistrian, B. Effects of severe dietary restriction on male reproductive hormones, *Jour. of Clin. Endoc. and Metab.* 1986, Vol. 62, No. 2; 288-292.

Homard, J., McCulley, C., Shinebarger, M. and Bruno, N. Effects of exercise training on plasma androgens in men, *Horm. Metab. Res..* 26 (1994); 297-300.

Jackson, J., Waxman, J. and Spiekerman, M. Prostatic complications of testosterone replacement therapy, *Arch. Inter. Med.*, Vol. 149, Oct. 1989, 2305-2366.

James, W. Prostatic cancer, coital rates, vasectomy and testosterone, *Jour. Biosci. Sci.* (1994) 26, 269-272.

Kalin, M. and Zumoff, B. Sex hormones and coronary disease: A review of clinical studies, *Steroids,* 1990, Vol. 55, Aug., 330-352.

Marin, P., Hollmang, S. and Jonsson, L. The effects of testosterone treatment on body composition and metabolism in middle-aged obese men, *Int. J. Obesity* 1992; 16; 992-997.

Matsumoto, A. Andropause – are reduced androgen levels in aging men physiologically important?, *WJM*, Editorial Nov. 1993, Vol. 159, No. 5, 618-620.

Matsumoto, A. Effects of chronic testosterone administration in normal men, safety and efficacy of high dosage testosterone, *J. Clin. Endoc. Metab.* 1990; 70, 282-287.

Morley, J., Perry, H. and Kaiser, F. Effects of testosterone replacement therapy in old hypogonadal males, a preliminary study, *Jour. Am. Geriatrics Soc.* 1993, 41, 149-152.

O'Carroll, M. and Bancroft, J. Testosterone therapy for low sexual interest and erectile dysfunction in men: A controlled study, *Br. J. Psychiatry*, 1984; 145: 146-151.

Opstad, K. and Aakvaag, A. The effect of sleep deprivation on the plasma levels of hormones during prolonged physical strain and calorie deficiency, *Europ. Jour. of Applied Physiology*, 1983, 51; 97-107.

Petrow, V. The dihydrotestosterone hypothesis of prostate cancer and its therapeutic implications, *The Prostate* 9; 1986; 343-361.

Phillips, G. Relationship between serum sex hormones and the glucose-insulin lipid defect in men with obesity, *Metabolism*, Vol. 42, No. 1, Jan. 1993, 116-120.

Phillips, G., Jing, T.Y. and Pesnick, L. Sex hormones and hemostatic risk factors for coronary heart disease in men with hypertension, *Journal of HPT* 1993, 11:699-702.

Phillips, G., Yano, K. and Stemmermann, G. Serum sex hormone levels and myocardial infarction in the Honolulu heart program, pitfalls in prospective studies on sex hormones, *Jour. Clin. Epidemiol.* Vol. 41, No. 12, 1988, 1151-1156.

Simon, D., Presiosi, P., Roger, M. and Nahoul, K. Interrelation between plasma testosterone and plasma insulin in healthy adult men, *Diabetologia*, 1992, 35: 173-177.

Singer, F. and Zumoff, B. Subnormal serum testosterone levels in Male Internal Medicine Residents, *Steroids*, 1992, Vol. 57, Feb, 86-89.

Skolnick, A. Is "male menopause" real or just an excuse?, *JAMA* Nov. 11, 1992, Vol. 268, No. 18, pg. 2486.

Stearns, E., MacDonnell, J. and Kauffman, B. Declining testicular function with aging, hormonal and clinical correlates., *American Journal Med.* 1974: 57:761-766.

Swerdloff, R. and Wang, C. Androgen Deficiency and Aging in Men, *West. J. Med.*, 1993, 159:579-585.

Swerdloff, R., Wang, C., Hines, M. and Gorski, R. Effect of Androgens on the Brain and Other Organs During Development and Aging, *Psychoneuroendocrinology*, 1992, Vol. 17, No. 4, 375-383.

Tenover, J. Effects of testosterone supplementation in the aging male, *Journ. Clin. Endo. and Metab.* 1992, Vol. 75, No. 4, 1092-1098.

Tenover, J., Matsumoto, A., Plymate, R. and Bremner, W. The effects of aging in normal men on bioavailable testosterone and luteinizing hormone secretion: Response to clomiphene citrate, *Journ. Clin. Endoc. and Metab.* 1987, Vol. 65; No. 6, 1118-1126.

Tsthouras, R., Martin, F. and Harman, S. Relationship of serum testosterone to sexual activity in elderly men, *Journal of Gerontology* 1982; 37: 288-93.

Vermeulen A. and Kaufman, J. Editorial: Role of the hypothalamo-pituitary function in the hypoandrogenism of healthy aging, *Journ. Clin. End. and Met.* 1992, Vol. 75, No. 3, 704-705.

Vermeulen, A. Clinical review of androgens in the aging male, *Journal Clin. Endoc. and Metab.* 1991, Vol. 73, No. 2, 221-224.

Vermeulen, A. The male climacterium, *Annals of Medicine*, 25: 1993, 531-534.

Vermeulen, A., Kaufman, J. and Giagull, V. Influence of some biological indexes on sex hormone-binding globulin and androgen levels in ageing or obese males, *Journ. Clin. Endoc. and Metab.* 1996, Vol. 81, No. 5, 1821-1826.

Weksler, M. Hormone replacement for men, *BMJ*, April 6, 1996.

Wheeler, G., Wall, S., Belcastro, A. and Cumming, d. reduced serum testosterone and prolactin in male distance runners, *JAMA*, July 27, 1994, Vol. 252; No. 4, 514-516.

Yesavage, J., Davidson, J., Widrow, L. and Berger, P. Plasma testosterone levels, depression, sexuality and age, *Biol. Psychiatry* 1985:20;199-228.

Zumoff, B., Trooxler, R. and O'Connor, J. Abnormal hormone levels in men with coronary artery disease, *Arteriosclerosis* 2: Jan/Feb 1982 ,58-67.

BENIGN PROSTATIC HYPERTROPHY

Boyle, P. New insights into the epidemiology and natural history of benign prostatic hyperplasia. *Progress in Clinical and Biological Research*. 386; 3-14, 1994.

Chyou, P.H., Nomura, A., Stemmerman, G. and Hankin, J. A prospective study of alcohol, diet, and their lifestyle factors in relation to obstructive uropathy. *The Prostate*. 22:253-64, 1993.

Fitzpatrick, J. and Lynch, T. Phytotherapeutic agents in the management of symptomatic benign prostatic hyperplasia. *Urologic Clinics of North America*. Vol.22, No.2, 407-12, May 1995.

Guess, H. Epidemiology and natural history of benign prostatic hyperplasia. *Urologic Clinics of North America*. Vol. 22, No.2, 247-61, May 1995.

Isaacs, J. Etiology of benign prostatic hyperplasia. *Eur. Urol:* 25 (suppl 1);6-9, 1994.

Krezesli, T., Borkowski A., Witeska A. and Kuczera J. Urtica dioica and Pygeum africanum in the treatment of benign prostatic hyperplasia: Double-blind comparison of two doses. *Clin. Ther.;* 15(6): 1011-20, Nov-Dec 1993.

Lee, C., Kozlowski, M. and Grayhack, T. Etiology of benign prostatic hyperplasia. *Urologic Clinics of North America*. Vol. 22, No. 2, 237-46, May 1995.

Lepor, H. Alpha blockade for the treatment of benign prostatic hyperplasia. *Urologic Clinics of North America*. Vol.22, No. 2, 375-86, May 1995.

Lepor, H. The treatment of benign prostatic hyperplasia: A glimpse into the future. *Urologic Clinics of North America*. Vol. 22, No.2, 455-59, May 1995.

Martin, F. and Murphy, P. Treatment options for benign prostatic hyperplasia. *Canadian Family Physician;* 43:1395-1404, 1997.

McConnell, J. Benign prostatic hyperplasia: Hormonal treatment. *Urologic Clinics of North America.* Vol. 22, No. 2, 387-400, May 1995.

Netter, A. Effect of zinc administration on plasma testosterone, dihydrotestosterone and sperm count. *Arch. Androl.* 69-73, 1981.

Nicholson, H. and Jenkin, L. Oxytocin and prostatic function. *Advances in Exp. Med. and Biol.* 395:529-38, 1995.

Shapiro, E. and Lepor, H. Pathophysiology of clinical benign prostatic hyperplasia. *Urologic Clinics of North America.* Vol. 22, No. 2, 285-90, May 1995.

Sikora. Ginkgo biloba extract in the therapy of erectile dysfunction. *Journal of Urology.* 141, 188A. 1989.

Verlag, G. Inhibition of 5 a-reductase and aromatase by PHL-00801 (*Prostatonin*), a combination of PY 102 (*Pygeum africanum*) and UR 102 (*Urtica dioica*) extracts. *Phytomedicine.* Vol.111 (2), 121-28, 1996.

TESTOSTERONE DECREASES WITH AGE, BPH INCREASES WITH AGE

Cunha, G. et al. The endocrinology and developmental biology of the prostate, *Endoc. Rev.,* 8:1987, 338.

Gleason, P. et al. Possible etiologic factors in the development of BPH, *Journal of Urology,* Vol. 49, June 1993, 1586-1592.

Grayhack, J. et al. Pathogenesis of BPH in alternate methods in the treatment of benign prostatic hyperplasia, Springer-Verlag, NY, 1993, 13.

Lee, C. et al. Etiology of Benign Prostatic Hyperplasia. *Urologic Clinics of NA,* Vol. 22, No. 2, May 95, 237-246.

OTHER GROWTH FACTORS INFLUENCING BPH

Lee, C. et al. Etiology of benign oratatic hyperplasia, *Urol. Clinics of North America,* Vol. 22, No. 2, May 95, 236-246.

Sherwood, E.R. et al. Basic fibroblast growth factor: A potent mediator of stromal growth in human prostate. *Endocrinology* 130: 1992, 2955.

Steiner, M.S. Role of peptide growth factors in the prostate: A review. *Urology* 42:99, 1993.

Sutkowski, D.M. et al. Interaction of epidermal growth factor and transforming growth factor B in human prostatic epithelial cells in culture. *Prostate* 21: 133, 1992.

INCREASED ESTROGEN EQUALS INCREASED BPH

Berry, S. et al. Effect of age, castration and testosterone replacement on the development and restoration of canine benign prostatic hyperplasia. *Prostate* 9: 1986, 295.

Cook, P.S. et al. Estrogen receptor expression in developing epididymis, efferent ductules, and other male reproductive organs. *Endocrinology* 128: 1991, 2874.

Lee, C. et al. Etiology of benign prostatic hyperplasia. *Urologic Clinics North America*, Vol. 22, No. 2, May 1995, 237-246.

Trachtenberg, J. et al. Androgen and estrogen receptor content in spontaneous and experimentally induced canine prostatic hyperplasia. *J Clin. Invest* G5: 1980, 1051.

INCREASED SHBG EQUALS INCREASED BPH

Juniewicz, P.E. et al. Requirement of testis in establishing sensitivity of canine prostate to develop benign prostatic hyperplasia. *J. Urol.*, 152:1994, 996.

Lee, C. et al. Etiology of benign prostatic hyperplasia, *Urologic Clinics of North America*, Volume 22, Number 2, May 1995, 237-246.

Rosner, W. Plasma steroid-binding proteins. *Endocr. Metab. Clinics of North America*, Volume 20, 1991, 697.

Sutkowski, D.M. et al. Effect of spermatocele fluid on growth of human prostatic cells in culture. J. *Androl.* 14:1993, 233.

INCREASED ENDOTHELIN AND DECREASED NITRIC OXIDE EQUALS INCREASED BPH

Kobayashi, S. et al. Localization of endothelin receptors in the human prostate. *J. Urol.* 151: 1994, 763.

Kobayashi, S. et al. The binding and functional properties of endothelin receptor subtypes in the human prostate. *Mol Pharmacol.* 45: 1994, 306.

Lepor, H. The treatment of BPH; a glimpse into the future. *Urologic Clinics of North America*, Vol. 22, No. 2, May 1995, 455-459.

Takeda, M. et al. Pharmacological and physiological evidence of nitric oxide synthase activity in human and canine prostates. *Urolog. in Press.*

PROSTATE CANCER AND PROSTATITIS

Ask-Upmark, E. Prostatitis and its treatment. *Acta Med Scan.* 181: 355-7, 1987.

Cassin, B.F. and Pontes, J.E. Carcinoma and intraepithelia prostate in young male patients. *J Urol.* 150 (2 Pt. 1): 379-85, Aug. 1993.

Chodak, G.W. Questioning the value of screening for prostate cancer in asymptomatic men. *Urology.* 42:116, 1993.

Coffey, D.S. The molecular biology, endocrinology, and physiology of the prostate and seminal vesicles. In *Campbell's Urology,* 6th Edition, ed. Walsh, P.C., Retik, A.B. et al. W.B. Saunders Co., Phil., PA, 221-24, 1992.

Corral, D., Pisters, L., von Eschenbach, A. treatment options for localized recurrence of prostate cancer following radiation therapy. *Urol Clin North America.* Vol. 23, No. 4. 677-84. Nov. 1996.

Hanks, G. Long–term control of prostate cancer with radiation: past, present, future. *Urol Clin North America.* Vol. 23, No. 4. 605-16. Nov. 1996.

Krahn, M.D., Mahoney J.E., Echman, M.H. et al. Screening for prostate cancer: A decision analytic view. *JAMA.* 272: 773, 1994.

Mann, C.C. The prostate-cancer dilemma. *The Atlantic Monthly.* 102-18, Nov. 1993.

Meares, E.M. Jr. Prostatitis and related disorders. In *Campbell's Urology,* 6th Edition, ed. Walsh, P.C., Retik, A.B. et al. W.B. Saunders Co., Phil., PA, 807-22, 1992.

Nelson, W., Simons, J. New approaches to adjuvant therapy for patients with adverse histopathologic findings following radical prostatectomy. *Urol Clin North America.* Vol. 23, No. 4. 685-96. Nov. 1996.

Palmer, J., Chodak, G. Defining the role of surveillance in the management of localized prostate cancer. *Urol Clin North America.* Vol. 23, No. 4. 555-56. Nov. 1996.

Petrow, V. The dihydrotestosterone (DHT) hypothesis of prostate cancer and its therapeutic implications. *The Prostate.* 9:343-361 (1986).

Schroder, F.H. Androgens and carcinoma of the prostate. *Testosterone: Action, deficiency, substitution.* ed. Nieschlag, E. and Behre, H.M. 245-60, 1990.

Sokoll, L. and Chan, D. Prostate-specific antigen: Its discovery and biochemical characteristics. *Urol Clin North America.* 24:253, 1997.

INDEX